# Contested Property Claims

Property relations are such a common feature of social life that the complexity of the web of laws, practices, and ideas that allow a property regime to function smoothly are often forgotten. But we are quickly reminded of this complexity when conflict over property erupts. When social actors confront a property regime – for example by squatting – they enact what can be called 'contested property claims'. As this book demonstrates, these confrontations raise crucial issues of social justice and show the ways in which property conflicts often reflect wider social conflicts. Through a series of case studies from across the globe, this multidisciplinary anthology brings together works from anthropologists, legal scholars, and geographers, who show how exploring contested property claims offers a privileged window onto how property regimes function, as well as an illustration of the many ways that the institution of property shapes power relationships today.

**Maja Hojer Bruun** is Associate Professor of Anthropology at the Department of Learning and Philosophy, Aalborg University, Denmark. Her work in the Contested Property Claims research group focuses on urban commons and how ownership is practiced in everyday life through relations of care, stewardship, belonging, and identification.

**Patrick J. L. Cockburn** is Assistant Professor at the Department of Philosophy and History of Ideas, Aarhus University, Denmark, and post-doctoral researcher with the Contested Property Claims research group (funded by the Carlsberg Foundation and the Danish Council for Independent Research). He works on the political philosophy of economic practices and institutions and is the author of the forthcoming book *The Politics of Dependence: Economic Parasites and Vulnerable Lives* (Palgrave Macmillan).

**Bjarke Skærlund Risager** is a PhD Fellow in the Department of Philosophy and History of Ideas, Aarhus University, Denmark. Part of the Contested Property Claims research group, he writes about social movements and activism from an interdisciplinary perspective. His research has been published in *Globalizations*, *International Journal of Sociology and Social Policy*, *Interface: A Journal For and About Social Movements*, and elsewhere; it can be followed on au.academia.edu/BjarkeRisager.

**Mikkel Thorup** is Professor with Special Responsibilities at the section for intellectual history at the Institute of Culture and Society, University of Aarhus, Denmark. His main interests concern the history of political and economic thought, and he directed the research project of Contested Property Claims behind this book. Recent books include *Pro Bono?* (Zero Books 2014), *The Total Enemy* (Wipf & Stock 2015), and the edited volume *Intellectual History of Economic Normativities* (Palgrave 2016).

## Social Justice

Series editors: Sarah Keenan, *Birkbeck College, University of London, UK*, Davina Cooper, *University of Kent, UK*, and Sarah Lamble, *Birkbeck College, University of London, UK*

*Social Justice* is a theoretically engaged, interdisciplinary series exploring the changing values, politics and institutional forms through which claims for equality, democracy and liberation are expressed, manifested and fought over in the contemporary world. The series addresses a range of contexts from transnational political fora to nation-state and regional controversies to small-scale social experiments. At its heart is a concern and inter-disciplinary engagement with the present and future politics of power as constituted through territory, gender, sexuality, ethnicity, economics, ecology and culture.

Foregrounding struggle, imagined alternatives and the embedding of new norms, *Social Justice* critically explores how change is wrought through law and governance, everyday social and bodily practices, dissident knowledges, and movements for citizenship, belonging, and reinvented community.

www.routledge.com/law/series/RCSOCJ

**Most recent titles include:**

**Sensing Law**
*Sheryl Hamilton, Diana Majury, Dawn Moore, Neil Sargent and Christiane Wilke (eds.), 2017*

**Revaluing Care in Theory, Law & Policy**
*Rosie Harding, Ruth Fletcher and Chris Beasley (eds.), 2017*

**Law Unlimited**
*Margaret Davies, 2017*

**Contested Property Claims: What Disagreement Tells Us about Ownership**
*Maja Hojer Bruun, Patrick J. L. Cockburn, Bjarke Skærlund Risager and Mikkel Thorup (eds.), 2018*

**Forthcoming:**

**Regulating Sex After Aids: Queer Risks and Contagion Politics**
*Neil Cobb*

# Contested Property Claims

## What Disagreement Tells Us about Ownership

Edited by
Maja Hojer Bruun, Patrick J. L. Cockburn, Bjarke Skærlund Risager and Mikkel Thorup

Routledge
Taylor & Francis Group
LONDON AND NEW YORK

First published 2018 by Routledge

2 Park Square, Milton Park, Abingdon, Oxfordshire OX14 4RN
52 Vanderbilt Avenue, New York, NY 10017

*Routledge is an imprint of the Taylor & Francis Group, an informa business*

First issued in paperback 2019



*British Library Cataloguing-in-Publication Data*
A catalogue record for this book is available from the British Library

*Library of Congress Cataloging-in-Publication Data*
Names: Bruun, Maja Hojer, author. | Cockburn, Patrick J. L., author. | Risager, Bjarke Skµrlund, author.
Title: Contested property claims : what disagreement tells us about ownership / Maja Hojer Bruun, Patrick J.L. Cockburn, Bjarke Skµrlund Risager.
Description: Abingdon, Oxon [UK] ; New York : Routledge, 2017. | Includes bibliographical references and index.
Identifiers: LCCN 2017032025 | ISBN 9781138550896 (hardback) | ISBN 9781351362108 (adobe reader) | ISBN 9781351362092 (epub) | ISBN 9781351362085 (mobipocket)
Subjects: LCSH: Right of property. | Possession (Law) | Property.
Classification: LCC K721.5 .B79 2017 | DDC 346.04/32—dc23
LC record available at https://lccn.loc.gov/2017032025

ISBN: 978-1-138-55089-6 (hbk)
ISBN: 978-0-367-26437-6 (pbk)

Typeset in Galliard
by Apex CoVantage, LLC

# Contents

# Contributors

**John Angus** is an artist, designer, printmaker, researcher, and curator based in Lancaster, England. He was director of a contemporary art gallery, Storey Gallery, for 20 years. He has recently taken this organisation in a new direction as StoreyG2 to deliver art projects exploring local issues of global significance, currently landownership. He studied genetics at Liverpool and Birmingham Universities.

**Sulayman Mpisi Babiiha** is a long-serving lecturer in the Department of Development Studies at Gulu University. Since 2007, at the end of the 20-year insurgency in the region, he has been engaged in research on post-war rural and community development in the Acholi sub-region. He is currently pursuing a PhD degree in Development Studies at Gulu University with affiliation to University of Copenhagen focusing on sustainable livelihoods in post war local communities in the Acholi sub-region.

**Nicholas Blomley** is Professor of Geography at Simon Fraser University in Vancouver, Canada. A geographer, he has a general interest in law and a particular interest in property in land. He has traced the work of property in many conflicts and social relations, including gentrification, urban gardening, the municipal regulation of panhandling, and Indigenous-state treaties. He is currently engaged in team-based research on the use of 'area restrictions' included in bail and sentencing conditions imposed in the context of criminal proceedings involving marginalized groups of people and is also part of a large collaborative project exploring the liquidation of Japanese–Canadian property after WWII.

**Maja Hojer Bruun** is Associate Professor in anthropology at the Department of Learning and Philosophy, Aalborg University. Her work in the Contested Property Claims research group focuses on urban commons and how ownership is practiced in everyday life through relations of care, stewardship, belonging, and identification.

**Patrick J. L. Cockburn** is Assistant Professor at the Department of Philosophy and History of Ideas, Aarhus University, and post-doctoral researcher with the Contested Property Claims research group (funded by the Carlsberg

Foundation and the Danish Council for Independent Research). He works on the political philosophy of economic practices and institutions and is the author of the forthcoming book *The Politics of Dependence: Economic Parasites and Vulnerable Lives* (Palgrave Macmillan).

**Michael Fabris (Krebs)** is currently pursuing his PhD in geography at UBC. He also completed his Masters in geography at UBC and has a BA from SFU. His doctoral research focuses on the role of land-based practice in the formation of Indigenous identity in urban and rural reserve environments. An Indigenous student of Blackfoot and European descent, Mike lives on the unceded Skwxwu7mesh, Tsleil-Waututh, and Xʷməθkʷəy̓əm territories of Vancouver.

**Neil Gray** is Director of Operations at the Urban Studies Foundation, University of Glasgow. His recent research focuses on a critical examination of the right to the city thesis; a spatial re-reading of Italian autonomous Marxism; and the stigmatisation, devalorisation and revalorisation of housing and vacant and derelict spaces. He is currently editing a book on Glasgow's seminal 1915 rent strikes and their relevance for contemporary housing struggles.

**Marie Kolling** is a post-doctoral researcher at the University of Southern Denmark and holds a PhD in anthropology from the University of Copenhagen. She has conducted extensive fieldwork in Brazil concerning urban marginality and the interplay between housing, mechanisms of social exclusion, and political economy. She recently produced the documentary film *De Andada* [Moving], which has been screened at ethnographic film festivals worldwide.

**Manissa M. Maharawal** is an Assistant Professor in the Anthropology Department at American University in Washington, DC. She is a member of the Anti-Eviction Mapping Project – a data visualization, data analysis, and narrative collective documenting the dispossession and resistance of Bay Area residents. She also co-founded AEMP's oral history sub-project, Narratives of Displacement and Resistance, with Erin McElroy. Her research and writing has been supported by the Wenner Gren Foundation, the Andrew Mellon Foundation, and the American Council of Learned Societies.

**Miguel A. Martínez** is Professor of Sociology at the IBF-Institute for Housing and Urban Research, Uppsala University (Sweden). He was previously affiliated with the University Complutense of Madrid and City University of Hong Kong. Since 2009 he is a member of the activist-research network SqEK (Squatting Europe Kollective). He is interested in urban sociology, social movements, and participatory-activist methodologies. Most of his works are available at www.miguelangelmartinez.net.

**Bill Maurer** is Professor of Anthropology and Law at the University of California, Irvine. He is the author of *How Would You Like to Pay: How Technology Is Changing the Future of Money* (Duke, 2016), among other works. His research concerns money, finance, and payment technologies and infrastructures.

**Erin McElroy** is a doctoral candidate in feminist studies at University of California, Santa Cruz, and founder of the Anti-Eviction Mapping Project, a data visualization, data analysis, and oral history collective documenting the dispossession and resistance of San Francisco Bay Area residents upon gentrifying landscapes. With Manissa M. Maharawal, Erin also cofounded the AEMP's narrative sub-project, Narratives of Displacement and Resistance. At UCSC, Erin's work mobilizes feminist science studies, critical race studies, and post-socialist analytics to theorize Silicon Valley techno-utopics and its dispossessive landscapes. Erin's work has been supported by the Creative Work Fund, the Kala Institute, the Blum Center on Poverty, and Cota-Robles and Foreign Language and Area Studies Fellowships.

**Julaina A. Obika** is a Senior Lecturer and Researcher at the Institute of Peace and Strategic Studies, Gulu University. She holds a Bachelor's degree with a specialization in gender and development and a Master's degree in conflict transformation and management. She is finalizing her PhD study, which has focused on land and trust in gender relations in the post-conflict Acholi region, where land conflicts are widespread.

**Tayanah O'Donnell** is a Postdoctoral Research Fellow with the University of Canberra, Australia. She undertook her PhD (recently submitted) at the Institute for Culture and Society, Western Sydney University. She has lectured in law and the social sciences at the Australian National University and Western Sydney University, worked as a solicitor in Sydney, Australia, and spent 2009 as a researcher for Justice Sheahan AO in the Land and Environment Court of New South Wales.

**Ben Adol Otto** is a PhD finalist in Gulu University under the Trust Land Project in the Institute of Peace and Strategic Studies (IPSS). He holds a master's degree of arts in culture and environment in Africa (CEA) and a degree in organizational studies and communication skills. His current research is on traditional institutions and post-war governance in the Acholi sub-region, which is undergoing recovery characterized by widespread land conflicts.

**Shiri Pasternak** is Assistant Professor in Criminology at Ryerson University. Her book *Grounded Authority: The Algonquins of Barriere Lake Against the State* is published by the University of Minnesota Press.

**Maria Persdotter** is a PhD student in urban studies at Malmö University, Sweden, and Roskilde University, Denmark, and a member of CRUSH, a strong research environment for urban and housing studies. Her research concerns the governance of homeless Roma EU citizens in Malmö, Sweden, bridging critical migration and urban studies.

**Libby Porter** is Vice Chancellor's Principal Research Fellow at the Centre for Urban Research, RMIT University. Her work concerns the processes and politics of displacement and dispossession as a consequence of urban planning and development. Her current activities are focused on the possibilities of decolonising urban geography and planning.

**Bjarke Skærlund Risager** is a PhD Fellow in the Department of Philosophy and History of Ideas, Aarhus University, Denmark. Part of the Contested Property Claims research group, he writes about social movements and activism from an interdisciplinary perspective. His research has been published in *Globalizations*, *International Journal of Sociology and Social Policy*, *Interface: A Journal For and About Social Movements* and elsewhere; it can be followed on au.academia.edu/BjarkeRisager.

**Mikkel Thorup** is professor with special responsibility at the section for intellectual history at the Institute of Culture and Society, University of Aarhus, Denmark. His main interests concern the history of political and economic thought, and he directed the research project of Contested Property Claims behind this book. Recent books include *Pro Bono?* (Zero Books 2014), *The Total Enemy* (Wipf & Stock 2015), and the edited volume *Intellectual History of Economic Normativities* (Palgrave 2016).

**Estair Van Wagner** is an Assistant Professor at Osgoode Hall Law School where she teaches Property Law and is co-director of the Environmental Justice and Sustainability Clinic. Before joining Osgoode, she taught at Victoria University of Wellington in New Zealand. Her research interests include the relationship between property law and land use decision making, public participation in land use decisions, critical perspectives on property law and theory, feminist and Indigenous legal theory, and environmental justice.

**Michael Whyte** is Emeritus Associate Professor with the Department of Anthropology at the University of Copenhagen. He has carried out research in Uganda since 1969 on kinship and social organization, agricultural development, food security, and HIV/AIDS. He contributed chapters to the polygraph *Second Chances: Surviving AIDS in Uganda* (S.R. Whyte, 2014); since 2008 he has been involved with capacity development at Gulu University. In 2013 he became part of the TrustLand research project, based at the Institute for Peace and Strategic Studies at Gulu University.

# Preface

This collection is about the social institution of property and what disputes, disagreements and conflicts can tell us about ownership. With the concept of 'contested property claims', we emphasise that property is always unstable. Property regimes have to be constantly enacted and negotiated to be maintained; they are the result of social struggles and, in a world in flux, they will bring about new struggles. People do not just *have* property rights, formal, customary or political, but they also have to have the ability to claim and defend their rights in front of states, cities, courts or other authorities. In these struggles, actors adopt or invent different registers of speech and action, sometimes far from property law and legal systems. Every property regime implies normative commitments and values, but justice does not always happen, and seldom for all. Time and the movement of people and landscapes can challenge existing property regimes and lead to new types of conflict.

The collection reflects the research project *Contested Property Claims: Moral Reasoning about Property and Justice in Practice, Debate and Theory* that we editors have worked on between 2013 and 2017. The research project was guided by three central research questions: How do social actors configure property claims as moral problems? What kinds of justifications or critiques do different social actors produce as they reason about these contested property claims in specific social contexts? How do they argue about the justice of these contested claims in relation to the justice of dominant property regimes? The research project has been an interdisciplinary endeavour right from the beginning, and it integrated four studies from different disciplinary areas: an anthropological study of a contemporary social controversy over property, an intellectual history study of property arguments in ideological and social context, a philosophical study of theories of legitimate expropriation and appropriation, and a sociological and human geographical study of property struggles by social movements. This multidisciplinary project gave us the possibility of studying moral reasoning about property as an aspect of on-going social practice, political struggle, and theoretical argumentation. These ideas are reflected in this collection that extends the collaboration with perspectives from law, socio-legal studies, urban studies and development studies. The approaches to property taken by scholars from these disciplines often converge, but they also sometimes pull in different directions. We wish to thank our anonymous peer reviewers, the series editors, Sarah Keenan, Sarah Lamble and Davina Coopers, and the editorial staff from Routledge for providing helpful comments and suggestions that have helped to bring the collection together.

The volume grew out of the conference *Contested Property Claims*, held in Aarhus in December 2015. Apart from papers that were originally presented at the conference, the collection also includes contributions from scholars who did not participate in this event. We would like to thank those other scholars who participated in this conference, our seminar series and workshops and helped make them such successful and inspirational events. A particular thanks goes to Nicholas Blomley and Bill Maurer, who gave keynotes at the conference and have written a foreword and afterword (respectively) for this volume.

Moreover, our project has sought to integrate agendas and perspectives from practitioners, activists and artists. This was visible during our two conferences on *Contested Property Claims* and *The Right to the City – The Struggle for the City*, especially the latter, where almost all panels and streams where organised by practitioners, activists, artists and researchers together. Some panels took up local issues of urban planning, others presented international struggles, and all of them sparked off interesting debates and brought about new perspectives on questions of property. Thus, we decided to maintain this practice, and we are happy that John Angus, who also presented his work at the *Contested Property Claims* conference, has written one of our two intermezzo chapters, which have the character of political 'interventions'. Angus documents the contemporary art project *Landed (Freeman's Wood)*, undertaken by the small art organisation StoreyG2 based in Lancaster, North West England. Manissa M. Maharawal and Erin McElroy from the Anti-Eviction Mapping Project in the San Francisco Bay Area contribute with an activists' account of the political situation in the United States of America after the election of real estate mogul Donald Trump as president.

We would like to thank the Danish Council for Independent Research (grant number DFF 1319–00077: Contested Property Claims) and the Carlsberg Foundation (grant number 2012–01–0596) that generously funded the Contested Property Claims project. We also want to thank the School of Culture and Society at Aarhus University and the staff that helped organise our activities.

Aarhus, May 2017
Maja Hojer Bruun, Patrick J. L. Cockburn,
Bjarke Skærlund Risager and Mikkel Thorup

# Foreword

## How property matters

*Nicholas Blomley*

*In the Foreword, Nicholas Blomley challenges the idea that property is a simple and uncontested phenomenon. Property is not merely an individual affair, a relation between the subject and object. It entails a relation between people, often mediated by institutions and often of an asymmetrical kind. The asymmetries lead to contestation and struggle.*

The thesis behind this book, that property is a site of contention, is, from one quarter, a puzzling one. A dominant view treats property – private property in particular – as a valuable allocation device, forestalling conflicts over valued resources. Property serves defensible moral values – notably, the liberty of individuals. Property promises clarity and certainty: if everyone knows what everyone has, then conflict is minimized. All of these claims rest on a view of property itself as a transparent and straightforward set of arrangements.

> What is property? One might think that this is a simple question. Property is about rights over things and the people who have those rights are called owners. Owners are free to use their property as they wish. They have the right to exclude others from it or grant them access to it. They have the power to transfer title – to pass the powers of ownership to someone else. They are also immune from having their property taken away from them without their consent [. . .]
>
> (Singer, 2000, pp. 3–4)

This, however, is an overly constrained model of property (Singer, 2000; Blomley, 2004). One immediate problem, as any lawyer will tell you, is that property is much more than 'rights over things'. If I own X, it is tempting to think of my claim purely as a relation between me and X. However, what such a claim effectively means is that I am to be given priority when it comes to the use of X. You do not get to use X unless I invite you. Thus, property entails relations between people, not just things. But, of course, the relation is more complex than that. I only have an effective right in X if I am able to call upon a powerful institution, such as the state, to sustain my claim to X. Rather than the state being somehow outside property, in other words, it is integral to it. So property is not a purely private, individual affair but necessarily entails the state and thus wider social and political relations.

When we make decisions about who is to have what sort of property rights, what the extent of those rights are, and how those rights are to be backed up, we make crucial decisions about how power is to be allocated within society. When we organize and distribute property rights, in other words, we organize and distribute social privileges and powers. Property rights in that sense are not apolitical and private but are 'collective, enforced, even violent decisions about who shall enjoy the privileges and resources which this society allocates among its citizens' (Underkuffler, 2003, p. 146). The decision to allocate individual rights in land, for example, is a momentous one. Private property rights protect individual control and exclusivity. Therefore, because of the rivalrous nature of land, to provide property protection to one person is to deny that right to others. 'Dominion over things is also *imperium* over our fellow human beings', noted the legal realist Morris Cohen (1927, p. 13), a point that Bill Maurer expands on in the afterword of this volume. Property law does more than protect people in their possessions. It determines what people shall acquire. Protecting the property rights of the landlord means giving the landlord the right to collect a rent. Property rights determine the future distribution of such goods. Under capitalism, such relationships become deeply asymmetrical and locked in as a status quo. Property rights thus help organize and sustain dominant and entrenched relations of power, structured in relation to class, gender and race (Bhandar, 2014). More generally, decisions regarding who can own, what can be owned and what claims are to be acknowledged and sustained by the collective are profound ones and have long been the grounds for contestation (Banner, 2011), as is evidenced in struggles ably documented in this volume, including indigenous claims to land (Pasternak and Fabris), environmental law (Van Wagner and O'Donnell), and urban conflicts (Gray and Porter, Kolling, Persdotter, and Martínez).

So property entails a set of relations between owners, nonowners and the state. A property regime, in this sense, needs to be thought of as organizing a set of relations, enabling certain possibilities, while closing off others. Put another way, particular property arrangements hook people up or deny them access to particular networks and resources of more or less stable and enduring form (Blomley, 2014). As Macpherson puts it, rather acidly, 'A system of property rights is an instrument by which a society seeks to realize the purposes of its members, or *some* of the purposes of *some* of its members' (1978, p. 13, my emphasis). These systems matter. While they can be exclusionary, they can also be valuable and productive. Property should not be thought of simply in terms of the power of the private owner to exclude but also needs to be explored in relation to those who assert the right to 'not to be excluded' (Blomley, 2016). Many claims – such as those of the seventeenth-century English commoner, the sit-down striker in 1930s Michigan and the contemporary anti-gentrification activist in inner-city Vancouver – can be thought of through this lens.

For property is a dynamic social institution. As social systems can serve to organize and secure a particular set of relations, so they can also remake them, often in destructive and unjust ways. States have long organized and remade property to serve various ends. This can occur through foundational moments, as in the case of colonial dispossession (making possible a settler property regime) or in more inclusive ways, such as the creation of state-owned housing, the recognition of labour unions or the formalization of the 'right to roam', for example. Such inclusionary moments, of course, are not moments of largesse but again derive from longstanding forms of social struggle and contestation.

Such arrangements, however arranged, matter beyond the ways in which they structure access to material resources. Property is caught up in identity formation in complex and often contested ways, for example. Western liberal societies encode private property as a marker of masculine identity, responsibility, citizenship, purity, authenticity and self-possession (Davies, 2007). The link between 'propriety' (that which is 'proper') and property is not coincidental. But by extension, those who are deemed less valuable – marked by hierarchies of race, gender and class – are often seen as problematic in relation to private property, as less 'proper'. This can work in quite subtle ways: the distinction between renters and owners is one particularly important means by which property's identities are assigned and policed. Note the manner in which homeowners are assumed to live in 'communities', while renters live in 'units of housing', for example, and the consequences this has for urban democracy.

Property also serves as a means by which we inhabit, produce and are shaped by the spaces and places we occupy. The landscape we navigate is a propertied one: it can affirm understandings of our right to occupy and use particular places. It can provide a form of security, a means by which we can anchor ourselves. To remake property relations is to remake the relations that make space and place. Contests in and through space often implicate property relations for good reason. Indigenous–state treaty making in British Columbia, for example, entails not just a metaphoric space of reconciliation but also a struggle over the geographies of land (Blomley, 2014).

Property is also a site of memory in several senses (Peñalver, 2011). Property law and property institutions, like land titles offices, help organize and police memory in particular ways, opening up certain memories and closing others. Titling does not just record, in that sense, it also arbitrates. Property more generally is a site for storytelling that also helps organize memory and make it meaningful. John Locke's famous account of property is a story, and a highly conditional one (Rose, 1990). Notions of urban space as more or less revitalized, for example, mobilize stories of property's desired unfolding. But people also narrate their lives in and through property, shaping their identities and the places they occupy. The memories of property are thus often sites of contestation (Maandi, 2009).

Property, in all these senses, matters. In sustaining or disrupting relations, property constitutes wealth, identity and our relations to place and time. As Singer notes, '[p]roperty is a social institution that is fraught with tensions. It resolves but also creates conflict, builds and undermines expectations, promotes and threatens liberty, demands and resists regulation' (2000, p. 55). It is not surprising, then, that property becomes a site of politics and contestation.

Nicholas Blomley

## References

Banner, S. (2011). *American property: A history of how, why, and what we own.* Cambridge, MA: Harvard University Press.

Bhandar, B. (2014). Critical legal studies and the politics of property. *Property Law Review, 3*(3), 186–194.

Blomley, N. (2004). *Unsettling the city: Urban land and the politics of property.* New York, NY: Routledge.

Blomley, N. (2014). Making space for property. *Annals of the Association of American Geographers, 104*(6), 1291–1306. Retrieved from http://dx.doi.org/10.1080/00045608.2014.941738

Blomley, N. (2016). The right to not be excluded: Common property and the struggle to stay put. In A. Amin & P. Howell (Eds.), *Releasing the commons* (pp. 89–106). London & New York, NY: Routledge.

Cohen, M. R. (1927). Property and sovereignty. *Cornell Law Quarterly, 13*, 8–30. Retrieved from http://heinonline.org/HOL/LandingPage?handle=hein.journals/clqv13&div=8&id=&page=

Davies, M. (2007). *Property: Meanings, histories, theories.* Abingdon: Routledge.

Maandi, P. (2009). The silent articulation of private land rights in Soviet Estonia: A geographical perspective. *Geoforum, 40*(3), 454–464. Retrieved from http://dx.doi.org/10.1016/j.geoforum.2009.03.003

Macpherson, C. B. (1978). The meaning of property. In C. B. Macpherson (Ed.), *Property: Mainstream and critical positions* (pp. 1–14). Toronto: University of Toronto Press.

Peñalver, E. M. (2011). Property's memories. *Fordham Law Review, 80*, 1071–1088. Retrieved from http://heinonline.org/HOL/LandingPage?handle=hein.journals/flr80&div=38&id=&page=

Rose, C. M. (1990). Property as storytelling: Perspectives from game theory, narrative theory, feminist theory. *Yale Journal of Law and the Humanities, 2*, 37–57. Retrieved from http://heinonline.org/HOL/LandingPage?handle=hein.journals/yallh2&div=9&id=&page=

Singer, J. (2000). *Entitlement: The paradoxes of property.* New Haven, CT: Yale University Press.

Underkuffler, L. S. (2003). *The idea of property: Its meaning and power.* Oxford: Oxford University Press.

# Introduction

## Disagreement as a window onto property

*Patrick J. L. Cockburn, Maja Hojer Bruun, Bjarke Skærlund Risager, and Mikkel Thorup*

*The editors' introduction explains the key concept of 'contested property claims', situates the book within the contemporary field of property scholarship, and outlines the individual chapters. The introduction draws out commonalities between the individual studies and also highlights the diversity of issues of social justice at stake in disagreements and conflicts involving property.*

### The idea of contested property claims

In the summer of 2016 a squatted house in Berlin was evicted by the police, resulting in massive street clashes but also a demonstration under a banner claiming 'We need to evict the police who have illegally occupied our house'. This reversal of roles was probably more carnevalistic than anything else. It fails to establish a counter-claim to the house that will have lasting effects in this local context, and the participants know this. But it does show us how social actors can and do re-describe the rights and roles of property relations as they try to mobilise to their advantage the social forces that maintain the institution of property, in this case by using an inverted version of the 'official' language of illegal occupation, to challenge both the existing property distribution and the property regime as such.

In contemporary societies people generally acquire and defend property within a property regime based on trade, contracts, inheritances, and welfare state redistributions. The institution of property is, however, never a closed legal and social system functioning according to a consistent set of principles but is always open to reconfiguration and interruption (Katyal & Peñalver, 2007; Rose, 2000; Singer, 2000). Thus, as the example illustrates, property regimes do not always run smoothly. They are not merely accepted but also contested, ignored, circumvented, and strategically manipulated. Behind them lie histories of appropriation and expropriation, and from within they are constantly challenged by those who point to the social injustices that they can produce. Such challenges can aim to undermine a dominant property regime altogether (i.e. toppling a hegemonic mode of imagining and instituting property), but they can also simply aim to influence how a dominant regime distributes rights and responsibilities in specific contexts, thus using powerful institutions (e.g. courts) and languages (e.g. the idea of 'rights' or 'ownership') against other claim-makers. Whether radical or reformist, general or specific, attempts to mobilise a vision of property in order to reproduce or reorganise property relations are what we in this book call 'contested property claims'.

This concept of 'contested property claims' brings together two key ideas. *First*, the idea that property is established through processes of communication between social actors (Rose, 1994). In the words of Carol Rose, 'property takes some persuading in order to happen at all' (2006, p. 11). These persuasions or mutual recognition among social actors are performed not only verbally and linguistically but also through other kinds of actions, including practices of care, stewardship, and belonging that establish property boundaries, inclusions, and exclusions. *Second*, this communication can be, and often is, deeply confrontational and does not always lead to mutual recognition – at least not immediately. Such confrontations include occupation, enclosure, squatting, resistance, and protest. By thinking of property as established in communicative processes of persuasion, none of the violence, struggle, or battles of ideas that can surround property relations should disappear from view. The audiences that need persuading may exactly be those in a position to apply force (e.g. the state) and those who will be subject to that force (e.g. squatters). Property claims can be made both to mobilise and to challenge the forces that maintain property, and such claims will often be contested ideologically, legally, and practically.

This anthology examines a range of contexts in which such contested property claims are at work, and it asks what we might learn about the concepts and phenomena of property and ownership from these claims. The various chapters illustrate lessons in the politics of property. They show how normative ideas, alliances of interests, and practical performances interlink to stabilise a property regime and what happens where these links are challenged and loosened and contestation and conflict replace consensus or hegemony. Contested property claims are thus a window onto the politics of property at a given moment in a given social context, showing how social actors reason about and perform property when challenged to do so and what social justices and injustices are produced through property relations.

These forms of communication, both verbal and non-verbal, are resources both for naturalizing and for contesting property arrangements. They are skewed to the advantage of the established social powers, as is evident in the Berlin eviction example, but they are not fixed or determined in support of these powerful institutions and groups. The language of law can be countered by that of custom or that of politics by one of morality. Who owns a given piece of land? The legal owner? The old residents who have an emotional attachment to the place? The neighbours who have always used part of it as a pathway? The community who wants to preserve an old building on the site? The local council making development or preservation plans? Competing claims coming from different property languages can counter what would at first seem a clear-cut case of legal ownership.

Conflict and contestation are, however, not only windows onto property relations but sometimes also the events that drive the transformation and development of property ideas, practices, and laws themselves. The idea of the 'property outlaw' points to 'the powerful, and at times ironic, role of the lawbreaker in the process of fostering the evolution of property' (Katyal & Peñalver, 2007, p. 1098). Even more radically, Lucy Finchett-Maddock (2016) has argued that it is ultimately impossible to separate property resistance from property law, to conclude where the one ends and the other begins. Contested property claims are ubiquitous in the contemporary world as ever more conflicts over property emerge and political struggles are increasingly framed as questions of property relations and property rights. Using Karl Polanyi's (2001, p. 79) term, we might say that there is a 'double movement' in the global political economy today. On the one hand, exclusive private property rights are attached to ever more phenomena like genes, tradable quotas in rights to pollute or fish, internet domain names, and so on. On the other hand, a growing number of local, national, and international grassroots organizations and non-governmental organisations (NGOs) aim to counteract, regulate, and reduce private property rights.

Counter-movements include both the establishment of immaterial, cultural, intellectual, and creative commons and claims to physical space through squatting, guerrilla gardening, 'Reclaim the Streets', 'Occupy Wall Street' or other events to establish community ownership. These and many other contestations tell us much about *how* property regimes are contested but also about *what* property regimes exist, how they operate and develop, and how the everyday functioning of any property regime is always pushing up against social values that it works against (equality, for example). These frictions expose the way in which even relatively stable property regimes institute a form of claim making that is ultimately temporary and unstable, maintained in the face of challenges and the promises of alternative property regimes. Behind the surface of legality and normality, a property regime is itself, in essence, a contested form of claim making that requires constant ideological and practical shoring up.

'Offenders' and 'trespassers' have historically played an important role in the development of property law, which is often formulated and legitimated with reference to these threats, as is evident for instance in work on the criminalisation of squatting (Fox O'Mahony, Fox O'Mahony, & Hickey, 2015; Manjikian, 2013). But property regimes develop as much through resistance as through policing; outright theft and property destruction; the small manipulations of dominance, as detailed by James C. Scott (1990), the hidden manuscripts of property resistance where critiques and evasions are articulated but in a language or setting that is not so dramatic as outright resistance or refusal; the quiet encroachments of the ordinary detailed, for instance, by Asef Bayat (2013) whereby spaces, utilities, or functions are used by people for whom they were not intended, like when the street is used for begging, shoe shining, and prostitution or when homeless people build shacks on sidewalks; the symbolic and physical appropriations of property where space and things are modified by graffiti, posters, behaviour, re-arrangements to stake a claim of ownership to what one does not legally own, like when homeless people turn a public place into 'their' spot or skateboarders take over part of a park; political interventions in property regimes from 'reclaim the streets' bike demos to appropriations of parking lots as small community parks or theft from supermarkets to give to the poor in 'Robin Hood redistributions'. All of these actions are at work, in parallel to the more explicit political battles of redefining who gets to keep what and why, in shaping the property relations that we live with in society.

## Ways to think about property: from bundles of *rights* to bundles of *relations* to performative property *practices*

Discussing contested property claims warrants a reflection on the question: what counts as property? The very definition of property, as Nicholas Blomley highlights, is carefully policed (Blomley, 2008). Only certain relations are named 'property' and particular social actors recognised as owners. In most property theory and popular discourse it is *law* that stands at the centre of our explanations of what property 'is': a set of *legal* relations. In such accounts, property owners can be private individuals, corporations, or states, but they are all legally defined subjects. Furthermore, in what Joseph Singer (2000) calls the 'ownership model of property' and Chris Hann (1998) the 'dominant liberal paradigm', property is envisaged as the *rights of owners* to do what they want with what is theirs as long as they do not harm others. This ignores, for example, the obligations that property produces, such as the duties that rest on landlords (Alexander, 2009a). The dominant emphasis on law and the rights of owners has meant that claims not voiced in the language of law or through the institutions of the legal system may fail to register in public and theoretical debate as 'property claims' at all: they 'do not look like property to us, and we have tended to ignore them' (Rose, 1998 in Blomley, 2008, p. 321).

When property theorists like Singer and Hann refer to 'models' or 'paradigms' of property that they want to criticise, they are in fact referring not to a consistently worked-out theory in a specific text or tradition but a background set of assumptions about the nature of property that they believe inform a wide range of social actors in capitalist democracies: both ordinary people on the street and *some* (probably most) political and legal theorists. We need to do some unpacking here to understand what is going on in criticisms of such models. Thomas C. Grey (1980) famously pointed out in his essay on 'The Disintegration of Property' that in modern times ordinary persons' understandings of what property *is* have diverged radically from the technical understandings of property developed in legal theory and practice. On the one hand is the widespread 'commonsense' view of property as essentially consisting in *things*: the property is the thing owned. On the other hand is the legal conception of property as a complex bundle of rights that regulate *the relations between people with respect to things.*

This legal conception was most famously unpacked by Honoré (1961) as eleven 'incidents' of ownership including the right to use, the right to manage, the right to income from a thing, and more. Grey saw the 'commonsense' view as increasingly detached from the realities of ownership (as viewed by the courts) and predicted that the umbrella concept of property, which legal systems have used to gather together specific rules of access and control of resources, would 'disintegrate' under the accumulated pressure of circumstances. While Grey's prognosis was extremely important, the concept of 'property' has clearly not loosened its hold on public life and the legal imagination. And while Grey was right to point out the differences between the 'common' view and the 'technical' view, he may also have overlooked an important feature that they share: what they share is the focus on *the rights of owners*.

This brings us back to our idea of an 'ownership model' or a 'liberal paradigm' of property. Singer and Hann are criticising views of property – whether widespread or narrowly theoretical – that make the rights of owners into the key point of reference both for *describing* property as a social institution and for *normatively* judging social arrangements. There are two basic ways to take issue with this focus on the rights of owners: one is to question the focus on *rights*, the other is to question the focus on *owners*. As we outline in this section, critical scholarship on property by legal scholars, anthropologists, and geographers has done both of these things.

In legal scholarship 'progressive property' theorists have tried to shift the centre ground of US legal debate about property by emphasising the plurality of social goods that every property regime serves (Alexander, 2009a, 2009b, 2011; Alexander, Peñalver, Singer, & Underkuffler, 2009). By arguing that the law of property in the US already incorporates many normative considerations *other than* the rights of owners (such as the obligations of owners and the rights of non-owners), progressive property theorists are challenging a powerful stream of legal interpretation that has focussed on the right to exclude as the 'core' of property (Claeys, 2009; Epstein, 1985; Smith, 2009). This progressive reconstruction of the meaning of 'property' within the American legal tradition certainly challenges the centrality of the rights of owners to our thinking about property, but it remains limited to an analysis of the powerful languages of property: those ideas and arguments used in courts and the historical canon of political culture (e.g. the debates at the time of American independence; see Underkuffler, 1990).

By contrast, anthropologists have often examined both formal and informal forms of ownership and undertaken detailed empirical examinations of the diverse ways in which property is organised, understood, and enforced. Bronislaw Malinowski's (1935) account of the Trobriand land tenure system remains a classic. Land tenure involves the relationship of people to soil 'in the widest sense' and thus it includes magic, mythology, history, custom, personhood, citizenship, and kin relations. Anthropologists such as Max Gluckman (1965) and Franz and Keebet von Benda-Beckmann and Melanie Wiber (2006) have adapted the metaphor of property as a bundle of rights (developed from Henry Maine, through

Wesley Hohfeld and Tony Honoré) and explored how property rights are bundled in different ways. In ethnographic analyses from different parts of the world many forms and senses of owning fall outside legal definitions of property rights; such forms and senses of ownership are thus not based in law but build on other sources of authority including cultural traditions, social norms, and religious or community authority figures. While Honoré argued that ownership was properly the full bundle of rights and powers (use, exclusion, etc.), alternative views of ownership have emphasised that the bundle can be disaggregated into several 'sticks' or layers in which rights of use, access, and control may not be assigned to the same party: the party widely regarded as the 'owner' may not even have the right to alienate and sell the property.

Instead of limiting the investigation to property *rights* anthropological property theories often speak of property *relations* (Benda-Beckmann, Benda-Beckmann, & Wiber, 2006; Hann, 1998). Anthropologists have particularly highlighted how different notions and practices of belonging can constitute ownership and property relations: this is the case, for example, when people get access to resources through membership of different communities. In many cases persons and things mediate belonging. This is the case when people belong to one another through what belongs to them, as when they live together in a house or village or work together in the same workplace (e.g. Edwards & Strathern, 2000). Based on a study of the property regime at Summerhill School Davina Cooper (2007) distinguishes between two property registers, that of belonging and that of belonging*s*. *Belongings* identify a subject–object relationship whereby an object, space, or other resources are held by the property owner, who exercises rights and powers over it. The relation is a propertied relationship between a subject and an object and is characterized by severability, fungibility, and commodification. In contrast, *belonging* cannot be understood as propertied in a legal sense but is constituted by a social norm that attaches importance to a particular constitutive relationship between part and whole – in the same sense that a child belongs to a family. As constituted by relationships of belonging*s*, property sets up boundaries between those who belong within a larger entity, a whole, and those who are excluded. Attaching ownership to something, through patenting for instance, structures relations between persons; in the case of a patent, all the people whose work went into producing scientific results are not included as owners: the ownership has created boundaries between those who belong and do not belong (Strathern, 1996). In Strathern's relational ontology social life is a flow of persons and things, and property is a way of stopping or 'cutting' this flow, just as 'the force of "law" cuts into the limitless expanse of "justice", reducing it and rendering it expressible' (ibid., p. 522).

Thus, by decentring rights and owners, relational conceptualisations of property take us by degrees further and further from the 'ownership model' identified by Singer and the 'dominant liberal paradigm' identified by Hann. As we note later, this does not imply that either rights or owners become unimportant for our descriptions and normative judgements about property: it would be absurd to imagine that we could do without these ideas in the description of contemporary property relations, and it would overlook the important ways in which these ideas have been normatively re-appropriated by those who want to challenge the status quo of property regimes in capitalist democracies. But what is important to remember is that these focal points have all too often kept us from viewing property from those subject positions that the formal laws of property treat as secondary or ill defined: these are views of property from the 'margins' (van der Walt, 2009), from the 'outside' (Fox O'Mahony, 2014), and from the 'propertyless' (Waldron, 2009). These perspectives from the periphery of property law and practice help to show how one group's security (e.g. rights to exclude) may be another group's insecurity (e.g. the likelihood of removal or eviction).

It is important to remember that viewing property as social relations does not imply social equality or justice per se. Hierarchy, inequality, patriarchy, and other unequal relations of power are also produced through social relationships. For example, Cheryl Harris (1993) famously claimed that whiteness can be seen as property, and Sarah Keenan (2015) has developed this idea by arguing that whiteness is a (non-biological but culturally and politically upheld) racial category that, *via part–whole relations of belonging*, gives whites certain privileges and access to resources (see also Maharawal & McElroy, this volume). This hints at the double meaning of the word 'property' as being an object one can own as well as a quality a person or a thing can possess.

We also find a relational conceptualisation of property in human geography, but one that inserts property relations into geographical context. Legal considerations of property have most often ignored space in favour of the inter-subjective dimension of property (Blomley, 2016). But property in land is inherently spatial. Its value and utility are most often proportionally linked to its spatial extension and the location of its place in wider space. In line with the 'ownership model', property is now often understood as a space from which the owner has the right to exclude others (Blomley, 2016; McDonagh & Griffin, 2016). But what is left out of such 'everyday' views of property and has been recaptured by geographers is the fact that such spaces only constitute property within wider, and sometimes fragile, networks of power, law, capital, and people. To reconstruct and understand these networks, geographers like Blomley (2011) have drawn extensively on theories of space as relational (e.g. Lefebvre, 1991; Massey, 2005).

One example of the spatio-relational aspect of property is found in Blomley (2011) who, following Strathern (see earlier), renders the geography of property as the effect of an ongoing negotiation of its 'cuts' and 'flows'. These refer to two dimensions of property that are at once necessary and contradictory and that are linked to two different conceptualizations of space. By 'cutting' Blomley refers to the act of loosening the object of property from its surroundings and the structures and networks in which it is embedded so that it is given boundaries. The same is the case for the subject – the owner – whose individuality (through possession) is shielded off and protected by rights and law enforcement. This process gives meaning to all three constituent parts in the statement 'I own this', and it further determines the truth value of this statement within the property regime this process unfolds. According to Blomley, this process takes place in a perceived pre-political space that unproblematically can be cut up and on which boundaries can be drawn, objects contained, and people excluded. This purely instrumental conceptualisation of space turns property into a zero-sum game: the subject of property either owns the object or she doesn't.

This Blomley juxtaposes with the flows of property which go beyond its cuts and boundaries. From this potential for overflowing, contestation arises: while some flows work in the favour of the property owner – such as the influx into a city neighbourhood of potential renters of the owner's property which drives up demand and rent – other flows can cause contestation – such as when new urban planning forces people to give up the claim to their property and vacate (Gray & Porter, this volume) or when Indigenous practices of ownership conflict with settler-colonial imperatives of private property (Krebs, this volume; Pasternak, this volume). The flows of property mean that contestation is always internal to any given property regime: 'The cuts are provisional, at best. The cadastral grid hangs loosely upon the land. Its governmental effects do not materialize, or are contested by other, prior geographies of possession, reliant less on boundary and stasis than on flow and line', as Blomley (2011, p. 213) writes. The present collection on contested property claims deals with cases where the inherent contradiction and contestation of the cuts and flows of property surface.

With the conceptual shift of emphasis from rights to relations to relational cuts in space, property comes to look more and more like a social institution (or set of practices and ideas) that is in constant motion and flux. Not only are the value and purpose of property open to contestation in courts (the 'progressive property' point), but the social relations through which property is enacted in lived reality are part of a much wider and ever-changing fabric of human interaction (the anthropological point), and the 'flows' of property are constantly disrupting attempts to 'cut up', settle, and stabilise the world of property (the geographical point). All of this opens a *processual* or *performative* perspective on ownership: property relations are not static but need to be communicated, performed, or claimed – actively made and repeated – in order to function. The social and symbolic systems, sometimes more narrowly called property regimes, are dynamic, and in many cases contested claims and conflicts change the systems over time. All of this contingency in property relations is the backdrop against which contested property claims can happen. Social actors do not just 'fit into' a property regime that was there before them; they are in fact responsible both for making challenges to a property regime and for keeping such regimes going by performing them in the right way (see Blomley, 2013).

This idea of 'performativity' directs our attention to the practices that produce property and to a number of important features of these practices.

First of all, the performance of property is often citational, re-iterative, and imitational. As an example of this, Blomley describes the performative power of building a fence, for instance between two gardens, that must not be seen as an original act but as a citation of innumerable fences, borders, and other markers of ownership, physical or symbolic, that have delimited property over time. More than this, the performance of property is not only citational but also re-iterative and takes repeated work. Such a performative approach to property invites us to analyse different property practices, acts, and claims (see also Strang & Busse, 2011). Based on the chapters in this book, we can add that practices can also be imitational, for instance when squatters imitate the performances of legal owners (Martínez, this volume; Persdotter, this volume). Of course, these citations or imitations can and do often fail: squatters' claims to use-rights are rejected in evictions, and sometimes it is even difficult to get recognised as a *squatter* in the sense aimed for (see Kolling, this volume).

Second, the performance of property entails a relation between actors and audiences. As Carol Rose argues in *Property and Persuasion* (1994), ownership is established through culturally and historically specific systems of communication and recognition through which people act and negotiate property relations: 'It is not enough, then, for the property claimant to say simply, "It's mine", through some act or gesture; in order for the statement to have any force, some relevant world must understand the claim it makes and take that claim seriously' (Rose, 1994, p. 18). In this way, claims have to find resonance, and, as noted, this often means citing or imitating previous manifestations of property.

Third, studies like Cooper's (2007) discussed earlier, draw attention to the heterogeneity of the elements and logics that comprise property performances. Property performances are hybrid composites formed out of both formal and informal rules, specific material settings, and verbal and non-verbal actions. Explicit property utterances and everyday property practices coexist in complex ways and may diverge significantly from one another without property performances disintegrating under the strain (Cooper, 2007, p. 660). In fact, sometimes such divergences between the official and the unofficial sides of property are exactly what we need to grasp in order to understand the 'work' that social actors do in performing property. The idea that property performances are hybrid can also be extended in a number of directions: we can investigate the range of 'actors' who perform, going beyond human to non-human actors that play roles in the everyday performance of property (e.g. the role of wildlife in planning disputes; see Van Wagner, this volume); we can investigate how such performances of property can not only stabilise the social world but, on the contrary, may be subversive (Keenan, 2015); and we can look at how the 'becoming' of property, through its performance, is part of a broader 'becoming-world' constituted by developing technologies, environments, and social practices (see Maurer, this volume).

## What kinds of conflict? What kinds of contestation?

What is clear from all of the examples listed and from the cases discussed in this volume is that various property *conflicts* can have significantly different stakes from one another, and the forms of *contestation* in these conflicts can take many forms.

### *What, then, are some of the stakes of property conflicts?*

Property conflicts often intersect with struggles over racial, gendered, economic, and cultural inequality and oppression. This is obvious, for example, in the claims of Indigenous peoples against the property regimes established by colonial powers around the world (Krebs, this volume; Pasternak, this volume) or in the struggles fought by movements against racialised displacement (Maharawal & McElroy, this volume). Historically, women's property rights have also been restricted by law (e.g. laws of coverture), and even when this is no longer formally the case (in most societies today) property laws and practices can remain implicitly gendered, for example in the ways that ownership is structured within marriages and distributed in the event of divorce and the way in which women's claims to property can be integrally connected to their place in wider family structures (Obika, Otto, Babiiha, & Whyte, this volume). In their study of property claims in post-conflict Uganda, Julaina A. Obika and colleagues examine the way in which the status of being a mother to children within a clan lineage can be a more important starting point for making property claims than the idea of an 'individual' owner. Another example of such intersections of identity and property is the way in which women and African Americans, in particular, were made targets of predatory lending during the recent American housing bubble (Davidson & Dyal-Chand, 2010; Dymski, Hernandez, & Mohanty, 2013; Wyly, Moos, & Hammel, 2012). In Persdotter's study (this volume) of the eviction of a settlement in Malmö, Sweden, we see how a local property conflict is in fact embedded in the wider issue of the rights of Roma people in Europe. Specifically, we see how the conflict gets linked in racialising ways to notions of dirt and propriety.

What all of the examples illustrate is that property conflicts may be integral parts of wider social tensions and struggles, sometimes revolving around social identities that have been marginalised, oppressed, or actively attacked.

While these are examples of particular social groups seeking to redress historical injustice, conflicts over property can also be about determining the rights and duties of more abstract social entities such as 'government'. For some legal theorists, particularly from liberal and libertarian traditions of political thought, private property should first and foremost be understood as marking and maintaining the boundary line between the powers of government and the freedoms of individual citizens (Epstein, 1985). The problem of government 'takings' (forced transfers of property) has produced a vast field of scholarship in the context of US property law but also on restorative justice in many countries around the world (for a recent turn in this debate, see Atuahene, 2016). Neil Gray and Libby Porter (this volume) illustrate individual owners' attempts to defend their private property against the efforts of local government to evict them in the course of a programme of neighbourhood renewal and gentrification and conclude that citizens' rights are not universal or absolute but easily evaporate under the sovereign decision.

Property disputes can also be about the balance of power between private property–owning citizens and the wider public, as we see for example in court cases regarding the planning and development of cities and coastlines (on Australian cases, see O'Donnell, this volume). Rights of access to beaches, countryside, rivers, reefs (for surfing and fishing), public urban space, and more are very much about the balance of power between various kinds of owners (public, private, state, and collective) and various kinds of non-owners (shoppers in a mall in contrast to homeless people).

Finally, when thinking about these various kinds of conflict, we need to remember that the parties to property conflict are often asymmetrical in a number of ways that influence how a conflict unfolds. While collective subjects such as communities making property claims may be loosely defined and have few legally enforceable property rights, they may find themselves in confrontation with other collectives such as limited liability corporations that are not only sharply defined but have clear packages of legally enforceable property rights. These conditions of asymmetry are thoroughly unpacked in Van Wagner's study (this volume) of aggregate mining in Ontario, Canada, and local community resistance to these land uses.

This discussion outlines a number of the stakes of property conflicts, but we need also to pay careful attention to the many kinds of *contestation* and strategizing that take place in these conflicts.

By engaging in political rather than strictly legal strategies and tactics, social groups can challenge property regimes from outside of the institutions (e.g. courts) that constitute, regulate, and reproduce these regimes. Social groups can also make their property claims within the dominant power structures (e.g. using planning law against private property law) and using the prevailing language of a legal order (e.g. 'rights' or 'ownership'). In fact, the use of the concept of 'rights' to make property claims that contest the legal regime of property relationships is common. One of the most prominent such subversive uses is captured by the idea of 'the Right to the City'. The Right to the City was coined by Henri Lefebvre (1996) and has become a rallying cry for many activists as well as a fruitful entry point for many academics in the study of urban life. As mentioned, there is a large body of anthropological literature that discusses property as relationships of belonging. Claiming the Right to the City is also a way of establishing a relationship of belonging, and indeed identification, where the message conveyed by claimants is that 'We belong here; the city belongs to us'. Belonging to/in the city establishes property relationships that are partly based in emotions and affect, partly based in needs and interests. Whereas (as noted) property rights are often defined as the right to exclude others from one's property, the Right to the City is the right *not* to be excluded from the city. It is to have 'a right to an equitable usufruct of cities within the principles of sustainability, democracy, equity and social justice' (Lefebvre in Susser & Tonnelat, 2013, p. 110).

The discourse and oppositional practices of those who argue for the Right to the City are just one manifestation of a re-appropriation of the powerful language of property. Sometimes such re-appropriations are a way of building oppositional tactics that appeal to the dominant norms of a property regime while nonetheless resisting their current consequences. In other words, contestations can mix legal with extra-legal claim making. For example, what we see in both Kolling's and Persdotter's studies (this volume) are social groups anticipating the viewpoint of both a general public and the state authorities and conforming to the norms that might make their property claims *recognisable* from the point of view of the authorities. In Kolling's case, this is the attempt by squatters to organise their own eviction from a piece of land in the hope of being re-housed with more secure forms of tenure (see what follows). In Persdotter's Malmö study, the Roma residents facing eviction tried to make their settlement conform to standards of care and cleanliness that are culturally associated with property ownership (see what follows). In both cases, we see something like 'inverse governmentality' (Nielsen, 2011): the attempt to reorder things and actions precisely with a view to being captured and managed by governmental processes in the desired way.

The fact that much of property politics occurs outside of the formal frameworks of legal systems should not distract from the extent to which legal property regimes contain their own internal tensions and contradictions. As noted, the recent work of 'progressive property' scholars in the United States has shown that private property as imagined and instituted in US law serves many social ends that can be in conflict with one another, including, for example, security, efficiency, and personal and political autonomy (Alexander, 2011). These valued ends can and do come into conflict with one another in decisions about what rights and duties private property bestows on owners and non-owners. Where these internal tensions in the legal regime of ownership become problematic, it is up to courts and legislatures to decide which vision of property will be incorporated into law and enforced. Not only that, but there can also be important clashes between branches of law – such as planning law, environmental law, and the private laws of property – which courts and legislatures must put into hierarchies (see Van Wagner, this volume). There are thus forms of contestation *within* the power structures of a given legal order.

## Lessons about ownership: outline of the chapters

When illustrated in specific socio-legal contexts, the various forms of conflict and contestation discussed here reveal important features of the working of ownership: its meanings and consequences for both owners and non-owners; the forms that it can take, from legally enforceable rights of exclusion to emotional or cultural bonds (that actors may experience but states may not register); and the many fronts of social tension and struggle in which it plays a role. In what follows we outline the individual contributions to the volume that we have grouped into two sections within the book: Squatting and Eviction in the first part and Land Rights and Conflicting Laws in the second part.

One of the lessons developed by a number of the studies in this volume is that neither can we completely capture the complexity of property disputes through the lens of 'rights', nor can we do without the language of 'rights' if we want to understand the dynamics of these disputes. For example, Gray and Porter's study (Chapter 1) of the eviction of home owners in Glasgow in the course of an urban renewal programme shows that ownership rights may be central to a dominant property regime in a capitalist society but may nonetheless be little protection against governments determined to bypass them. While the defence of private property against governments tends to be regarded as a conservative project, Gray and Porter's argument suggests that sometimes *more inclusion*, in terms of who can live in a neighbourhood of a city, requires more powers of *exclusion*, keeping the government from evicting a neighbourhood with a view to gentrification.

Rights are also important in broader political ways in Kolling's study (Chapter 2) of citizens' attempts to gain secure state housing by moving to and squatting in an area of Salvador da Bahia, Brazil, where they hoped to be evicted and rehoused under an official housing programme. The study shows the complex and counter-intuitive manoeuvring of one group of actors who live outside a dominant property regime (by squatting) in the hope of being given security within it (in state housing). The residents' strategy can be seen as an attempt to claim a right to have rights: that is, to place themselves in a situation in which their right to be housed can be effectively asserted. Kolling employs the idea of a 'housing hierarchy' to explain that the squatters chose to take a step 'down' from renting or living with friends and family to the squatter settlement but that they did so in the hope of taking two steps 'up' by being evicted and rehoused with secure tenure. The case shows how these actors anticipated the application of government policy: the squatters needed to possess a house that should be replaced, but they also needed to live in a place they were likely to be evicted and to do so at the right time. Social rights such as the right to housing, and thus rehousing, that are safeguarded in Brazil's progressive urban legislation can thus be seen as a kind of property (cf. Reich [1964] on the 'new property' implied in welfare state regimes): rights that citizens have vis-à-vis the state and that they claim through various political tactics, sometimes successfully and sometimes not. All of this took place against the backdrop of a city government's attempts to make a park attractive and accessible to the general public by removing those who were squatting there. The interlinking of inclusion with exclusion is thus important at several layers in this case.

Moving on from rights, Kolling's chapter is also important for the way that it shows the interplay between the situation on the ground (people squatting and organising their housing in particular ways) and the legal and administrative structures that view and categorise this situation in ways that matter for the unfolding of the dispute. Similar to the way in which the Brazilian squatters anticipated the actions of the local government, the Malmö squatters in Persdotter's study (Chapter 3) sought to make their encampment conform to ideological expectations about what ownership practices look like, for example by clearing rubbish at the site of the camp: establishing a situation on the ground that might support recognition of a legal right to stay. In the end, however, one of the crucial lessons of the case is that the city government could circumvent the process of reclaiming the property for the official owner by simply *translating the conflict* into a problem about hygiene and living conditions. Environmental law could thus do the work that the assertion of property rights could not (so easily), and the government's use of this legal framework also helped to legitimise the intervention as 'humanitarian' (no one should have to live in conditions like this) rather than exclusionary (the reaffirmation of property rights).

Martínez's study on political squatters (Chapter 4) is also about the way political demands are strategically translated into legitimate claim making and the limits to that approach when it is not, as in Kolling's and Persdotter's cases, an attempt to gain property rights within the existing system, but an attempt to challenge or dismantle the capitalist-individualist property regime as such. Martínez documents the various ways in which different squatters manoeuvre within a moral and legal field not of their own making and how the choice of specific kinds of property (e.g. private or state) and of specific forms of building (e.g. residential or institutional) interlinks with different legitimation strategies. Of particular importance to his story is what happened to the possibilities of 'legitimate' squatting once new groups of middle-class, respectable citizens started squatting and mobilising on housing issues in Spain after the financial crisis. Those voicing radical demands and practising alternative lifestyles walk a fine line in their attempts to gain some legitimacy from the community, media, courts, and other established authorities while at the same time resisting complete co-optation.

Located in between our two main sections are two intermezzo chapters that have the character of 'interventions' that document and publicise specific projects of resistance to what has been identified as property injustices. These two chapters connect our two main structural themes of squatting and eviction, discussed already, as well as land rights and conflicting laws, discussed below. The two chapters (5 and 6) document an artist and an activist intervention into disputed land and property issues. Curator John Angus narrates an art project developed as a response to an enclosure of a plot of land used by generations of people on the edge of Lancaster, England. Angus not only shows a classical land dispute between private companies hedging in what people have hitherto seen and used as common land, he shows also how art projects can tell stories of different property uses and conflicts, all the way from what happens locally on the ground to the murky goings-on in the world of global finance. The intervention is an example of the roles art can play in commenting on and intervening in property conflicts. Intervening in a more explicitly political way is our activist intervention, the San Francisco–based Anti-Eviction Mapping Project using public data, storytelling, and visualisations to document and protest the dispossessions of residents, making visible on a structural and communal level what are otherwise hidden or unnoticed individual experiences. Co-founders and co-directors of the project, Manissa M. Maharawal and Erin McElroy, scrutinise the relation between 'real estate mogul' and now-President Donald Trump's recent rise to power and the struggle against dispossession and for housing. Unfolding the intersection between racialisation and property, the authors argue that Trump represents the newest development in a long history of a racist private property regime in America. We can view the mapping project as a way of taking personal experiences of eviction and translating them into the context of broader political conflicts.

The idea of 'translations', present in Kolling, Persdotter as well as Martínez, is also helpful for understanding a number of the other studies of land rights and conflicting laws. Van Wagner's chapter (7) studies disputes over the siting of mines in Ontario, Canada, and illustrates how land ownership is a legal category that structures planning processes in a way that reflects not only substantive governmental aims (economic development) but also embedded hierarchies of social actors who are given various roles and degrees of power in planning processes. Ownership rights are important in these planning processes, not only because they distribute rights and duties at any one point in time but also because they structure the planning process *over* time: they give 'chronological power'. Owners are given not only the power to initiate different phases of a development project but also to alter the physical environment in ways that can bypass regulations (e.g. protecting the landscape or wildlife) before these regulations can be used by opposition groups as a form of resistance to development. Thus ownership rights are translated into a set of privileges within planning processes. But counter-translations are going on too: activists resisting mining developments can sometimes translate the conflict into the domain of environmental law by countering property claims with laws that protect endangered species on the land in question. As in Pasternak and O'Donnell's contributions, what we see here are non-human actors becoming involved in disputes about land and property.

For O'Donnell (Chapter 8), the primary non-human actor in the story is the Earth's changing climate. Following Mariana Valverde's (2015) idea of the 'chronotopes of law' and emphasising the problems of applying a bundle-of-rights view of property to changing landscapes, the chapter highlights both the spatial and temporal dimensions of property disputes. It shows how changes to the coastal landscape in Australia through continuous erosion and dramatic weather events (flooding) force courts and policy makers to incorporate the temporality of planetary climate change into their approaches to planning and property law. What happens when the balance of public interests in access to a beach and private rights in coastal properties is suddenly rearranged by a storm event that changes the coastline in question? What happens when the long-term city planning of local governments to deal with inevitable sea-level rises clashes with the shorter-term interests of private property owners who don't want to relocate or find themselves in a planning zone with strict development bylaws? O'Donnell illustrates that the temporality of long-term climate change, of recurrent weather events, and of the individual lifetimes of property owners will continue to be extremely difficult to align in a way that avoids conflict.

While the future weighs heavily on the property conflicts sparked by climate change, the past certainly weighs heavily on the property conflicts generated by colonisation. In Shiri Pasternak's and Mike Krebs's chapters (9 and 10, respectively) ideas and laws of private property are analysed as part of the politics of settler colonialism. Both chapters examine the Canadian state's ongoing attempt to govern Indigenous people by laying settler-colonial power structures over Indigenous tenure systems, particularly through property law. In her study of the Algonquin of Barriere Lake in Quebec, Pasternak argues that colonial systems of property rights that regulate practices like hunting have certainly imposed drastic changes on the practices of Indigenous people, limiting the flexibility of a social system that allowed cooperation between hunting parties and collective organisation. The development of systems of hunting licences that require the mapping and dividing of territory has been a governmental technique reflecting an instrumental view of the natural world as consisting of resources that need to be exploited or preserved. Thus, for Pasternak, the primary question is not whether colonial property systems have been imposed on a pre-existing property system (a topic that has occupied generations of anthropologists) but what role colonial property practices have played in the gradual extension of Canadian legal *jurisdiction* over territory occupied by Indigenous people. Through this optic, property is part of the machinery of government. When Indigenous hunting practices become reconceptualised as rights to a particular 'trapline', something bigger is at stake: this is an important step in the process of 'corrupting' the Indigenous peoples' capacity to govern their lives according to an ethic of 'care' that embraces 'other-than-human worlds' – an ethic that bureaucratic regimes of ownership cannot replicate or sustain.

While the chapter by Krebs also takes settler-colonial jurisdiction as an entry point for his study, he ultimately places this in a wider context of genocide. Krebs discusses the most recent attempt by the Canadian state to implement a private property regime on Indigenous reserves through the First Nations Property Ownership Act (FNPOA): legislation the federal government proposed and then withdrew after widespread opposition by First Nations communities. Why, Krebs asks, does this struggle over property forms on reserves continue? And what can conflicts over property rights between Indigenous people and the Canadian state tell us about the underlying dynamics of dispossession and resistance in settler-colonial contexts? To answer these questions, Krebs first demonstrates how, despite its similarity with past attempts to privatise First Nations reserve lands, the FNPOA represents a re-articulation of these older proposals as a type of 'recognition' politics, in which the implementation of fee simple property regimes is cast as 'restoring' pre-colonial property rights regimes. Second, Krebs analyses the development of property rights in Canada as a tool of dispossession, drawing on contemporary discussions within geography and Indigenous studies concerning Karl Marx's theory of 'primitive accumulation'. He finally looks at how conflicts over First Nations land and property rights provide an important site from which to analyse how both the formation of colonised subjects and the continued existence of Indigenous subjects are inseparable from relationships with land. Krebs argues that the FNPOA illuminates the process of settler-colonial *resubjection* as part of the continued Canadian project of genocide, whereby attempts to reconfigure Indigenous relationships with land must be understood as attempts to eliminate the Indigenous subject position altogether.

Shifting from issues of cultural and racial difference to issues of gender, Julaina A. Obika, Ben Adol Otto, Sulayman Mpisi Babiiha, and Michael Whyte's chapter (11) looks at land disputes in northern Uganda Acholi after two decades of war. According to customary land tenure, there is no individual ownership to clan land in Acholi, but land is held in trust from generation to generation and cannot be sold. Use rights to land can also be achieved through kinship, clanship, inheritance, and marriage but also through use, for instance when women work on gardens and thereby establish ownership of the land. The chapter focuses on *both* the customary *rights* that clan members have in land through social relationships *and* their social *abilities* to bring forward their claims and get access to land. When people began to return to their homes from the camps for the internally displaced, their (re)claims to land were also claims to particular sets of relationships, of belonging to a family or clan. Land and belonging cannot be separated, and the authors open up the new conflicts, struggles, and dilemmas that are inherent in the integration of land and belonging and were fuelled when the war ended. Women's situations are especially precarious: they get access to land via relations to men in patrilineal Acholi society (e.g. marriages and fatherhood), and their belonging to patrilineal clans can easily be contested, because many of these relations were not formalized during the war. The authors discuss several cases of women claiming different social statuses – as daughters to their natal homes, wives or widows of clansmen, and/or mothers of clan children – and navigate between them to get access to land and gardens that they can work on for subsistence.

Finally, in the afterword Bill Maurer speculates about the future directions of property regimes and how new technologies of accounting and greater societal changes like climate change are reconfiguring how to own, what to own, and how to manage and distribute property. New lines of conflicts and regimes of distribution are in the making, some the result of intentional struggles, as many of the chapters elaborate upon; others are thrust upon us by changes in technology and by the Anthropocene, as O'Donnell discusses with respect to climate change.

## Conclusion

The chapters in this collection show people engaged in property conflicts and making property claims in a wide range of legal, social, political, and geographical contexts. They illustrate how conflicts over property give us an entry point into studying the process of subject formation, of capital accumulation, and of the assertion of territory, sovereignty, and nationhood. They also show how property conflicts can intersect with wider social problems concerning race, gender, poverty, marginalisation, and the environment. While they contain their own lessons about ownership, their common lesson is that legal title only ever gives a partial answer to the question: who is the owner? The point here is not to suggest that struggles over ownership are ubiquitous. In most societies that are not suffering from war or widespread civil strife, there is significant consensus on property, not on the justice of its current distribution, but on how to 'read' the signs of ownership that are there. All of the examples of conflict and contestation documented in this book should make us marvel at this degree of consensus. Contrary to those who insist that the meanings of property and ownership are conceptually simple and historically stable (influentially, Epstein, 1985), these conflicts show that such consensus is not inevitable or universal but the outcome of an immense accumulation of habits and authority structures.

The politics of property is not simply about the legitimacy or illegitimacy of private property nor only about the injustices of unequal distributions of property; it is also about what exactly can be claimed in the name of 'ownership' – and by whom. It is about the tension between sources of authority in a society: between different parts of legal codes, between informal custom and formal law, and most profoundly between morality and political power.

In one sense, the 'ownership model' – widespread in contemporary culture and theory but increasingly under attack in various forms of scholarship and activism (including in this book) – is right to put law, owners, and exclusion at the centre of our understandings of property: in societies with strong states and private property regimes we tend to be able to identify 'owners' without much difficulty, and if we do have difficulty figuring such things out, the police and courts are on hand to educate us. But where we go wrong with such models is when we slide from a pragmatic understanding of property to a dogmatic one: contested property claims may be voiced 'outside' of the current property order and its powerful institutions, but they are claims on the future of property and cannot be ignored.

## References

Alexander, G. (2009a). The social obligation norm in American property law. *Cornell Law Review*, *94*, 745–819.

Alexander, G. (2009b). Reply: The complex core of property. *Cornell Law Review*, *94*, 1063–1071.

Alexander, G. (2011). Pluralism and property. *Fordham Law Review*, *80*, 1017–1052.

Alexander, G., Peñalver, E., Singer, J. W., & Underkuffler, L. S. (2009). A statement of progressive property. *Cornell Law Review*, *94*, 743–744.

Atuahene, B. (2016). Dignity takings and dignity restoration: Creating a new theoretical framework for understanding involuntary property loss and the remedies required. *Law & Social Inquiry*, *41*(4), 796–823.

Bayat, A. (2013). *Life as politics: How ordinary people change the Middle East.* 2nd version. Stanford, CA: Stanford University Press.

Benda-Beckmann, F., Benda-Beckmann, K., & Wiber, M. G. (2006). The properties of property. In F. Benda-Beckmann, K. Benda-Beckmann, & M. G. Wiber (Eds.), *Changing properties of property* (pp. 1–39). Oxford: Berghahn Books.

Blomley, N. (2008). Enclosure, common right and the property of the poor. *Social & Legal Studies*, *17*(3), 311–331. Retrieved from http://doi.org/10.1177/0964663908093966

Blomley, N. (2011). Cuts, flows, and the geographies of property. *Law, Culture and the Humanities*, *7*(2), 203–216. Retrieved from http://doi.org/10.1177/1743872109355583

Blomley, N. (2013). Performing property: Making the world. *Canadian Journal of Law and Jurisprudence*, *26*, 23–48.

Blomley, N. (2016). The territory of property. *Progress in Human Geography*, *40*(5), 593–609. Retrieved from http://doi.org/10.1177/0309132515596380

Claeys, E. R. (2009). Response: Virtue and rights in American property law. *Cornell Law Review*, *94*, 889–947.

Cooper, D. (2007). Opening up ownership: Community belonging, belongings, and the productive life of property. *Law & Social Inquiry*, *32*(3), 625–664.

Davidson, N. M., & Dyal-Chand, R. (2010). Property in crisis. *Fordham Law Review*, *78*, 1607–1660.

Dymski, G., Hernandez, J., & Mohanty, L. (2013). Race, gender, power, and the US subprime mortgage and foreclosure crisis: A meso analysis. *Feminist Economics*, *19*(3), 124–151. Retrieved from http://doi.org/10.1080/13545701.2013.791401

Edwards, J., & Strathern, M. (2000). Including our on. In J. Carsten (Ed.), *Cultures of relatedness* (pp. 149–166). Cambridge, MA: Cambridge University Press.

Epstein, R. (1985). *Takings: Private property and the power of eminent domain*. Cambridge, MA: Harvard University Press.

Finchett-Maddock, L. (2016). *Protest, property and the commons: Performances of law and resistance*. Oxon & New York, NY: Routledge.

Fox O'Mahony, L. (2014). Property outsiders and the hidden politics of doctrinalism. *Current Legal Problems*, *67*(1), 409–445.

Fox O'Mahony, L., O'Mahony, D., & Hickey, R. (Eds.) (2015). *Moral rhetoric and the criminalisation of squatting: Vulnerable demons?* Oxon: Routledge.

Gluckman, M. (1965). *The ideas in Barotse Jurisprudence*. New Haven, CT: Yale University Press.

Grey, T. (1980). The disintegration of property. In J. R. Pennock & J. W. Chapman (Eds.), *Property: Nomos XXII* (pp. 69–85). New York, NY: New York University Press.

Hann, C. M. (1998). Introduction: The embeddedness of property. In C. M. Hann (Ed.), *Property relations: Renewing the anthropological tradition* (pp. 1–47). Cambridge, MA: Cambridge University Press.

Harris, C. I. (1993). Whiteness as property. *Harvard law Review*, *106*(8), 1707–1791.

Honoré, A. M. (1961). Ownership. In A. G. Guest (Ed.), *Oxford essays in Jurisprudence* (pp. 107–147). Oxford: Oxford University Press.

Katyal, S. K., & Peñalver, E. M. (2007). Property outlaws. *University of Pennsylvania Law Review*, *155*, 1095–1186.

Keenan, S. (2015). *Subversive property: Law and the production of spaces of belonging*. Oxon & New York, NY: Routledge.

Lefebvre, H. (1991). *The production of space*. Oxford & Malden, MA: Wiley-Blackwell.

Lefebvre, H. (1996). *Writings on cities*. (E. Kofman & E. Lebas, Eds.). Oxford & Malden, MA: Wiley-Blackwell.

Malinowski, B. (1935). *Coral gardens and their magic: A study of the methods of tilling the soil and of agricultural rites in the Trobriand Islands*. New York, NY: American Book Company.

Manjikian, M. (2013). *The securitization of property squatting in Europe*. New York, NY & London: Routledge.

Massey, D. (2005). *For space*. London: Sage.

McDonagh, B., & Griffin, C. J. (2016). Occupy! Historical geographies of property, protest and the commons, 1500–1850. *Journal of Historical Geography*, *53*, 1–10. Retrieved from http://doi.org/10.1016/j.jhg.2016.03.002

Nielsen, M. (2011). Inverse governmentality: The paradoxical production of peri-urban planning in Maputo, Mozambique. *Critique of Anthropology*, *31*(4), 329–358.

Polanyi, K. (2001). *The great transformation: The political and economic origins of our time*. Boston, MA: Beacon Press.

Reich, C. (1964). The new property. *The Yale Law Journal*, *73*(5), 733–787.

Rose, C. (1994). *Property and persuasion: Essays on the history, theory, and rhetoric of ownership*. Boulder, CO: Westview.

Rose, C. (1998). The several futures of property: Of cyberspace and folk tales, emission trades and ecosystems. *Minnesota Law Review*, *83*, 129–182.

Rose, C. (2000). Property and expropriation: Themes and variations in American law. *Utah Law Review*, *1*, 1–38.

Rose, C. (2006). Introduction: Property and language, or, the ghost of the fifth panel. *Yale Journal of Law and the Humanities*, *1*, 1–28.

Scott, J. C. (1990). *Domination and the arts of resistance: Hidden transcripts*. New Haven, CT: Yale University Press.

Singer, J. W. (2000). *Entitlement: The paradoxes of property*. New Haven, CT: Yale University Press.

Smith, H. E. (2009). Response: Mind the gap: The indirect relation between ends and means in American property law. *Cornell Law Review*, *94*, 959–989.

Strang, V., & Busse, M. (Eds.) (2011). *Ownership and appropriation*. Oxford: Berg Publications.

Strathern, M. (1996). Cutting the network. *The Journal of the Royal Anthropological Institute*, *2*(3), 517–535.

Susser, I., & Tonnelat, S. (2013). Transformative cities: The three urban commons. *Focaal: The European Journal of Anthropology*, *66*, 105–132. Retrieved from http://dx.doi.org/10.3167/fcl.2013.660110

Underkuffler, L. (1990). On property: An essay. *The Yale Law Journal*, *100*, 127–148.

Valverde, M. (2015). *Chronotopes of law: Jurisdiction, scale and governance*. Oxon & New York, NY: Routledge.

van der Walt, A. J. (2009). *Property in the margins*. Oxford: Hart Publishing.

Waldron, J. (2009). Community and property – for those who have neither. *Theoretical Inquiries in Law*, *10*, 161–192.

Wyly, E., Moos, M., & Hammel, D. J. (2012). Race, class and rent in America's subprime cities. In M. B. Aalbers (Ed.), *Subprime cities: The political economy of mortgage markets* (pp. 242–289). Malden, MA, Oxford & West Sussex: Wiley-Blackwell.

# Part I

# Squatting and eviction

Chapter 1

# The right to the city and its limits

## Contested property claims, urban exceptionality, and the fight for relational space in Glasgow's Commonwealth Games 2014

*Neil Gray and Libby Porter*

*This chapter takes up a critical discussion of the celebrated 'right to the city' thesis to examine the significant constraints that can emerge from a rights-based approach. The chapter explores a property conflict ignited by the 2014 Glasgow Commonwealth Games and its related urban renewal projects, in which the state used a Compulsory Purchase Order, a kind of emergency measure for property, to evict one family. Alongside a critical stance on the political implications and possibilities of invoking the right to the city, the chapter seeks to go beyond rights and recognition claims by combining a relational view of property and space with an empirical narration of one family's struggle to keep their property while confronting a state determined to evict them.*

### Introduction

In this paper we scrutinise the limits of the celebrated 'Right to the City' (RttC) concept by way of a vigorously contested compulsory purchase order (CPO) on the site of the athletes' Games Village for Glasgow's Commonwealth Games 2014 (CWGs 2014). We chart the dramatic story of how the Jaconelli family challenged displacement and inadequate compensation claims; the vagaries of the judicial process, and ultimately the sanctioned state violence of CPO procedures – a process of contestation that involved six years of 'staying put' (cf. Hartman et al., 1982) in a rundown, abandoned housing estate while facing the full brunt of local state and media defamation. Dalmarnock on the River Clyde, the site where the eviction took place, has now undergone a transformation from a working-class residential community of primarily social housing to an athletes' Games village, to a mixed-tenure housing 'village' construed as a central plank of the Games housing 'legacy'. This process has significantly shifted the tenure composition of the area from social to private.

Charting the mechanisms of this process and, crucially, the disagreements over its realisation, we question the very basis of rights claims per se. In particular, as scholar-activists, we make a critical intervention into debates over the celebrated RttC thesis, which has become inspirational for urban struggles worldwide. The thesis very usefully promotes a specifically urban or spatial politics which we strongly support, yet the concept and everyday application of rights is subject to three significant constraints that leave it vulnerable to critique as a practical mode of urban contestation. First, the notion of rights often remains too chimerical for practical use; second, the notion of citizenship, from which active rights are derived, is neither universal nor absolute; third, the use of state exceptionality, of which CPOs are an exemplary tool, means individual rights are easily usurped by threatened, implied or actual state violence.

Over and above a critique of rights discourse, we also focus on forms of contestation that might circumvent co-option into individual 'possessory' rights by going beyond 'absolute' conceptions of property (Porter, 2014). Such possessory and absolute conceptions view the spaces of properties as objective, bounded, technical and asocial, thus masking the politics of property's spatiality and its foundation in political economy. Following Massey (2005), we challenge readings that assume absolute notions of property, working towards a more 'relational' conception of property that views the spaces of property as the product of social interrelations and as themselves generative of space (cf. Blomley, 2014a; Keenan, 2010). This characterisation provides an intensely social, and thus more political, conception of space with which to apprehend struggles against displacement and state exceptionality. The deepening politicisation of the Jaconelli family over time, the main subjects of our case study, charts a tendential shift from an absolute to a relational conception of property (even if an absolute conception remained a practical necessity). Such a shift questions assumptions underlying individual property claims while suggesting how a politics of space, and of housing in particular, might be construed and conducted in an era that has seen a marked privatisation of housing in the UK and elsewhere.

Our argument proceeds by laying out the policy and planning context for the CWGs 2014, shifting modalities of property ownership in Glasgow, a narrative description of our CPO case study and an account of the scholar-activist methodology that has informed this chapter. We then present our three-fold critique of rights discourse and practice before illustrating, through our case study, the limits of rights talk in urban contestation and what disagreement tells us about ownership when it is configured as relative and not absolute. Finally, we argue for forms of spatial activism and critique beyond rights and possessory politics through a notion of relational rather than absolute space.

## The grounds of contestation

In 2008, the Dalmarnock neighbourhood in the East End of Glasgow was chosen as the main site for the CWGs 2014 Athletes' Village and primary sporting arenas. Like other urban areas targeted for mega-events and associated regeneration, Dalmarnock has long been subject to de-industrialisation, disinvestment and territorial stigmatisation (Gray & Mooney, 2011; Gray & Porter, 2015). Until the 1970s, it was a relatively thriving and populated area, comprising classic Glaswegian red-sandstone tenement flats with a significant proportion of public housing. However, through the 1970s and 1980s, planning blight and disinvestment accelerated, with resident displacement gathering pace in the 1990s before the land was transferred to Glasgow City Council (GCC) for 'area-based regeneration'. By the mid-2000s, the area had become largely derelict, characterised by under-maintained (though structurally sound) tenement buildings, abandoned shops and large areas of vacant land following phased demolition. Dalmarnock was thus an exemplary candidate for urban property development: a large-scale mega-event to catalyse investment, huge areas of derelict land with little current but much potential market value, a riverside setting and close proximity to the city centre and a seemingly fragmented, impoverished and stigmatised population lacking resources for neighbourhood resistance.

While most residents had been decanted from Dalmarnock by 2008, the Jaconelli family remained in their home, surrounded by advancing dereliction. Unlike most of their neighbours who socially rented, the Jaconelli family owned their small flat and were not eligible for relocation into social housing nearby (Porter et al., 2009). The case study, then, illuminates a wider problem in the UK where individual private property owners in predominantly social housing estates are excluded from the general maintenance and relocation rights procedures that social housing agencies are obliged to comply with. Caught in a vortex of falling property prices, urban abandonment and a ratcheting up of Games-related hype, the Jaconelli family prepared to defend their home, with extremely limited resources, against the juggernaut of Games-led urban regeneration.

Rejecting top-down narratives of positive urban transformation, the Jaconelli family refused desultory compensation offers and campaigned loudly about a lack of consultation and the destruction of a neighbourhood. Their objections to the CPO were heard but lost at a public hearing in 2009. Fighting eviction notices, the Jaconelli family signed up a prominent local housing rights lawyer to represent their case. When further legal appeals failed, they took the decision to barricade themselves into their home in protest, attracting intense media interest and the support of dozens of local people, students, activists and members of the Glasgow Games Monitor 2014 (GGM 2014), which the authors co-founded.[1] After six years alone on a derelict site without services, they were violently evicted in March 2011 and waited a further two years for compensation. Another claim at the European Court of Human Rights, finally considered in 2015, was ultimately unsuccessful.

With specific reference to the themes of disagreement and contested property claims, we draw here on our extensive experience in local campaigns around the CWGs 2014. Our involvement with GGM 2014 began in late 2008, seeking to provide accessible critical information on the Games and a basis for direct action solidarity. Our engagement involved: legal assistance, eviction support, direct action, media activity, blogging, extensive primary and secondary literature research and dissemination, leading public walks and numerous events, the production of our own photographic and documentary archives and interviews with those affected (Gray & Porter, 2015; Porter et al., 2009; http://gamesmonitor2014.org). Before discussing this situated engagement in relation to our case study, we review the limits of rights discourse as we see it.

## Beyond false premises and promises: the limits of rights discourse

The Right to the City (RttC) slogan has become something of a clarion call in critical urban geography since its formulation by Henri Lefebvre in 1968 (Lefebvre, 1996 [1968]; Mitchell, 2003; Purcell, 2002; Harvey, 2008, 2012; Mayer, 2009; Attoh, 2011; Merrifield, 2011, 2013). It is 'an immediately understandable and intuitively compelling slogan' (Marcuse, 2009, p. 189) that has helped establish urbanisation in political consciousness, just as Lefebvre intended. But here we probe some of the limits underlying the 'cry and demand' for the right to the city (Lefebvre, 1996 [1968], p. 158) as a call for practical political action. Through a three-fold critique of rights discourse we scrutinise the RttC slogan as 'empty signifier', the universal notion of rights-bearing citizenship and the sovereign power of exceptional decision making. Underpinning this survey is an understanding that rights claims cannot simply proceed from the premises of political economy. Political economy does not question the foundational basis of private property – which is the material summary expression of alienated labour – but 'takes for granted what it is supposed to explain' (Marx, 1977 [1844], pp. 61–62). It expresses the material processes through which private property passes after the fact – including its languages, laws and *rights* – rather than explaining how these formulas 'arise from the very nature of private property' (ibid p. 61). For us, rights claims tend to forestall radical urban struggle because they tacitly accept absolute conceptions of space that presuppose a positivist, asocial view of private property. Probing the way rights claims operate in urban struggles more closely, then, allows us to uncover the power-laden relationship between property, economics and law and to consider how this nexus might be disrupted and potentially overcome.

### *The Right to the City as empty signifier*

As Attoh (2011, p. 674) observes, Lefebvre's definition of rights in *The Right to the City* was 'sketchy at best', raising basic questions over how rights are defined, whose rights are being identified and for whose benefit. While the capaciousness of the RttC term may lend itself to urban solidarity and a certain urban political consciousness, ultimately such 'strategic fuzziness' tends to obscure complex and highly particular socio-economic contradictions (ibid, p. 679). To clarify, we are not suggesting that Lefebvre was a willing proponent of liberal human rights. In many other works, including *The Sociology of Marx*, also published in 1968,

Lefebvre expresses an unequivocal Marxist critique of such rights. Yet in *The Right to the City* he is much more ambiguous around this question. What concerns us here is the moderating influence of how the RttC slogan is sometimes taken up today, obscuring a deeper critical scrutiny of the viability of contemporary rights claims.

For Harvey (2008), one of Lefebvre's chief supporters, the RttC term has too often become an 'empty signifier' or mere 'chimera' due to the abstraction of its terms (Harvey, 2012, pp. xv–xvi), an opacity which has often left cognate urban literature and practice theoretically and politically underdeveloped (Purcell, 2002). Since the 'rights agenda' is so indeterminate, Merrifield (2013, p. 119) argues, it tends to stir 'the bleeding hearts' of liberals and reactionaries as much as those of pro-revolutionaries. Indeed, it is now a basic banality to say that the slogan has long been recuperated by multiple state agencies and NGOs for purposes that deviate strikingly from Lefebvre's radical intentions (Mayer, 2009; De Souza, 2010). Even the celebrated codification of the RttC into law, as has occurred in the case of Brazil's City Statute, does not finalise the protection of poor citizens. As Kolling (this volume) demonstrates, the RttC in this case is conflated, contra Lefebvre, with an ideology of bounded homeownership. Moreover, the promise of social housing under this codification has led some movements to risk attaining 'possession through dispossession' (by deliberately locating squatter settlements in certain places targeted for eviction so that resettlement might be initiated). Yet the state did not finalise the administrative procedures of issuing formal property title documentation, thus perpetuating precarity and rightslessness. In such ways, Lefebvre's conception suffers from dissipation and domestication: the 'social force' that Lefebvre posited as a 'necessary (but not sufficient)' condition for a new urban life (Lefebvre, 1996 [1968], p. 156) is now routinely eclipsed by institutional and reformist measures and the pseudo-participatory mechanisms of state mediation (De Souza, 2010).

There is of course a long tradition of criticism towards rights under the banner of citizenship. Marx (1844) observed how the second French 'Declaration of the Rights of Man and of the Citizen' (1793) was only a declaration of rights for 'man' in the singular; the liberty of man as an isolated monad (see also Agamben, 1998; Ranciere, 2010). This right of *self-interest*, Marx argued, reflected an abstracted view of citizens under the universal equivalence of exchange, an abstraction from real differences in wealth, privilege, power, occupation and kinship. Ultimately, he observes in *Capital* Vol. 1 (1990, p. 344), the question of rights is not guaranteed by civic membership but rather by a relation of power: 'Between equal rights force decides'.

Yet it is difficult to abandon rights entirely. Within socio-legal theory, there has been much debate between those who see rights as abstract, disempowering and obfuscatory and those who see them as a potentially empowering and necessary feature of emancipatory struggles (Herman, 1993). Schematically, for the latter camp, rights are viewed as an important bulwark against attacks on current living conditions and a progressive 'ideal' against which the behaviour of powerful actors can be measured (Brown, 1995; Mitchell, 2003). They provide a political yardstick that allows power relations, previously understood as 'common sense', to be reframed as inherently political and conditional (Blomley & Pratt, 2001, p. 152). They provide a vocabulary for 'naming, blaming and shaming' (Felstine, Abel, & Sarat, 1980, p. 631), and their abstraction and instability might paradoxically offer the potential for resignification by those not included in their alleged universality (Brown, 1995). Indeed, the critique of rights has often been seen as a white privilege denied to racialised subjects excluded from political membership and civic belonging (Williams, 1991). Yet for those predominantly situated in the former camp, such positions, however morally compelling, may inadvertently assume and obscure what must be critiqued, thus yoking the question of freedom through rights to the very institutions *producing* inequality and exclusion (see Tushnet, 1984; Fudge & Glasbeek, 1992; Brown, 1995).

### The myth of the universal citizen

Once we examine the acquisition of rights more closely we see that the erasure of certain kinds of bodies is structured into the very model of liberal 'citizenship'. The hollowness of liberalism's universal promise, Brown (1995, p. 164) contends,

> inheres not only in its depoliticisation of invidious social powers, not only in its often cruel celebration of fictional sovereignty, but in its emergence out of and sustenance of female difference and subordination.

This feminist problematic is replicated in 'other' subjectivities, albeit with important differences. Contemporary promises of legal liberalism, Hartman argues, do not ultimately challenge the economy and discourse of racial production and subordination but instead seek 'redress within its confines' (1997, p. 234, n.8). Zizek (2009b, p. 125) reminds us that the chimera of liberal freedom is not only applicable to gendered, racialised and other marginalised subjects. It applies, albeit unevenly, to *all* citizens since it always already contains its 'obscene underside': 'the legal-ideological matrix of freedom-equality is not a mere "mask" concealing exploitation-domination, but the very form in which the latter is exercised'.

Regarding the production of space, which we understand, following Lefebvre (1991 [1974]), as a general condition underpinning urban life under contemporary capitalism, Keenan (2010) observes that extant planning systems typically privilege a liberal subject that produces space in its own image while systematically marginalising subjects determined as different from an allegedly universal norm, a process that becomes perfectly clear in settler-colonial contexts, for example (see Moreton-Robinson, 2015; Porter, 2014). The *cost* of 'recognition' within this order is that dispossessed subjects (cf. Coulthard, 2014) must make themselves legible to a colonial sovereign state, which regulates the legitimacy and decidability of any claims on the basis of Anglo-Australian law, thus 'ensnaring citizen-subjects in a web of devastating, calculated dependence' (Porter, 2014, p. 400). Similar limits within the recognition paradigm, albeit with distinct path-dependent trajectories, have been recognised in land disputes in Israel (Yiftachel, 2002), Canada (Blomley & Pratt, 2001; Simpson, 2014; Blomley, 2014b), Cambodia (Springer, 2013) and elsewhere, troubling emancipatory notions of universality within allegedly liberal democratic regimes.

As Merrifield (2013, pp. 120–122) contends, the fundamental problem with rights is that they are founded on the principle of recognition, on the mutual acknowledgement of adversaries. This is the logic passed down from readings of Hegel's 'master–slave dialectic' (1977), where the independent consciousness (for itself) and the dependent consciousness (for another) can recognise themselves only by recognising one another (as both equal and separate). The problems of reification and separation that can ensue from this recognition (Fraser, 2000; Coulthard, 2014), were countered by Marx with the notion and practice of organised struggle and appropriation by social force rather than recourse to (mis)recognition of rights under a reified sovereign state – the typically under-examined 'stage' of recognition. Relatedly, the fundamental import of Agamben's (2005) 'state of exception' thesis, which is integral to our argument here, is not only its critique of authoritarian exceptionality but its calling into question of the sovereign state *tout court*.

### *The state of exception as usurper of rights and citizenship*

For Agamben (1998), the capture of bare life in the nexus of citizenship, rights and law is essential to the establishment and reproduction of sovereign state power. Indeed, the French Declaration of Rights represents for him 'the originary figure of the inscription of natural life in the juridico-political order of the nation-state' (1998, p. 126), a biopolitical process of naturalisation under state sovereignty (*bios*) on the one hand and of separation and abstraction from natural life (*zoe*) on the other. The same bare life that epitomised the totalitarian states of the twentieth century, Agamben argues, was central to the inscription of human rights at the birth of democracy. The biopolitical development and vocation of the nation-state in the nineteenth and twentieth centuries (including Nazism and fascism), he contends, cannot be understood without comprehending how natural life vanishes into the figure of the citizen, becoming the origin and ground of sovereign state power and the state of exception – which can decide who is inside and who is outside the national state (ibid, pp. 126–133).

The link between sovereign state power, bare life and the law is most dramatically revealed in the state of exception. Exceptionality has, of course, been widely scrutinised in extreme warlike situations such as Guantanamo Bay, the US War on Terror and the military response to 9/11. Yet Agamben (2005, p. 14) shows us that the state of exception is in fact a 'normal technique of government', modifying legalistic and political forms in civil life as well as military life. For us, the lens of exceptionality illuminates the increasingly quotidian suspension of legal planning procedures, particularly in relation to 'spectacular' mega-events (see Swyngedouw, Moulaert, & Rodriguez, 2002; Shin, 2012; Guillamon, 2012; Sanchez & Broudehoux, 2013). We have focused previously on CPOs as an increasingly applied tool of exceptionality in urban regeneration and Games events (Gray & Porter, 2015), and here we develop that work with a more specific focus on property rights and rights in general. As part of our threefold critique of rights, we argue that exceptionality undermines liberal rights profoundly and therefore the RttC and rights claims conceived via absolute space.

## The limits of contesting property through rights claims

The crux of this case lies in a contested claim over belonging and ownership in a highly complex field of land and property law, that of compulsory purchase. Compulsory purchase ('eminent domain' or 'expropriation' in other contexts) is the power reserved by a state to acquire land title without the consent of the private owner. Relatively few planning or legal practitioners in the UK specialise in this narrow sub-field, and there is no specific legal or planning aid available to those subjected to its regulatory implementation. That regulatory system at first sight gives the appearance, as legal systems often do, of fairness before the law. In Scotland and the UK, the system is touted as a 'last resort' to be used only after negotiated attempts to settle between the purchasing authority and the landowner fail. In this case, however, there was no attempt by the purchasing authority, GCC, to consult with those they would finally expropriate.

The Jaconelli family ultimately developed a vocal critique of Games-related urban regeneration, but at the outset they largely supported it (see, Porter et al., 2009). They had struggled along for years in a declining neighbourhood, so they were hopeful of neighbourhood investment. What they initially objected to was their exclusion not only from the formal public policy process but from the wider benefits that regeneration purported to bring. When a blanket CPO was advanced in 2008, formal objections were submitted by Margaret Jaconelli (on behalf of her family), other local shop owners affected[2] and one of the authors of this paper (Porter), plus a petition with 220 names. These objections triggered a public hearing. But it was not possible to advance the case that the objectors sought to bring: to hold Glasgow City Council accountable for lack of due process and claim their rights of belonging in their neighbourhood. The only grounds on which contestation could be made was the suitability of the site for the proposed development and the necessity of compulsory purchase orders (CPOs) for acquiring the properties. The state did recognise the objectors as private owners, contesting that their loss of ownership could only be adequately compensated through market-based mechanisms. However, these rights to private property were routinely set against the 'public good' claims being made for the CWGs. Such rights, so the argument in the media ran, could not impede the rights of the broader citizenry to benefit from the public good, framed as 'Legacy', which the CWGs might catalyse.

The objectors disputed the transgression of their citizenship rights by the state via their property rights, as citizens are normally encouraged to do. Yet they were also contesting a different, less quantifiable kind of ownership: their sense of belonging, their relationship to their neighbours and neighbourhood, their 'right to stay put', their right to a home (not just 'a house' or 'unit') and their right to a livelihood. Additionally, they disputed the assumed *necessity* of their displacement (note that the land in which their buildings once stood remains vacant at the time of writing, more than two years after the CWGs), calling into question a central shibboleth of state exceptionalism, as we will shortly see. The somewhat inevitable quashing of their case at public hearing unleashed the next phase of the CPO process, known as vesting. Once served with the General Vesting Declaration papers, the Jaconelli family were placed in the 'zone of indistinction' that characterises spaces of exception: outside the law's protection yet subjected fully to its violence (Agamben, 2005; Gray & Porter, 2015). Now classed as 'trespassers', or illegal occupiers, in the terms of the General Vesting Declaration, their 'bare life' was placed at the very threshold of the citizenship contract (Agamben, 1998). The use of mundane administrative law to re-classify people from social subjects to legal objects in a fraught discursive politics of legal technicalities can be seen in other cases, such as in the description by Persdotter (this volume) of the classification of people literally as trash in order to justify their removal.

But the contest was not over. While the bureaucratic steps involved in securing the titles may have been relatively straightforward in the abstract, displacing recalcitrant bodies was more difficult. Yet this process also reveals the chimerical nature of 'rights' for those without the power to implement them. The case for eviction was heard in Glasgow Sheriff Court, where those declared as 'trespassers' were summonsed. Margaret Jaconelli represented herself, supported by one of the authors (Porter). By this stage the inadequacy of access to appropriate legal support and expertise for those subject to CPOs was strikingly apparent. Weeks of phone calls and meetings failed to find a lawyer or surveyor suitably qualified in CPO legislation to take on the case. Many refused approach because they worked for the Council on other cases. The sense that this was a small club of experts quietly disavowing (or working in the service of) dispossession was egregious. Yet despite the limits of self-representation noted here, the Jaconelli family's legal contestation led to a stay of execution by the Sheriff. They then managed to secure the services of a prominent housing rights lawyer, who launched an appeal to the Sheriff-Principal. The Jaconelli family were not present in court when that appeal was quashed, since by then they refused to leave their home for fear they would not be allowed to return. The phone call from the lawyer at the Sheriff's Court heralded a stark choice: to stay put and face an inevitably brutal eviction or to give up and leave. Surrounded by their family, activist supporters and members of the media, the Jaconelli family chose to stay put, barricading themselves into their tenement flat.

Outside, supporters, including the authors, gathered their few resources. Press releases and calls for support were sent out, and news and television crews arrived in droves. Family and supporters camped out in their cars at night to keep watch. Meanwhile, Glasgow City Council worked hard to stigmatise the family, illegally leaking misinformation about unpaid council tax and the nature of the offers made to the family (see Gray & Porter, 2015). Helicopters circled, and nearby CCTV cameras fixed on the flat. Sheriff's officers arrived twice to serve papers and were twice prevented by peaceful protest, supporters linking hands, standing shoulder to shoulder barring the way. In the pre-dawn hours of 24 March 2011, they returned with more than eighty police officers and fifteen riot vans, clearing the streets of supporters, cutting the power and taking a sledgehammer to the doors and windows. By eleven a.m., the Jaconelli family were finally evicted by force, their remaining belongings smashed and left in a heap on the street.

This narrative, bounded and localised though it may appear, has much to teach us about contestation and property rights, starkly demonstrating the necessity yet insufficiency of rights claims. It was rights that provided the yardstick against which the actions of powerful state actors could be measured and called out and towards which certain kinds of claims could be advanced. Rights provided recourse to forms of legal procedure and compensation, which finally came years later.[3] Rights claims offered the potential to produce accountability, even though that attempt largely failed in this case. Moreover, the legal property rights of the Jaconelli family were not so easy to wrest from them; that required state exceptionality and the exercise of legal force by the police, ultimately costing the public purse much more than paying fair compensation after reasonable consultation. We accept, then, that it would be unwise to abandon rights claims entirely. However, our threefold critique of rights helps illustrate the limits of rights discourse in such disagreements.

First, the public discourse, driven by the proponents of the Games development and their partners in the media, vilified those subject to CPO as profit-seeking individuals 'holding out' for higher private gains to the detriment of the Games 'Legacy'. This was made possible by a top-down discourse of 'public good', driven by the axioms of development and growth, illustrating clearly how 'fuzzy' rights claims can be marshalled discursively by powerful state actors as much, if not more, than those of the disenfranchised (see Attoh, 2011; Merrifield, 2011, 2013). Moreover, the defence of private property rights in this case, however necessary given the terms being contested, served to reinforce the position of individualised and abstracted citizens under the universal equivalence of exchange relations (Marx, 1844, 1977 [1844]). As Porter (2014) argues, claiming recognition on the basis of property rights tends to co-opt struggle into the language of individual *possession*, mitigating the possibility of a broader, collective 'social force' that might question the domination of private property *per se*. To some extent this was the case in Dalmarnock, though it should be noted that the Jaconelli family became increasingly vocal about relational injustice in and around the Athletes' Village site, as we will shortly show.

Second, the case reveals the limits of citizenship as a subject identity through which a rights-claim can be advanced. Once those made subject to the CPO had been deemed 'trespassers', following the General Vesting Declaration, they were pushed to the threshold of citizenship and those relations of civility, duty of care and protection associated with the citizen–state social contract. We have shown the limits of citizenship primarily on race and gender terms, but there is also a *classed* construction of which bodies can belong where and through which registers of belonging. If emancipation and equality are really assured through universal citizenship, then the profound unevenness and inequality between the treatment of different bodies and subjects in this case should not have been feasible. This case, by contrast, reveals that citizenship is by no means a guarantor of equality. Most pertinently, while the Jaconelli family were made subject to CPO, after minimal consultation, through the exceptional auspices of Section 42 of the Commonwealth Games Act (2008), this option was not pursued by Council with regard to capital-rich adjacent landholders. There, financial agreements with the GCC led to massive profits for assorted individuals and companies at huge expense to the public purse (Gray & Porter, 2015).

Third, under the presumption of necessity, which functions as a moral concept to release a particular case from the application of the law (Agamben, 2005), the state of exception usurps all rights. With the state of exception on the horizon, rights operate as a subterfuge, obscuring the unwritten order of things: the state's power over sovereign space. Yet the 'naïve' presupposition of 'pure factuality' that supports the principle of necessity, and thus the state of exception, Agamben argues, cannot be objectively determined. Instead, such factuality is ultimately based on the sovereign decision which is paradoxically anchored to the norms of the juridical order yet has authority to suspend it by means of a state of exception:

> far from occurring as an objective given, necessity clearly entails a subjective judgement . . . obviously the only circumstances that are necessary and objective are those that are declared to be so.
>
> (ibid, p. 30)

What is really going on in this case, we argue, is the state pushing certain classed bodies to the threshold of citizenship and paradoxically using the expropriation of individual property rights to maintain the hegemony of private property *in general*. With the production of a reimagined space of 'improvement', powerful state actors erased working-class relations of belonging by stigmatising them and casting them out of place (Keenan, 2010, 2015). The meaning of rights evaporated because these subjects had been removed to a 'zone of indistinction' by the sovereign decision, a threshold bereft of the law but at the same time turned over to it: '*Being-outside, and yet belonging*, this is the topological structure of the state of exception' (Agamben, 2005, p. 35, italics in original). Reduced to bare life, they became fully subject to the violence of sovereign power while having no recourse back to that sovereign power as the protector of their citizenship and bodies.

Ultimately, the state of exception provided the justificatory architecture for the violence of sovereign power to be wielded in the visceral form of forced eviction. As many have noted, violence is fundamental to both the establishment and maintenance of law (Benjamin, 2009 [1921]; Arendt, 1970; Agamben, 1998; Zizek, 2009a). 'Violence is not aberrant', Blomley observes, 'but central to the law. It is not exceptional, but quotidian' (2003, p. 130). Indeed, violent home evictions and displacements are escalating across Europe due to the everyday workings of land and property markets, where the right to property trumps all other rights (EAC, 2016).[4]

In the UK context, Cooper and Paton (2015) observe an 'unprecedented growth in evictions' as 'tenants are increasingly being removed from their properties to release the value of the land'. According to the Ministry of Justice, there were 42,728 repossessions by county court bailiffs in England and Wales in 2015, the highest annual figure since the data series began in 2000.[5] For Cooper and Paton, such figures represent a deployment of systemic state violence that is vastly disproportionate to the support offered to those evicted while also indicating the wider relevance of individual CPOs and evictions at a time when land and property development has become a primary mode of capital accumulation in the UK and beyond. As we have noted, the possessory rights claims in our case study, however legitimate, may have partially worked to foreclose the quite different claims and practices that were also being made and undertaken. Yet these broader relational struggles around the wider effects of Games-related development and displacement betoken a political praxis beyond rights claims. To these we now turn.

## Conclusion: toward a praxis beyond rights

This case reveals the limits of contesting claims to place, space and a life through the frame of rights and ownership. Rights incite claiming subjects to constitute themselves as individuated citizens only recognisable if they claim their rights as possessive individuals to absolute space. Such (mis)recognition breeds reification (of state, subject and space) and reinforces the status quo (Fraser, 2000; Porter, 2014). Worse, rights and citizenship can easily evaporate under the sovereign decision and are far from universal or absolute. Yet the core promise of rights cannot easily be critiqued away, since in these regressive times they set in motion material political processes and demands and offer at least a formal means of recognising the *limits* of political emancipation through liberal democracy (Brown, 1995). Therein, perhaps, lies the ambivalence of Lefebvre's 'Right to the City' thesis, which seems to contradict his otherwise radical critique of liberal democracy. The challenge, as we see it, is to locate a praxis *beyond* rights, one that does not fully disavow their importance in locating forms of injustice and exploitation but registers their reification as a problem to be overcome. For us, displacing or relegating the privileged place of rights in urban contestation rather than debating their relative merits forces us to consider organised struggle and our own capacities first and foremost. For rights, if they ever come, typically only follow on from the threat of organised social struggle (Mitchell, 2003). In this concluding section, we offer some possible ways of conceiving such praxis.

Collective resistance to evictions emerging across Europe (EAC, 2016), including the rise of 'eviction watches' in the UK (Cooper & Paton, 2015), offers inspiration for the current conjuncture. Many of these struggles mobilise notions of the right to housing and to the city, but it is not rights in their concreteness alone that motivate these struggles because, as we have noted in this paper, and as these activists are all too aware, rights are always already bound to the very institutions that *produce* evictions and displacement. This bounding is achieved through what Ranciere (2010, p. 57) calls the 'privatisation of rights': the implicit restriction of the space of citizenship to a 'definite set of institutions, problems, agents and procedures'.

A praxis beyond such privatised rights may have strong resonances (albeit qualified by important differences) with what Audra Simpson (2014) conceptualises as the politics of refusal in a context of persistent settler-colonial dispossession and disavowal. This political alternative to (mis)recognition, deployed insistently by Kahnawake Mohawk people, she argues, is 'a political and ethical stance that stands in stark contrast to the desire to have one's distinctiveness as a culture, as a people, recognized' (ibid, p. 11). By refusing the frame of recognition, rights or liberal citizenship, democratic praxis is thus configured as *dissensus* (or 'disagreement') forming a *disjunction* from formal institutional coordinates. This dissensual disjunction, Ranciere (2010) contends, is the proper form of democracy conceived as an open and unlimited process of political contestation.

Such a politics, we argue, necessarily entails moving from 'absolute' to 'relational' conceptions of property and space (Keenan, 2010, 2015; Blomley, 2014a; Coulthard, 2014). An 'absolute' view regards space as *a priori* and asocial, and thus calculable and geometric; a 'relational' view regards space as meaningful only in relation to human practice (Blomley, 2014a). A relational view of space enables attention to be diverted away from the absolute notion of a 'thing' (such as a property title) or heavily bounded spatiality toward the network of connections that 'hold up' (or do not) certain types of belonging or ownership in space (Keenan, 2015).

In the case of the Jaconelli family, an initial absolute bounded view of space, fixed understandably on compensation for possessory rights to their home, was undermined in the process of their disagreement with the City Council, leading to an understanding that property rights, and rights in general, do not necessarily protect all citizens. This was confirmed by the use of exceptional law, underwritten by the violence of the state. This led the Jaconelli family to an increasingly politicised, relational view of space that conceived their home as a key site within a much larger contest over land and property relations in Dalmarnock and the East End of Glasgow due to the CWGs and the Clyde Gateway regeneration project. Through their own investigative research and exposure to other investigations (including that of the authors), they began to link their struggle for possessory rights to wider campaigns against gentrification, the closure of a day care centre for a CWGs Bus Park, issues of land speculation, public corruption and public subsidies for land remediation leading to private gain. This was reflected in an active presence, both physical and vocal, at public meetings, marches and demonstrations, numerous mainstream and independent media statements and active solidarity with others subjected to evictions and displacement.[6]

A crucial aspect of property and planning law and of the logics of urban policy is the violence each wields in the severing of relational networks and connections. For example, the boundaries that delineate the inside and outside of 'yours' and 'mine' in modern property law also delineate the boundaries of rights. Conceiving lived spaces in such absolute property terms, as the rights approach does, displaces attention from the controller and the controlled to a depoliticised depiction of the territory or object itself (Blomley, 2014a). What this case teaches us is that the logic of private property itself must be challenged if we are to go beyond possessory rights and the trap and costs of recognition. Short-circuiting a politics of depoliticisation through individuated rights requires a relational understanding of space. The 'social force' that Lefebvre (1996 [1968]) posited as a 'necessary (but not sufficient)' condition for a new urban life must be central to that understanding.

## Notes

1 http://gamesmonitor2014.org
2 In this chapter we have decided to focus only on the Jaconelli family. For more detail on the shopkeepers see, Gray and Porter (2015).
3 Initially offered only £30,000 for their home, they were finally awarded £90,000 compensation.
4 The acronym, EAC, is of our own making for brevity's sake.
5 www.gov.uk/government/uploads/system/uploads/attachment_data/file/499083/mortgage-and-landlord-possession-statistics-october-to-december-2015.pdf
6 http://gamesmonitor2014.org/category/jaconelli-family/

## References

Agamben, G. (1998). *Homo sacer: Sovereign power and bare life*. Stanford, CA: Stanford University Press.

Agamben, G. (2005). *State of exception*. Chicago, IL: University of Chicago Press.

Arendt, H. (1970). *On violence*. New York, NY: A Harvest Book.

Attoh, K. A. (2011). What kind of right is the right to the city? *Progress in Human Geography*, *35*(5), 669–685.

Benjamin, W. (2009 [1921]). On the critique of violence. In *One-way street and other writings* (pp. 1–28). Trans. J. A. Underwood. London: Penguin Books.

Blomley, N. (2003). Law, property, and the spaces of violence: The frontier, the survey, and the grid. *Annals of the Association of American Geographers*, *93*(1), 121–141.

Blomley, N. (2014a). Property, law and space. *Property Law Review, 3*, 229–235.
Blomley, N. (2014b). Making space for property. *Annals of the Association of American Geographers, 104*(6), 1291–1306.
Blomley, N., & Pratt, G. (2001). Canada and the political geographies of rights. *The Canadian Geographer, 45*(1), 151–166.
Brown, W. (1995). *States of injury: Power and freedom in late modernity*. Princeton, NJ: Princeton University Press.
Cooper, V., & Paton, K. (2015, 17 April). *Tenants in danger: The rise of eviction watches*. Retrieved from www.opendemocracy.net/ourkingdom/kirsteen-paton-vickie-cooper/tenants-in-danger-rise-of-eviction-watches
Coulthard, G. (2014). *Red skins, white masks: Rejecting the colonial politics of recognition*. Minneapolis: University of Minnesota press.
De Souza, M. L. (2010). Which right to which city? In defence of political-strategic clarity. *Interface, 2*(1), 315–333.
European Action Coalition for the Right to Housing and to the City (EAC). (2016). *Resisting evictions across Europe*. Brussels: Rosa Luxemburg Foundation.
Felstine, W. L., Abel, R. L., & Sarat, A. (1980). The emergence and transformation of disputes: Naming, blaming, claiming. *Law and Society Review, 15*(3/4), 631–654.
Fraser, N. (2000). Rethinking recognition. *New Left Review, 3*, 107–120.
Fudge, J., & Glasbeek, H. (1992). The politics of rights: A politics with little class. *Social & Legal Studies, 1*(1), 45–70.
Gray, N. & Mooney, G. (2011). Glasgow's new urban frontier: "Civilising" the population of "Glasgow East". *City, 15*(1), 4–24.
Gray, N., & Porter, L. (2015). By any means necessary: Urban regeneration and the "state of exception" in Glasgow's commonwealth games 2014. *Antipode, 47*(2), 380–400.
Guillamon, I. M. (2012). Olympic state of exception. In In Powell, H., & Marrero-Guillamón, I. (Eds.), *The art of dissent: Adventure's in London's Olympic State* (pp. 20–29). London: Marshgate Press.
Hartman, C., Keating, D., Legates, R., & Turner, S. (1982). *Displacement: How to fight it*. Berkeley, CA: National Housing Law Project.
Hartman, S. V. (1997). *Scenes of subjection: Terror, slavery, and self-making in nineteenth-century America*. New York, NY: Oxford University Press.
Harvey, D. (2008). The right to the city. *New Left Review, 53*(September–October), 23–40.
Harvey, D. (2012). *Rebel cities: From the right to the city to the urban revolution*. London: Verso.
Hatherley, O. (2010). *Guide to the new ruins of Great Britain*. London: Verso.
Hegel, G.W.F. (1977 [1807]). *The phenomenology of spirit*. London: Oxford University Press.
Herman, D. (1993). Beyond the rights debate. *Social & Legal Studies, 2*(1), 25–43.
Keenan, S. (2010). Subversive property: Reshaping malleable spaces of belonging. *Social & Legal Studies, 19*(4), 423–439.
Keenan, S. (2015). *Subversive property: Law and the production of spaces of belonging*. London: Routledge.
Lefebvre, H. (1991 [1974]). *The production of space*. London: Wiley-Blackwell.
Lefebvre, H. (1996 [1968]). The right to the city. In (trans. and ed. Kofman, E. and Lebas, L) *Writing on cities* (pp. 63–181). Oxford: Wiley-Blackwell.

Marcuse, P. (2009). From critical urban theory to the right to the city. *City, 13*(2–3), 185–197.
Marx, K. (1844). *On the Jewish question*. Retrieved from www.marxists.org/archive/marx/works/1844/jewish-question/
Marx, K. (1977 [1844]). *Economic and philosophic manuscripts of 1844*. London: Lawrence and Wishart.
Marx, K. (1990). *Capital*, Volume 1. London: Penguin Classics.
Massey, D. (2005). *For space*. London: Sage.
Mayer, M. (2009). The 'right to the city' in the context of shifting mottos of urban social movements. *City, 13*(2–3), 362–374.
Merrifield, A. (2011). The right to the city and beyond: Notes on a Lefebvrian re-conceptualization. *City, 15*(3–4), 473–481.
Merrifield, A. (2013). *The politics of the encounter: Urban theory and protest under planetary urbanization*. Athens: University of Georgia Press.
Mitchell, D. (2003). *The right to the city: Social justice and the fight for public space*. New York, NY: Guilford Press.
Moreton-Robinson, A. (2015). *The white possessive: Property, power and Indigenous sovereignty*. Minneapolis: University of Minnesota Press.
Porter, L. (2014). Possessory politics and the conceit of procedure: Exposing the cost of rights under conditions of dispossession. *Planning Theory, 13*(4), 387–406.
Purcell, M. (2002). Excavating Lefebvre: The right to the city and its urban politics of the inhabitant. *GeoJournal, 58*(2–3), 99–108.
Ranciere, J. (2010). *Dissensus: On politics and aesthetics*. London: Bloomsbury Publishing.
Sánchez, F., & Broudehoux, A. M. (2013). Mega-events and urban regeneration in Rio de Janeiro: Planning in a state of emergency. *International Journal of Urban Sustainable Development, 5*(2), 132–155.
Shin, H. B. (2012). Unequal cities of spectacle and mega-events in China. *City, 16*(6), 728–744.
Simpson, A. (2014). *Mohawk interruptus: Political life across the borders of settler states*. Durham, NC: Duke University Press.
Springer, S. (2013). Violent accumulation: A postanarchist critique of property, dispossession, and the state of exception in neoliberalizing Cambodia. *Annals of the Association of American Geographers, 103*(3), 608–626.
Swyngedouw, E., Moulaert, F., & Rodriguez, A. (2002). Neoliberal urbanization in Europe: Large-scale urban development projects and the new urban policy. *Antipode, 34*(3), 542–577.
Tushnet, M. (1984). An essay on rights. *Texas Law Review, 62*, 1363–1403.
Williams, P. J. (1991). *The alchemy of race and rights: Diary of a law professor*. Cambridge, MA: Harvard University Press.
Yiftachel, O. (2002). The shrinking space of citizenship. *Middle East Report, 223*, 38–45. Retrieved from www.merip.org/mer/mer223/shrinking-space-citizenship
Žižek, S. (2009a). *Violence*. London: Profile Books.
Žižek, S. (2009b). *First as tragedy, then as farce*. London: Verso.

Chapter 2

# Possession through dispossession

## In quest of property and social mobility in urban Brazil

*Marie Kolling*

*This chapter examines the housing struggles of squatters who settled in a public park and heritage site in Salvador da Bahia, Brazil, in order to be evicted by the state and resettled to state-built social housing. By analyzing the moral stakes in their quest for property and social mobility in relation to both the values attached to homeownership in Brazil and social housing policies that strongly shaped their strategy of gaining 'possession through dispossession', the chapter provides a nuanced understanding of squatters' contested property claims in contemporary Brazil and sheds new light on otherwise well-known issues of dispossession.*

In the northern zone of the city of Salvador da Bahia, Brazil, an urban rainforest and public park was re-opened in October 2014 in the peripheral and impoverished neighbourhood known as *Subúrbio Ferroviário* or Railway Suburb. In the 1980s, the park was one of the most visited sites in Salvador and a site of leisure and Sunday picnics, but in the nineties, increasing problems with security – including violence and robberies – made people stop visiting (IPE, 2013, p. 166, 168). During these decades, Salvador was undergoing rapid urbanisation, and informal settlements emerged in and around the park. For years a sign at the main entrance promised renewed government investment: 'São Bartolomeu Park. Soon the largest heritage site of the *Subúrbio* will be yours'. Nearly a decade after that sign was put up, it was replaced with a colourful sculpture with the name of the park. Located in a part of the city that offers its residents little access to public leisure areas, the park was revitalised in order to make it once again a popular place for the wider public to visit.

In order to return the park to the public, the state aimed to protect it by fencing it off. Hundreds of the families who had lived in the park for decades were evicted, as were local vendors who made a living selling refreshments to visitors, which was no longer permitted on the park premises. The revitalisation project not only concerned the restoration of the park and heritage site. It was part of an integrated plan for urban upgrading in the communities surrounding the rainforest[1] and resettlement schemes for the families who resided there. More than a thousand impoverished black families were displaced as a result of this urban development project; they were offered either financial compensation or resettlement to state-built social housing.

Salvador is the capital of the federal state of Bahia and a city of nearly three million inhabitants (IBGE, 2014). It was the first capital of colonial Brazil and has one of the highest percentages of people of Afro-Brazilian descent, at around 80 percent. According to the 2010 population census, the Railway Suburb has a population of more than 280,000 people and is among the areas of the city with the highest concentration of the black population (Pena & Bouças, 2015). Anthropological research on revitalisation projects has criticised the displacement of Salvador's black, low-income population 'in the public interest', as well as the use of the term *revitalise* in association with beautification rather than improving living conditions or spurring social change (Collins, 2008; Gledhill, 2013; Perry, 2004, 2013). Similarly, scholars have vigorously criticised the enclosure of urban commons as contested sites of exclusion and multiple property claims in Brazil and beyond (Blomley, 2004; Harvey, 2008).

In the Railway Suburb, the enclosure of São Bartolomeu Park and the dispossessions of residents and vendors indeed generated critique as it disrupted social networks and livelihoods and caused uncertainty and despair. But it also brought new hope for the future. In a context of pervasive urban poverty, the enclosure of the park brought the potential for gaining homeownership, which was otherwise unattainable for the majority of families in this part of the city. The resettlement schemes for families evicted from the park attracted newcomers who tried to take advantage of the enclosure, hoping that they, too, would be included in the urban development project and the government resettlement scheme and obtain a home of their own.

This chapter examines the housing struggles of these squatters who settled on the fringes of São Bartolomeu Park in 2012. Through an ethnographic account, it sheds new light on otherwise well-known issues of dispossession by way of presenting a case of urban poor who wished to be dispossessed as a means to improve their housing situation. The chapter shows how Brazilian social housing policy strongly shapes the strategies of urban poor. By analyzing the moral stakes in their housing struggles – in relation to housing policies and the values attached to homeownership in Brazil – it provides a nuanced understanding of property claims in contemporary Brazil and demonstrates the importance of understanding how such claims across the globe are shaped and differentiated by their local context.

I start the chapter by elaborating the notion of what I call *possession through dispossession*. Then I examine the ideology of private property that was embedded in the urban development project and promoted by the national government, which the squatters subscribed to and acted upon in their quest for property and social mobility. This section includes a discussion of the particularities of the state-built social housing they were making claims to. It is followed by an analysis of the importance of housing for social upward mobility and the centrality of housing for the squatters' dreams of a better future. Central to this analysis is what I call a *housing hierarchy* in which the squatters attempted to move up in the hierarchy by first moving down and becoming squatters. I then examine how the squatters attempted to make claims to resettlement through the urban development project and the contested nature of these claims. Finally, I describe the outcome of the squatters' struggle for housing and the dismal prospects of their housing dreams coming true.

## Dispossessions

The squatters in São Bartolomeu Park present a case of urban poor who wished to be dispossessed as a means to improve their housing situation. This is what I call *possession through dispossession*: only by giving up what they had by moving to the squatter settlement and then losing that too, when evicted by the state, could they hope to gain possession in the form of social housing of which they would become the rightful owners. As will become clear throughout the chapter, this was an aspirational project. The squatters knew they would eventually be evicted by the state, but they also knew that there was no guarantee that the state would agree to resettle them – this was a matter of negotiation. If they succeeded, they would not only gain possession in the form of housing; the squatters who had previously lived in rented housing were also able to save money by squatting, thus saving for other types of possessions for the new home, like new furniture and kitchen appliances.

This case differs from the extensive literature of the dispossessed in the Global South that shows how disenfranchised populations struggle to retain or reclaim their land under circumstances of political transition and land reforms (James, 2007; Lund, 2011; Visser & Spoor, 2011) or in the face of capitalist accumulation by dispossession (Harvey, 2003b; Levien, 2013; Steur, 2015; Steur & Das, 2009). As discussed by Harvey, urban development reproduces inequality in the city because the neoliberal economic policies that often drive urban development result in a centralisation of wealth and power in the hands of corporations and the already wealthy. This accumulation of capital occurs at the expense of the population in the areas of intervention as they are dispossessed of their wealth, homes or land (Harvey, 2003a). Harvey calls such processes of displacement 'accumulation by dispossession', which he argues lies at the core of urbanisation under capitalism (Harvey, 2003b).

In the case of the squatters in São Bartolomeu Park, it is the poor who – in quest of property and social upward mobility – aimed to 'accumulate possession' by staging their own dispossession. They sought to forge a situation of displacement that would render them eligible for a home of their own in state-built housing. By moving to the squatter settlement, some of the squatters had dispossessed themselves of their rented housing. Others had lived with relatives prior to joining the squatter settlement. They all considered themselves roofless but not homeless – a point I return to later in this chapter, as this was an important moral distinction in the narrative of the squatters' housing struggle as they became affiliated with the national squatter movement *Movimento dos Trabalhadores Sem-Teto* (the Roof-less Workers' Movement). Without inclusion in the urban development project, 'possession' could not be achieved. This inclusion did not hinge on an assessment of their housing needs in view of their situation of 'rooflessness' (Kellett & Moore, 2003) but on the state's willingness to expand the number of beneficiaries in the project and increase the construction of social housing.

## The dream of homeownership and housing politics

In 2003, a new government seized power in Brazil, led by a left-wing president, Luiz Inácio 'Lula' da Silva, from the Workers' Party, which remained in power until August 2016. During Lula's second term in office, housing politics became central to the Workers' Party's political agenda, and a national housing plan was presented in 2008. It aimed to reduce Brazil's massive housing deficit and give all Brazilian citizens 'access to dignified housing' (Magalhães, 2013, p. 16; Ministério das Cidades, 2009, p. 5). Dignified housing was first and foremost understood as homeownership and single-family homes, and the social housing was either built as high rises or attached multi-unit housing.

In Holston's article on self-built housing practices in the urban peripheries in Brazil (1991), he writes about 'the paramount importance of property ownership in the constitution of Brazilian society' (1991, p. 453). Since the 1930s, for the working class, 'a home of one's own is still an all-consuming struggle and lifelong ambition' (ibid). Holston points to state initiatives for making homeownership accessible for the working class in São Paulo since the foundation of the modern Brazilian state in the 1930s rather than promoting rented housing (ibid: 447, 455), and Bonduki (2002) explains how auto-constructed properties expanded rapidly in the peripheries of São Paulo in the 1940s due to the housing crisis in the city and failure of the social housing policies.

By 1980, homeownership had become the norm, with nearly 60 percent of the population in Brazil's metropolitan cities living in their own home (Lago & Ribeiro, 1993, p. 482). This 'all-consuming struggle' today extends to people on the lowest rungs of Brazilian society, and state-funded social housing programs promote and speed up this process by offering free or heavily subsidised housing to people with a low income; lower than the working-class described by Holston (1991). Social housing is publicly funded, planned and built by state agencies, but residents expand and reform their home over time so that social housing typically gains the appearance of self-built housing.

In 2009, the Workers' Party launched Brazil's biggest nationwide social housing program to date for the low-income population, aptly called *Minha Casa Minha Vida* – My House My Life (MCMV). Between 2009 and 2015, more than two million houses were built across Brazil and three million more houses were aimed to be delivered by 2018 (COHAB, 2015; Caixa Econômica Federal, 2015b). This housing program was one of the flagships of the Workers' Party electoral politics. During my fieldwork, advertisements on all major TV channels and on colourful billboards across the city of Salvador promoted the government's 'realising people's dreams of home ownership' through the social housing program.

## The particularities of social housing in Brazil

Social housing constitutes a particular type of homeownership in Brazil. Residents in state-built social housing are exempted from paying municipal tax, including the municipal land property tax, IPTU (Ministério das Cidades, 2010, p. 8). Moreover, residents are intended to own the house but not the land it is built on. Residents gain the legal right to the house they have been granted and the right to use the plot it is been built on (Ministério das Cidades, 2010). This particular provision of tenure rights in Brazil is called *regularização fundiária*, and one of the main objectives of the urban development project was precisely to 'regularise land ownership' (Conder & Sedur, 2009, p. 48; World Bank, 2013, 2014).

*Regularização fundiária* is a policy that was adopted in Brazil's progressive urban legislation, the City Statute, which is a federal law that was approved in 2001 and is an amendment to the Brazilian constitution of 1988. The City Statute aims to provide people of low income, living in informal settlements, with tenure rights nationwide (Lima, 2013, p. 5; Ministério das Cidades, 2010, p. 6). It lays out a set of principles, policies and specific instruments for how to create equal access to land and housing and establishes that the city and urban property must fulfil a social function (Caldeira, 2006, p. 105). The City Statute defines housing as a social right and also ensures the right to social housing for low-income populations (Santos Carvalho & Rossbach, 2010). The City Statute provides urban people with 'the right to the city', responding to the call by Gray and Porter (this volume) for practical uses of Lefebvre's concept, which it has gained in Brazil through this statute.[2]

In São Bartolomeu, the urban development project aimed to reduce informal housing by regularising informal settlements and providing social housing in alignment with the City Statute. The families from São Bartolomeu Park who were resettled to social housing were supposed to receive formal tenure rights to their new homes, but as the project ended, the new homeowners had, however, not received this documentation. Without formal tenure rights, the houses could not be sold in the formal real estate market. The new homeowners who either sold or rented out their house did so in the informal real estate market. The lack of regularisation was curious in view of the fact that the project was partly funded through loans by the World Bank, which also monitored the project. The World Bank has, for more than a decade, promoted the importance of providing poor populations with legal tenure rights and formal homeownership based on the ideas of the economist Hernando de Soto. He argues that providing the poor with land titling and access to property as capital, along with access to banking services and mortgage financing, can reduce poverty (Buckley & Kalarickal, 2006; Rao, 2013). Such correlation between formalisation of property rights and poverty reduction is, however, a contested hypothesis and criticised for the lack of supporting evidence and evidence to the contrary. Titling can result in both security and insecurity; it favours speculators and leads to an overall increase in class cleavage (Nyamu-Musembi, 2007; Rao, 2013).

The restrictions to tenure status of social housing and its lack of formal property status did not, however, concern the squatters. In what follows, I explore what was at stake for the squatters in their struggle for social housing. I first describe the squatter settlement and my first visit, where I met Dalva, the squatters' spokesperson. She became a key interlocutor as I attempted to understand their contested property claims.

## The 'new invasion'

The first social housing estate for families who were evicted from São Bartolomeu Park was inaugurated in May 2012. They had lived in a precarious slum, *Rua das Fontes*, built along a river that runs through the park, which had become more and more prone to flooding since the slum emerged in the late 1980s. When this slum was being demolished, the squatters built a new informal settlement next to it on the fringes of São Bartolomeu Park. The squatter settlement was referred to in São Bartolomeu as '*a nova invasão*'; 'the new invasion.' Deriving from the verb *invadir*, to invade, this term is commonly used in Salvador to describe when people occupy land that does not belong to them and which they do not have permission to use. As it was the most recent settlement in the area, it was therefore the 'new invasion'. All that could be seen of the squatter settlement from the main road, running through the community of São Bartolomeu next to the park, was a makeshift fence that the squatters had put up, which was made from scrap wood, road signs and anything else they had been able to find. Old discarded doors made up the two main entrances and were locked with chains and padlocks. This made it inaccessible for people who did not have any business there and a mysterious place that many residents of São Bartolomeu were wary of. The wariness was also due to the great number of squatters who were outsiders to the community and the drug sales points (*bocas*) allegedly located there. Outsiders and drugs were two attributes that invoked insecurity in an area plagued by drug trafficking and recurring shootouts between police and drug dealers.

The first time I had an opportunity to enter was with Ana, who had lived in *Rua das Fontes* and was resettled to the state-built social housing. Ana was a vegetable vendor, and one day, when I was with her in São Bartolomeu, she needed to collect money from squatters in the new invasion who had bought her produce on credit. I decided to go with her, and it was during this visit that I met Dalva.

As we walked through the narrow, muddy alleyways between the wooden, makeshift shacks, I quickly discovered that there were *bocas* in the settlement, as I had been warned. They were guarded by young men, who Ana told me to greet to show respect. At one point Ana stopped at a shack to collect her money. While Ana was talking to the woman, who did not have any money, a young man appeared in the alleyway. He had a gun in his hand and an expression of disapproval on his face, and he was looking straight at me. The people hanging out in the alley turned quiet, including Ana and the woman in the doorway, and for a few seconds the air grew thick with suspense as we awaited what he was about to do. But just as he approached me, a woman carrying a small child intervened and got in between us, and he lowered his gun. He then disappeared as quickly as he had appeared, and people resumed their conversations. Afterwards, Ana introduced me to the woman with the small child, Dalva.

At my next visit to the new invasion, I set up an appointment with Dalva, who met me in the main street in São Bartolomeu so I could enter the settlement with her. She showed me around the settlement, which consisted of some one hundred shacks. She introduced me to some of the people living there and invited me to see her own *barraco*, or shack, as she called it, which she had built herself. It consisted of several small wooden structures that faced a tiny courtyard, where laundry was extended and a few benches took up most of the small space. Dalva's source of income came from selling beer and snacks, and the courtyard served as a small bar area. When I was visiting that afternoon, the bar was lively, and young drug dealers came to hang out between shifts. When things quietened down, I talked to Dalva about their struggle and how and why the settlement emerged in the environmentally protected zone of São Bartolomeu Park.

*Figure 2.1* The squatter settlement in São Bartolomeu Park, November 2013

Photo: Marie Kolling

## Environmental protection as a window of opportunity

Dalva described the squatters' strategy to 'invade the land' inside the environmentally protected zone of São Bartolomeu Park. This way, according to Dalva, the state would have to evict them and resettle them in state-built social housing like all the other families who had been identified as living within this zone. In fact, they had strategically set up the squatter settlement next to a now-demolished slum, but on a different piece of land so they would constitute a new case of eviction. The demolished slum Dalva referred to was where Ana had lived, *Rua das Fontes*. The zoning Dalva referred to is part of the urban master plan for the city of Salvador that was approved by the municipality in 2008, prohibiting people from living in environmentally protected zones.

According to Dalva, the location of the land invasion was important, but as we shall see, it turned out that the timing of their occupation was even more crucial to the dispute. The location of the squatter settlement in a forest and public park that became a heritage site and an environmentally protected zone is key to understanding why families were evicted from their homes on these premises in the first place and why the squatters expected the state to also evict them. Therefore, in order to explain how it became a window of opportunity for the squatters, I briefly describe the enclosure of the park.

São Bartolomeu Park was legislatively turned into an area of environmental protection by the state of Bahia in 2001 because of its unique biodiversity and endangered species (Sedur & Conder, 2010, pp. 4–5). The park holds a special religious status for practitioners of the Afro-Brazilian religions, such as Candomblé, and has been a site of worship for more than a century (IPE, 2013, pp. 166, 172). The park also has historical importance because defining battles for Bahia's independence were fought there, and runaway slaves, *quilombolas*, resided there (IPE, 2013, pp. 1–2, 166; Serpa, 2006, p. 15). Because of its historical and religious importance, another law was passed in 2002 that turned it into an 'environmental and cultural heritage site in Salvador' (Conder, 2014; IPE, 2013, p. 50). It was in the context of this legislation, as well as the urban master plan, that enabled the state to intervene in the park after decades of abandonment in which it suffered from deforestation and degradation (ibid) and carry out evictions of both residents and vendors.

In order for the squatters to strengthen their position in negotiating their claims to housing and help put pressure on the state to agree to resettlement, they aligned themselves with the social squatter movement, the *Movimento dos Trabalhadores Sem-Teto* (the Roof-less Workers' Movement), also known in Brazil as the MTST. The MTST fights for housing rights for the urban poor across Brazil by occupying unused land or empty buildings in order to be granted the property for the squatter families or social housing elsewhere in the city.[3] By aligning themselves with the MTST, Dalva and the squatters in São Bartolomeu Park tried to gain visibility to the state, as the MTST is a nationwide and well-known squatter movement. This also took a symbolic form, as the squatter settlement in the local community was hidden from view except for the red flags of the MTST that could be seen through the trees of the forest from afar. By joining the movement, they became what Martínez (this volume) has labelled 'political squatters', although few of the squatters, and mainly Dalva, actually got involved with the movement by participating in meetings and marches in the city for better housing.

## In quest for property and social mobility: the housing hierarchy

As mentioned, formal tenure rights did not concern the squatters or residents like Ana who had already been resettled from the park. What mattered to the residents was that the house was *theirs*. If they received the house from the state, it was theirs in practical terms – socially and materially – regardless of whether they received documentation stating their entitlements to it in legal terms. From my conversations with Dalva and other squatters, it became clear that the desire was not about formal homeownership in legal or economic terms. It was about aspiring to a better life – a life that a home of one's own could bring, where one was freed from the financial burden of paying rent and where they were able to 'do housing'. The notion of *doing housing* is inspired by the work of John Turner, who approached housing as a verb and as a process (1972, p. 151). This concept captures the housing practices in Brazil's urban peripheries, where housing is an ongoing – and often lifelong – endeavour of engaging in refurbishing, expanding, decorating and maintaining (see Kolling, 2016).

Anthropological studies on homeownership in contemporary neoliberal economies have revealed that houses can represent multiple values that extend beyond economic or exchange value (Bruun, 2012; Han, 2012; Nielsen, 2011; Sjørslev, 2009, 2012). For Dalva and her fellow squatters, it was indeed the use value – having a decent home to live in – as well as the social and moral value connected to it that was at stake. Squatters repeatedly emphasised having a place to live which was theirs and where they did not have to pay rent, and rarely mentioned wishing to own a home they might be able to rent or sell. In contrast to Martínez's argument (this volume), this finding can be interpreted not so much as an act of aspiration to be included in the private property system in order to participate in or benefit from capitalism but rather as an aim to access the basic human right of a decent place to live within a particular social context. The distinction between property as capital (to sell, rent or leverage for loans) and property as use (to carry out daily life) is crucial to interpreting squatters' goals.

To elaborate the argument of the social and moral value attached to homeownership, and in order to understand why the squatters were willing to sacrifice so much since they were not homeless people but people in need of homes, as they repeatedly emphasised, I suggest that the struggles for better housing can be understood within what I call a *housing hierarchy*. Achieving homeownership was essentially about climbing the housing hierarchy and constructing a house and a respectable life. Melissa, who had received a house in the social housing, said, 'A house is a life'. Such a statement indicates the centrality of housing in people's lives and how much is at stake for those who do not have the house that enables this life.

At the top of the housing hierarchy in the Railway Suburb, and in the most desired position, was to live in a house of one's own, the *casa própria*. Below homeownership was renting. People could also be in an even worse situation than renting, namely to *morar a favor*, 'to live in favour', which means to stay with family or friends because one had nowhere else to live and otherwise would live on the street. It was to be homeless but managing to keep off the street. Below renting and living *a favour* with family or relatives was squatting on illegally occupied land or in abandoned buildings. At the very bottom of the hierarchy was to be without a home of any kind and live on the street. The housing categories in the housing hierarchy are to be understood not only as practical modes of living but also as moral categories of distinction vis-à-vis other poor people, as the specific categories were established among residents in relation to those from whom they wished to distinguish themselves.

Housing was paramount to the modes of distinction among the urban poor living in the Railway Suburb. The squatters distinguished between a house, *casa*, and their shacks, *barracos*. During one of my visits to the squatter settlement, I was corrected when I used the term *casa* to refer to the home of the family I was visiting. They told me it was not a *casa* but a *barraco* and pointed out its material construction of wooden poles, tarpaulin and the dirt floor. Whereas most of the housing in the area was in a precarious condition, it was predominantly made of bricks and therefore considered to be different from – and better than – shacks. This insight that Brazil's urban poor largely compare themselves within their own social class and that the modes of distinction are largely in accordance with their housing situations has also been put forth by Castilhos and Rossi (2009), Cavalcanti (2007) and Holston (1991). The squatters' aspirations of a better life and striving for higher positions within social hierarchies was not in comparison to the superior middle class but their own 'local class positioning' (Fehérváry, 2002, p. 394). By 'local', I refer to the part of the city where they live. In this manner, the categories of different modes of living that make up a local housing hierarchy may vary depending on the specific local context and its housing categories.

The attempt to gain possession through dispossession was a process that required Dalva and her fellow squatters to become squatters, thereby moving down in the housing hierarchy in an attempt to reach the desired top position: that of homeownership.

The head of the MTST in Bahia, Genivaldo, emphasised that the MTST viewed people who were either in a situation of having to pay rent or living *a favour* to be 'roof-less' people without a home, who therefore had a legitimate claim to 'dignified housing'. This was indeed the housing situation for the vast majority of the people living in the squatter settlement before moving to the settlement; they either lived in rented housing or *a favour*. In fact, Genivaldo repeatedly distanced the squatters from homeless people in the interview, who he portrayed as people with substance abuse problems and mental illness and as morally inferior to the squatters. Therefore, the MTST did not collaborate with homeless people's movements or organisations, he explained. To Genivaldo, homeless people – in Brazil called 'street residents' – were people who did not want to leave the street, whereas the squatters were organised and hardworking people who wanted to leave the squatter settlement for a house of their own. He was thus making claims to housing on moral grounds, as squatters were people with certain moral values that entitled them to a proper life, which entailed a proper home.

## The squatters' contested claim to housing

I now examine how the squatters tried to make the housing claims through the urban development project and the contested nature of this claim. From the state's point of view, the squatters had arrived long after all the houses in São Bartolomeu and in the park had been registered, and it had been decided which families were to receive new housing as part of the project. The state's thorough registration made it difficult to argue that a house had already been there before the registration started when in fact it had not.

During the registration process, all the houses in the area were photographed and measured, and they all received a number. The families residing there had filled out a questionnaire for a socio-economic demographic survey of the area. The state agencies in charge of the urban development project had also used date-marked aerial photos to document the number of shacks and houses in 2006, before the project started, and again in 2008. In these photos, all housing units were marked and given a number, and the residents had also been consulted in this process and asked to identify their houses. In this manner, it was thoroughly documented that the squatters had settled on the land after the project had started, and the state agencies therefore disagreed with their claim to the free social housing that was provided to the other families dispossessed of their homes in the park.

The squatters had settled, however, before a fence around the park had been completed, which was supposed to prevent people from building new informal settlements in the park. The fence was put up all the way around the park to limit access and improve the protection of the park. This entailed the construction of paved roads to enable security to patrol along its borders, which in turn meant demolishing houses built where pavement was envisioned by the urban planners. Once the fence and formalised park entrances were completed, both were patrolled by security personnel, and opening hours were instated. The fence was missing on the stretch with the padlocked doors of the squatter settlement. Some squatters found the symbolism of the incomplete fence an important testimony to the incomplete enclosure of the park and to their struggle that was deemed to still be worthwhile. As the squatters refused to leave, the dispute was taken to court.

The head of the MTST in Bahia, Genivaldo, evoked the right to 'dignified housing' that was on the political agenda of the Workers' Party, and so did Dalva. But they both hesitated in answering my questions about their claim to resettlement, since they had arrived after the urban development project had started. In one of my interviews with Dalva, as a way of answering my question, she spoke of the right to dignified housing and the squatters' right to a home from the state, affirming, 'Everyone has the right to a home of their own, the right to dream and be happy'. While this claim was dismissed by the project officials, this evocation of the right to a home of one's own resonates with the Workers' Party housing politics but also with the City Statute as described earlier. As Fernandes (2007) writes, this legislation has elevated Lefebvre's political notions of the 'right to the city' to a legal right. In view of this Brazilian law, designed to ensure the right to housing for the poor (Santos Carvalho & Rossbach, 2010), the squatters did actually have a right to housing. However, the squatters did not evoke their 'right to have rights' (Arendt in Butler, 2009), and the state conveniently ignored this aspect of the City Statute.

The strategy of squatting as a means to pressure urban governments to bring solutions to the massive housing deficits in Brazilian cities has been successful across Brazil in recent years (Bergamim, 2014). It had also worked previously in São Bartolomeu Park. The emergence of squatters, practically overnight, had occurred at another site in the park earlier in the project phase. Some one hundred squatters had been granted resettlement to social housing, which was lamented by project officials, who believed that it had set the precedent for the new invasion.

This time around, the squatters' claim to resettlement was dismissed. After three years of residing in São Bartolomeu Park, they lost the court case, and the state agencies were given permission to evict them from the park without providing resettlement. Due in part to losing the court case and in part to a worsening security situation because of drug trafficking in the settlement, many of the squatters moved voluntarily – including Dalva – at the end of 2014. They returned to rented housing or to living with relatives. The dream of homeownership, once again, seemed unlikely to come true. In the end, the squatters' strategy of moving down the housing hierarchy, enduring harsh living conditions in the settlement, bore no fruits, and the potentiality of possession through dispossession was eventually lost.

## Conclusions

This chapter has explored how an enclosure and revitalisation of an urban rainforest and public park generated hope in the urban periphery of the city of Salvador da Bahia for what is a lifelong dream of urban poor in Brazil: homeownership. The attempt of gaining possession through dispossession was a process that required moving down the local housing hierarchy by becoming squatters in an attempt to reach the desired top position of homeownership in the local housing hierarchy. In a context of precarity, where few opportunities existed, squatting was the means by which to act upon a rare opportunity to – hopefully – realise their dream of homeownership and bring an imagined and better future closer.

After losing the court case, the squatters in São Bartolomeu Park were enrolled and waitlisted in the federal social housing program My House My Life. The waitlist offers no guarantees that those on the list will ever receive housing. In fact, the head of MTST told me that it was exactly this waitlist that they had tried to circumvent by squatting. For how long would the program be expanded in the city? How many housing units would be built, how long would it take to build them, and how many – potentially thousands of – people were ahead of them on the waiting list? These were questions the squatters had no answers to. Additionally, unlike free housing given to those evicted from the park, houses provided through My House My Life are not offered entirely free of charge.

The squatters' housing struggle relates to broader issues of social justice, housing politics and promised futures in contemporary Brazil. With the removal of the Workers' Party from power in August 2016 through the controversial impeachment of the president, Dilma Rousseff, the promised futures of the Workers' Party collapsed. The liberal-conservative interim government (from 2016–2018) has instated austerity measures that affect a wide range of the Workers' Party social policies and social programs, and in this current political climate, the squatters are even more likely to be waiting in vain.

## Notes

1 The ecosystem of São Bartolomeu Park is referred to in Brazil as *mata atlântica* (IPE, 2013, p. 54).
2 The 'right to the city' was launched by Lefebvre in 1968. To Lefebvre, different groups struggle to establish their right to inhabit urban space, which is central to the realisation of full citizenship. He argued that cities can only fulfil their true potential if all inhabitants are able to participate in diverse appropriations of space on the basis of equal rights of participation and appropriation (Gledhill, 2013, p. 118). In Brazil, the right to the city has been appropriated by academia, policy makers, urban planners, politicians, and social movements and has become a slogan and often an 'empty signifier', as discussed by Gray and Porter (this volume).
3 The movement emerged in the late 1990s from the sister movement fighting for agrarian reform and land to workers in rural areas, the *Movimento dos Trabalhadores Rurais Sem Terra* (MST).

## References

Bergamim, G. (2014, 25 November). Invasões de sem-teto quase triplicam durante gestão Haddad. *Folha de São Paulo*. São Paulo. Retrieved from www1.folha.uol.com.br/cotidiano/2014/11/1552793-invasoes-de-sem-teto-quase-triplicam-durante-gestao-haddad.shtml

Blomley, N. K. (2004). *Unsettling the city: Urban land and the politics of property*. New York, NY: Routledge.

Bonduki, N. (2002). *Origens da Habitacao Social no Brasil: Arquitetura Moderna, Lei Do Inquilinato E Difusão Da Casa Própria* (3rd First). São Paulo: Estação Liberdade.

Bruun, M. H. (2012). *Social life and moral economies in Danish cooperative housing: Community, property and value*, PhD Thesis, University of Copenhagen.

Buckley, R., & Kalarickal, J. (2006). *Thirty years of world bank shelter lending: What have we learned?* Washington, DC: The World Bank.

Butler, J. (2009). Performativity, precarity and sexual politics. *AIBR: Revista de Antropología Iberoamericana*, *4*(3), i–xiii.

Caixa Econômica Federal. (2015b). *Números: Acompanhe o maior programa habitacional brasileiro*. Retrieved March 25, 2015, from http://mcmv.caixa.gov.br/numeros/

Caldeira, T. (2006). I came to sabotage your reasoning: Violence and resignifications of justice in Brazil. In J. Comaroff & J. L. Comaroff (Eds.), *Law and disorder in the postcolony* (pp. 102–149). Chicago, IL & London: University of Chicago Press.

Castilhos, R. B., & Rossi, C.A.V. (2009). Subindo o Morro: Consumo, Posição Social e Distinção Entre Famílias de Classes Populares. In S. Rocha and Angela da Jorge Ferreira da (Eds.), *Consumo da base da Pirâmide: Estudos Brasileiros* (pp. 49–74). Rio de Janeiro: Mauad X.

Cavalcanti, M. (2007). *Of shacks, houses and fortresses: An ethnography of Favela consolidation in Rio De Janeiro*. Chicago, IL: University of Chicago.

COHAB. (2015). *Minha Casa Minha Vida Cuiabá: Inscrições Abertas*. Retrieved from http://programahabitacional.org/

Collins, J. (2008). "But what if I should need to defecate in your neighborhood, madame?": Empire, redemption, and the "tradition of the oppressed" in a Brazilian world heritage site. *Cultural Anthropology*, *23*(2), 279–328. Retrieved from https://doi.org/10.1525/can.2008.23.2.279.C

Conder. (2014). *Governo do Estado entrega Requalificação do Parque São Bartolomeu*. Retrieved January 25, 2015, www.conder.ba.gov.br/index.php?menu=noticia&COD_NOTICIA=240

Conder, & Sedur. (2009). *Parte 2 – Política de Atendimento do Programa de Reassentamento Involuntário*. Companhia de Desenvolvimento Urbano do Estado da Bahia - CONDER & Secretaria de Desenvolvimento Urbano – SEDUR, Salvador da Bahia, Brazil.

Fehérváry, K. (2002). American kitchens, luxury bathrooms, and the search for a "Normal" life in postsocialist Hungary. *Ethnos*, *67*. Retrieved from https://doi.org/10.1080/0014184022000031211

Fernandes, E. (2007). Constructing the 'right to the city' in Brazil. *Social & Legal Studies*, *16*(2), 201–219. Retrieved from https://doi.org/10.1177/0964663907076529

Gledhill, J. (2013). Redeeming the promise of inclusion in the neo-liberal city: Grassroots contention in Salvador, Bahia, Brazil. In S. Abram & G. Weszkalnys (Eds.), *Elusive promises: Planning in the contemporary world* (pp. 117-135). New York, NY & Oxford: Berghahn Books.

Han, C. (2012). *Life in debt: Times of care and violence in neoliberal Chile*. Berkeley and Los Angeles, CA: University of California Press.

Harvey, D. (2003a). Debates and developments: The right to the city. *International Journal of Urban and Regional Research*, *27*(December), 939–941. Retrieved from https://doi.org/10.1111/1468-2427.00257

Harvey, D. (2003b). *The new imperialism*. Oxford & New York, NY: Oxford University Press.

Harvey, D. (2008). The right to the city. *New Left Review*, *53*, 23–40.

Holston, J. (1991). Autoconstruction in working-class Brazil. *Cultural Anthropology*, *6*(4), 447–465.

IBGE. (2014). *Salvador*. Retrieved August 19, 2015, from http://cod.ibge.gov.br/232MX

James, D. (2007). *Gaining ground: "Rights" and "property" in South African land reform*. London and Johannesburg: Routledge-Cavendish and Wits University Press.

Kellett, P., & Moore, J. (2003). Routes to home: Homelessness and home-making in contrasting societies. *Habitat International*, *27*(1), 123–141. Retrieved from https://doi.org/10.1016/S0197-3975(02)00039-5

Kolling, M. (2016). *New homes, new lives? Slum upgrading, consumption dreams and debt in Brazil*, PhD Thesis, University of Copenhagen.

Lago, L. C. do., & Ribeiro, L. C. de Q. (1993). A Casa Própria em Tempo de crise: Os Novos Padrões de Provisão de Moradia nas Grandes Cidades. In *Anais: Encontros Nacionais da ANPUR 5*.

Levien, M. (2013). The politics of dispossession: Theorizing India's "land wars." *Politics & Society*, *41*(3), 351–394. Retrieved from https://doi.org/10.1177/0032329213493751

Lima, A. (2013). O direito à cidade e as zonas especiais de interesse social: Um olhar sobre o município de Salvador. In *Anais: Encontros Nacionais da ANPUR*.

Lund, C. (2011). Fragmented sovereignty: Land reform and dispossession in Laos. *Journal of Peasant Studies*, *38*(4), 885–905. Retrieved from https://doi.org/10.1080/03066150.2011.607709

Magalhães, I. (2013). Planos Locais de Habitação na Estratégia da Política Nacional. In R. Denaldi (Ed.), *Planejamento habitacional: Notas Sobre a Precariedade e Terra nos Planos Locais de Habitação* (pp. 13–27). São Paulo: Annablume.

Ministério das Cidades. (2009). *Plano Nacional de Habitação*. Brasília, Brazil: Ministério das Cidades.

Ministério das Cidades. (2010). *Regularização Fundiária Urbana: como aplicar a Lei Federal n° 11.977/2009*. Brasília, Brazil: Ministério das Cidades.

Nielsen, M. (2011). Futures within: Reversible time and house-building in Maputo, Mozambique. *Anthropological Theory*, *11*(4), 397–423. Retrieved from https://doi.org/10.1177/1463499611423871

Nyamu-Musembi, C. (2007). De Soto and land relations in rural Africa: breathing life into dead theories about property rights. *Third World Quarterly*, *28*(8), 1457–1478. Retrieved from https://doi.org/10.1080/01436590701637334

IPE (Instituto de Pesquisas Ecológicas). (2013). *Plano de Manejo. Volume IV: Encarte 3: Análise do Parque São Bartolomeu*. Nazaré Paulista, Brazil.

Pena, J. S., & Bouças, R. L. de J. (2015). Racismo, luta e resistência da população negra na cidade segregada. *Sociedade Brasileira de Urbanismo*. Retrieved from https://sburbanismo.wordpress.com/racismo-luta-e-resistencia-da-populacao-negra-na-cidade-segregada/

Perry, K-K. Y. (2004). The roots of black resistance: Race, gender and the struggle for urban land rights in Salvador, Bahia, Brazil. *Social Identities*, *10*(6), 811–831. Retrieved from https://doi.org/10.1080/1350463042000324283

Perry, K-K. Y. (2013). *Black women against the land grab. The fight for racial justice in Brazil.* Minneapolis & London: University of Minnesota Press.

Rao, U. (2013). Tolerated encroachment: Resettlement policies and the negotiation of the licit/illicit divide in an Indian metropolis. *Cultural Anthropology*, *28*(4), 760–779. Retrieved from https://doi.org/10.1111/cuan.12036

Santos Carvalho, C., & Rossbach, C. (2010). *The city statute of Brazil: A commentary* (C. Santos Carvalho & C. Rossbach, Eds.). São Paulo: Cities Alliance and Ministry of Cities.

Sedur, & Conder. (2010). *Plano de Reassentamento Involuntário de População e Atividades Econômicas.* Comunidade Parque São Bartolomeu Pis Cobre. Salvador da Bahia, Brazil.

Serpa, A. (2006). Gestão territorial do sistema de parques públicos em Salvador, Bahia: contradições e paradoxos. *Revista Ra'e Ga – O Espaço Geográfico Em Análise*, *12*, 7–19. Retrieved from https://desenvrepositorio.ufba.br/ri/handle/123456789/1685

Sjørslev, I. (2009). Kald og drømmestof: Parcelhusets værdier. *Tidsskriftet Antropologi*, 59/60, 21–40.

Sjørslev, I. (2012). "Cash the equity and realize yourself": An anthropological approach to house values. *Housing, Theory and Society*, *29*(4), 382–400. Retrieved from https://doi.org/10.1080/14036096.2012.655381

Steur, L. (2015). Theorizing Thervoy: Subaltern studies and Dalit praxis in India's land wars. In A. G. Nilsen & S. Roy (Eds.), *New subaltern politics* (pp. 175–198). New York, NY: Oxford University Press. Retrieved from https://doi.org/DOI:10.1093/acprof:oso/9780199457557.003.0008

Steur, L., & Das, R. (2009). What's left? Land expropriation, socialist "modernizers," and peasant resistance in Asia. *Focaal*, *2009*(54), 67–72. Retrieved from https://doi.org/10.3167/fcl.2009.540105

Turner, J. (1972). Housing as a verb. In J. Turner & R. Fichter (Eds.), *Freedom to build, dweller control of the housing process.* New York, NY: Palgrave Macmillan.

Visser, O., & Spoor, M. (2011). Land grabbing in post-Soviet Eurasia: The world's largest agricultural land reserves at stake. *Journal of Peasant Studies*, *38*(2), 299–323. Retrieved from https://doi.org/10.1080/03066150.2011.559010

World Bank. (2013). *Brazil: Bahia poor urban areas integrated development.* Implementation Status & Results.

World Bank. (2014). *Implementation completion and results Report.*

Chapter 3

# The politics of legal technicalities

## An inquiry into the demolition of a Roma EU-migrant settlement in Malmö, Sweden

*Maria Persdotter*

*Social conflicts related to Roma – Europe's most persecuted people – are often mired in discourses of sanitation and framed around garbage, odour, and smoke. What happens when such elements are translated into objects of legal governance? This chapter explores the legal process that led to the expulsion of about two hundred Roma from a squatter settlement in Malmö, Sweden. Highlighting the role of legal technicalities, it suggests that the process hinged on the categorisation of the settlement as trash and on the power of the municipal authorities to supersede private property rights in order to enforce standards of health and sanitation.*

On 3 November 2015, about two hundred persons were expelled from a long-standing squatter settlement in Norra Sorgenfri, a formerly industrial neighbourhood in Malmö, Sweden. Most, if not all, of them were Roma from Southern Romania with low and precarious incomes and restricted rights to social benefits in Sweden. Once the police had ousted them from the site, a majority of them found themselves on the street with minimal access to shelter. Meanwhile, the expulsion restored more or less exclusive rights over the site to its private owner, a real estate speculator[1] with plans to turn it into a mixed-use residential development.

At a first glance, this appears to be a typical case of spatial exclusion, with the economic interests and exclusionary rights of the private property owner being upheld and reinforced to the detriment of an already extremely marginalised group of persons. There is much to be said for this. One commentator, for instance, attributed the expulsion to 'cynical urban renewal plans' that perpetuate the dispossession of poor and racialised communities while simultaneously celebrating a sanitised and 'deeply exotifying' vision of diversity (Malm, 2015). Others argued that the expulsion reflected a 'discriminatory logic' and linked it to a long history of institutionalised racism towards Roma and Travellers in Sweden (cf. Mendez, 2015).

While I am sympathetic to these perspectives, I would suggest that, precisely because the expulsion was so intensely politicised, it is important to understand how it came about in an administrative and legal sense. The contestation over the settlement in Norra Sorgenfri seems to provide a counterintuitive example of the ways in which contested property claims interlace with urban social conflicts and one that complicates the narrative of exclusion. For one thing, the expulsion did not come about on the basis of trespassing charges. In legal terms, it was not an eviction. Rather, it was the outcome of a series of attempts by the municipal environmental administration to do away with the settlement in order to address what the administration had defined as a 'nuisance' (*olägenhet*) and a 'major risk' to the 'health', 'safety' and 'wellbeing' of the squatters themselves as well as to the public at large (Miljönämnden & Malmö stad, 2015). Importantly, the injunction named the property owner as its legal subject and accused them of failing to uphold standards of property management pertaining to sanitation and habitability as these are set out in the Swedish Environmental Code.

The registrar at the Malmö Police Department made sure to remind me of this when I contacted them with a request to see some documents pertaining to the 'eviction'. Over the phone they told me that 'the police never participated in any eviction'. What they did was to 'assist the municipal authorities so as to allow them to execute a decision to demolish the settlement and clean the area' (personal communication, 18 November 2015). From the point of view of experience, this probably did not make much of a difference to the squatters, who saw several hundred policemen arrive in the dim hours of the morning to usher them off the site. However, the legal technicalities of the procedure were consequential to how the process unfolded. The squatters' dwellings and belongings were *legally* defined as trash, allowing municipal contractors to demolish and discard them while leaving the squatters with few opportunities for any sort of legal recourse.

Mariana Valverde (2009) calls for an engagement with the mechanisms of legal governance that pays close attention to the politics of legal technicalities. Following, amongst others, Michel Foucault, she argues for the importance of careful documentation and analysis of *how* exactly particular legal knowledges and practices work and *what their effects are.* This is important because the politics of legal technicalities are central to the legal governance and spatial regulation of poor and marginalised people, especially Roma (cf. Pusca, 2010; see also Sylvestre, Damon, Blomley, & Bellot, 2015). In this chapter, I give an account of the administrative process that resulted in the expulsion of the squatters. In doing so, I highlight the significance of a number of legal mechanisms specifically related to property eviction procedures and environmental administration that proved consequential for how it unfolded. I suggest that the expulsion of the squatters was not a simple case of spatial exclusion from private property but rather the outcome of a convoluted process that occasionally worked in the interests of the squatters but which ultimately undid any claims they might have had to the site.

The demolition of the settlement in Norra Sorgenfri was not an isolated event. Roma squatter communities are expelled on a routine basis, often away from the purview of the media and broader public. In 2015 alone, the Swedish authorities demolished or otherwise did away with more than eighty 'unauthorised settlements' across the country (cf. Kronofogdemyndigheten, 2015). The Norra Sorgenfri case was different in that it was and still is so intensely contested. This makes it complicated to generalise from the case. Following Bent Flyvbjerg's (2006) discussion of atypical cases,[2] I would suggest, however, that the Norra Sorgenfri case, precisely because it was and remains a somewhat unique case, gives a particularly illuminating example of the entanglements of property in the context of the legal governance of Eastern European Roma in Sweden.

The chapter begins with an overview of some theoretical perspectives on the role of spatial tactics and property regulations in the governance of homeless and otherwise marginalised Roma, followed by some brief notes on the local context and history of the settlement in Norra Sorgenfri. This sets the stage for a chronological account and analysis of the administrative and legal process that resulted in the demolition of the settlement. The chapter ends with a discussion on the entanglements and effects of property regulations and environmental law in the Norra Sorgenfri case.

## Perspectives on the spatial governance of marginalised Roma

Several studies have noted the centrality of spatial tactics of exclusion (Clough Marinaro & Sigona, 2011; Johansen, 2016; Levy, 2016; Pusca, 2010) and confinement (Picker, Greenfields, & Smith, 2015; Sigona, 2011) in the context of the contemporary governance of Roma and Travellers in Europe, as well as in the regulation of urban poor and homeless more broadly (cf. Doherty et al., 2008; Thörn, 2011). The motivation for such regulation, it is argued, ranges from deep seated anti-Roma racism (cf. Aradau, 2009; Sigona, 2011) to forms of punitive neoliberalism (cf. Wacquant, 2009, 2014) and revanchism (cf. Smith, 1996). To the extent that these studies engage explicitly with legal matters, they tend to treat legal mechanisms as instruments of external ideological and political processes. Following, amongst others, Sylvestre et al. (2015), I would suggest, however, that these 'technicalities' deserve attention:

> Spatial tactics are often justified by revanchist discourses of purification, such as broken windows and zero-tolerance narratives. It is thus tempting to characterize them as naked instruments of domination. But, when we take specific legal mechanisms and knowledge seriously, we uncover hidden logics, dynamics and rationales. To understand their effects demands that we treat them on their own terms, rather than simply reducing them to other logics.
> (Sylvestre et al., 2015, pp. 1362–1363)

It is useful to remember Boaventura de Sousa Santos's (1987) assertion that law is fundamentally a mapping exercise premised on the continual separation, classification and sorting of different social phenomena in ways that often appear to be politically neutral and technical. Put differently, different forms of law 'translate the same social objects into different legal objects' (Santos, 1987, p. 288; see also Valverde, 2009, pp. 140–141). Nicholas Blomley's work on the regulation of panhandling through the enactment of traffic law illustrates this point (2007a, 2010, 2011). As the title of one of his articles – 'How to Turn a Beggar into a Bus Stop' – powerfully captures, the enactment of traffic law works to translate the social object of 'the beggar' into a legal object not much different from a telephone pole or a bus stop. This has important implications for the rights situation of those who depend on begging for their livelihoods in that it tends to effectively undermine their access and use of public space and deflect rights-based arguments on their behalf (Blomley, 2007a). While the context and details are obviously different, I suggest that this observation is pertinent to the Norra Sorgenfri case and to the spatial governance of marginalised Roma more generally.

Indeed, Claudia Aradau (2015, p. 100) suggests that the main security discourse about the Roma in Europe today is a discourse of cleanliness framed around 'the materialities of daily life', such as electricity, garbage, housing, mud, toilets and water. Rather than relying on 'an explicit discourse of friend versus enemy', she argues, '[this discourse links Roma] to a series of more or less minor illegalisms such as theft, welfare fraud, and cultural difference [pertaining to] cleanliness and dirt' (Aradau, 2015, p. 98). It is crucial therefore to understand what happens when such discourses are taken up in practices of legal governance.

Writing on slum-removal processes in New Delhi, India, Asher Ghertner (2012) contends that popular discourses of dirt and disorder pertaining to slum settlements frequently travel into and gain legitimacy in practices of legal governance in ways that allow private grievances to be translated and expressed in terms of public interest and environmental welfare (2012, p. 3). This 'nuisance talk', Ghertner observes (2012, p. 8), tends to attribute various aesthetic annoyances and private grievances to particular objects (e.g. the slum), as well as to particular subjects (e.g. the slum dweller, or the beggar). In doing so, 'nuisance talk' frequently identifies these as causes rather than effects of urban decay. In a similar vein, Valverde suggests that the category of nuisance is fundamentally spatialising in that it locates and localises problems and solutions to specific sites and properties. Nuisance law, in the North American context, she argues, regulates only property and its uses (2011, p. 294). By definition, 'nuisances always have specific and usually local solutions' (2011, p. 296), and the protections it affords are not rights belonging to persons but 'privilege[s] that [flow] from one's links to property' (2011, p. 295).

## Property rights, proprietary duties

Indeed, to the extent that the 'Roma problem' in the European Union (EU) is frequently translated into a 'space problem' (Pusca, 2010), the legal governance of Roma is tethered to the scale of urban land relations and property. As such it is important to consider the specificities of property regulations. Blomley

(2004b, p. xv) notes that 'urban scholars have tended to underplay the importance of property as a set of political relations to urban social relations' and calls for an engagement with property that is attentive to its diverse politics. Specifically, he suggests that critically minded scholars should be careful not to reproduce hegemonic accounts of property in which property in land is taken to be synonymous with private property, defined as a bounded space over which a solitary owner exercises absolute exclusionary rights (see also Blomley, 2004a, pp. 636–637). This is the prevailing conception of property in classical economic theory as well as in contemporary neo-liberal discourse. However, it is morally impoverished and descriptively inaccurate (see also Singer, 2000, p. 71). Private property in its imagined ideal form simply does not exist. While celebrated for its ability to sustain autonomy and privacy by marking a boundary between the realm of private affairs and state power, private property is fundamentally embedded in state and collective forms of power and regulated in all sorts of ways (Blomley, 2004b, p. xvii).

Moreover, the classical conception of property is in perpetual tension with an alternative conception that sees property as an important material basis for the promotion of public interests and social order (Blomley, 2007b, p. 620; see also Rose, 1994, p. 59). This has been referred to by some as the proprietarian conception of property, and its roots stretch back to European feudal societies in which property relations were fundamental to the maintenance and reproduction of fixed social hierarchies (Alexander, 1998; Harding, 2002; Rose, 1994). Indeed, Donald Krueckeberg (1995, p. 302) notes that the word 'property' shares its etymological roots with the word propriety (from Latin and Old French *proprieté*) and suggests that although property today does not serve the same social functions as it did in feudal times, it nevertheless continues to be wedded to normative notions of conformity and correctness and to ideas about 'the public interest'.

As a set of legal relations, property, of course, involves responsibilities that reflect norms and principles of order, propriety and public good. This is acknowledged by legal property theorists such as Anthony Maurice Honoré (1961), whose 'incidents of liberal ownership' include – in addition to the rights to possess, use and manage – a number of prohibitions on harmful use. For Honoré, these prohibitions give legitimacy to ownership and guarantee the integrity of the liberal property regime as a whole. Honoré gives the example of a landowner who is allowed to build on the land but only in such a way that the building does not collapse onto the neighbour's land. As I have already mentioned, the administrative process pertaining to the settlement in Norra Sorgenfri hinged on a legal argument about such prohibitions. Put differently, it centred on 'proprietary duties' as opposed to 'property rights'.

In what follows I will provide some brief comments on the local context and history of the settlement in Norra Sorgenfri and show how private complaints over dirt and disorder were taken up by the authorities and translated in the language of the Environmental Code into a nuisance and a risk to the health and well-being of the squatters as well as the broader public. Furthermore, I will show how the enactment of environmental law to do away with the settlement came to activate property law and regulations in ways that exposed a complicated and convoluted relationship between hegemonic and proprietarian conceptions of property and between property rights and property duties.

## 'A good place to live'

Norra Sorgenfri is an industrial area wedged in between several residential neighbourhoods close to the city centre. From the late 1800s and until the mid-1980s, the area was dominated by a variety of industries, the municipal gasworks and a transit depot. While there are still some industries left in the neighbourhood, the municipal planning department has adopted a plan to redevelop Norra Sorgenfri into a mixed-use residential neighbourhood. Several lots in the area, however, are still vacant. A private real estate speculator (Industrigatan i Malmö AB) owns the particular lot where the Roma squatters lived. In the cadastre it is called *Brännaren 19*, but colloquially it is better known as 'the steppe' (*Stäppen*) or 'the vacant lot' (*Ödetomten*). Many of its former residents simply refer to it as 'the place'. Over the years it has been the site of a variety of informal activities, ranging from short-lived squatter settlements to guerrilla gardening projects and the DIY construction of a concrete skateboard park (Andersson, 2010).

The settlement in question was set up incrementally over the spring and summer of 2014. At first it consisted of a small group of tents and makeshift huts. Over time, however, more people moved into the community, and the settlement began to take on more of an established character. Many parked their vehicles and trailer homes on the site or used discarded construction materials, pallets and tarps to build small cabins that they furnished with salvaged woodstoves and furniture. While there was a steady turnover of people on the site, some stayed for well over a year. Looking back at life in Norra Sorgenfri almost a year after the settlement was demolished, former resident Gina Ionescu explains that '[it] was a good place to live. It was like a village. There was our trailer. There was the café. I feel sorry for this place' (quoted in Thornell, 2016).[3]

The settlement was not set up with an explicit political agenda. Still, it was from the very beginning an intensely politicised place. As previously mentioned, most of the persons who lived in the settlement were EU citizens from Southern Romania. The EU framework on freedom of movement sets out the right of all EU citizens to move and reside within another member state for up to three months. However, to be able to stay past the initial three-month period, one has to either be employed or be seen to have a genuine chance of obtaining work. Furthermore, one is expected to have 'sufficient resources for [oneself] and [one's] family members not to become a burden on the social assistance system of the [host state]' (see Directive 2004/38/EC of the European Parliament and of the Council). In Sweden, as in most other EU member states, EU citizens who do not meet these requirements are almost entirely restricted from accessing

*Figure 3.1* A picture of the settlement taken on 1 November 2015 during a protest, two days before the expulsion

Photo: Jenny Eliasson, Malmö Museer

social benefits and services. This places homeless EU citizens in a position in which they have minimal access to the kinds of services that are available to most other homeless individuals.

Following the accession of Bulgaria and Romania to the European Union (EU) in 2007, there has been a growing visibility of homeless and otherwise marginalised persons from these countries in cities and towns across Sweden. This has disrupted widespread understandings of Sweden as an egalitarian society in which extreme poverty and homelessness are a rare sight and stirred debates over questions of citizenship and migration, human rights and social justice (Hansson, 2014; Levy, 2016). Referred to in much of the mainstream media as 'Sweden's largest slum' (see for example Karlsson, 2015), the settlement in Norra Sorgenfri was an important locus of broader ongoing controversies over the presence and situation of homeless EU citizens in Sweden.

Arguably, the expulsion and subsequent demolition of the settlement marked a pivotal moment in the context of these debates. In the days leading up to it, the national coordinator for so-called 'vulnerable EU-citizens', Martin Valfridsson, proposed a 'zero-tolerance approach to unauthorised settlements' (Saarinen, 2015; see also SOU, 2016, p. 6). While many applauded this initiative (e.g. Magnusson, 2015), the expulsion also served to galvanise opposition to what many saw as a blatant refusal on the part of the authorities to address the humanitarian needs of homeless EU citizens. The squatters themselves organised a two-week protest camp outside city hall to demand an alternative site where they might live and respect for their rights as Roma EU citizens. Meanwhile, the United Nations Office of the High Commissioner of Human Rights (UN-OHCHR, 2015) issued a statement in which they criticised the expulsion on grounds that it violated a number of international human rights norms and reinforced the marginalisation of Roma in Europe.

## Nuisance allegations and questions of liability

How did this intensely politicised and contested expulsion come about then? It is interesting to note that it did not begin as a conflict over property. In fact, for many months, neither the property owner nor the authorities did anything to address the apparent breach of property rights directly. Rather, the municipal environmental administration initiated a case pertaining to the settlement in response to a number of nuisance complaints from nearby residents and business owners. While some expressed empathy and concern for the residents, others were outright disdainful. One person, for example, called in to voice their concern that 'Malmö [was] turning into a slum-city' and asked that the authorities 'do something about the pack'.[4] The owner of an adjacent business complained that the garbage situation on the site was getting out of hand and asked the municipal authorities to do something about the fact that 'a major social issue ha[d] landed in their neighbour's yard'. Many complained about smoke and foul odours or commented on the unsanitary conditions in the settlement – some even compared the squatters to animals. The following excerpt is somewhat typical of the kinds of emails and phone calls that the environmental administration received during the winter and early spring of 2015:

> I live close to [the settlement] and when I open my window at night I can feel its smell. It smells of smoke and chemicals. In one corner of the lot there is a toilet. I see and smell this every day. I have a dog, and I make sure to pick up after her. Meanwhile these people defecate out in the open. It is absurd!

Smoke, odours, litter, excrement. These are all categories of environmental law. The Swedish Environmental Code, which was adopted in its current form in 1999, is a composite of sixteen previously existing statutes, including the Environmental Protection Act, the Nature Conservancy Act, the Health and Safety Act and elements of nuisance law (Nilsson, 2010). The sections of the Environmental Code that deal with public health and safety issues, in particular, have a genealogy that traces back to the early 1900s and the formation of the national social state. Indeed, health and safety protections, especially as they related to the politics of housing provision and standards, were central to the constitution of the Swedish welfare state in the early to mid-1900s (cf. Molina, 1997). 'The

People's Home' (*Folkhemmet*), the foremost imaginary of the social democracy of the 1930s, emphasised the provision and management of appropriate housing (bright, clean, modern, spacious) as a two-pronged strategy to address the housing crises of the time and simultaneously create a respectable people. 'Dirt-Sweden' (*Lort-Sverige*), with overcrowding and poor living standards, was to give way to a new and improved social order.

Today, health protection and environmental administration is to a large extent a municipal responsibility (Nilsson, 2010). In 2008 it was revealed that the environmental administration of the City of Malmö had ignored signs and failed to take action against a major housing corporation notorious for its slumlord practices. Following this high-profile case, the municipality invested significant resources into monitoring and enforcing regulations pertaining to housing standards. The municipality also instituted a specialised unit to focus on proactive and pre-emptive housing inspections (Bubenko, 2014). Importantly, it was this unit that was tasked with investigating the situation in the settlement in Norra Sorgenfri.

Based on some of the complaints, as well as on observations made during a number of visits to the settlement, the Environmental Administration determined that there was a problem with littering on the site and proceeded to issue an injunction which ordered the property owner, Industrigatan i Malmö AB, to 'clean the site' and 'remove the litter' or face a fine of 50,000 SEK (c. €5,160) (Miljöförvaltningen & Malmö stad, 2015a). The injunction hinged on the pragmatic reasoning that since the littering was being carried out by a large number of people who were staying on the property temporarily and who could not easily be identified and submitted to administrative action, the property owner should be considered liable for failing to prevent it from appearing on the site. The property owner appealed the decision to the County Administrative Board (*Länsstyrelsen i Skåne*) and made the argument that, although the firm owned the land, they were not the de facto occupants and users of it, and therefore they should not be liable for the litter (Law Solution, 2015). The environmental administration, however, maintained that the property owner had failed to comply with the duty to observe prohibitions on harmful use, stressing that the property owner had failed to 'protect their property' by not properly fencing and guarding it. The County Administrative Board ultimately upheld the Environmental Administration's injunction but removed the requirement on the property owner to pay a fine, acknowledging that it would be practically complicated for them to abide by the injunction (Länsstyrelsen Skåne, 2015).

## Ineffective evictions and challenges of identification

In response to the actions of the Environmental Administration, the property owner turned first to the so-called Enforcement Authority (*Kronofogdemyndigheten*) and later to the police to have the squatters evicted. The fact that the settlement was located on private, as opposed to public, property mattered a great deal for how these requests were taken up and processed. While one might assume the integrity and scope of private property rights to be such as to make it easier to evict someone from private property than from public lands, it turned out in this case to be the other way around. Indeed, to evict the squatters from the site in Norra Sorgenfri proved complicated, not to say impossible.

When it comes to 'unauthorised settlements' on public lands, the police authorities can generally expel or remove someone in order to 'ward off a punishable act' under the Public Order Act (1993:1617) or the Police Act (1984:387) or based on municipal ordinances. In fact, during the time that the conflict over the settlement in Norra Sorgenfri was ongoing, the municipal authorities enlisted the support of the police to do away with a number of settlements located in parks and on state property. Often, they did so based on public order ordinances that make it an offence to pitch a tent on municipal land except for one designated campground at the outskirts of the city.

These pieces of public order law, however, generally do not apply in situations in which someone is seen to be trespassing on private land property. Trespassing is instead defined in the Swedish Penal Code (*Brottsbalken*, 4 ch 6 § 2, 3) as a crime punishable by fine or, in some rare cases, prison. The police have a mandate to act on the basis of the legislation. However, in most cases it is the Enforcement Authority (*Kronofogdemyndigheten*) that is primarily responsible for dealing with situations of trespassing.[5] The Enforcement Authority is a state agency responsible for debt collection and related matters, and it deals with public as well as private claims over taxes, custom duties, parking fines, library fees, rent payments and eviction requests.[6] As a basic principle of legal certainty, any request to the Enforcement Authority has to identify its subject, who can be natural or legal persons, by their name, and preferably also by their personal identity number.[7] The onus, importantly, is on the individual or firm making the request to supply this information. In situations in which a property owner seeks, for instance, to have a lease-holding tenant removed, this is usually never an issue. However, in the case of the Norra Sorgenfri settlement, the ambiguous legal status of the squatters, in combination with the fact that there was a steady turnover of persons on the site, meant that the requirement to specify the identities of the squatters became a stumbling block for the authorities, as well as for the property owner.[8]

After the owner was informed that the Environmental Administration had initiated a case related to their property, they turned to the Enforcement Authority with a request to have one of the squatters removed from the site. The request was formally approved. However, when the staff from the Enforcement Authority went to the settlement to inform this individual of their pending eviction, they found that the person had already left. Similarly, a few months later the Enforcement Authority approved a request to evict a person named 'Alexander Stoyan'. On site in the settlement, however, the staff was informed that although there was a person named Alexandru Stoian[9] living there, the name on his identity card was different from the one on the eviction order, and therefore he could not be evicted.

*Figure 3.2* A notice of eviction from the Enforcement Authority left in the chain-link fence surrounding the settlement in Norra Sorgenfri, spring 2015

Photo: Jenny Eliasson, Malmö Museer

In connection with their attempts to evict the squatters, the property owner also made requests to the police authority to use their powers to identify the squatters. The police, however, maintained that the issue should first and foremost be dealt with by the Enforcement Authority and insisted that it was not within their mandate to carry out any identity controls on the site (Häggström, 2015). Later, in April 2015, the owner filed an official report with the police, charging the squatters collectively with trespassing (case no. 5000-K435770). The police authorities responded to this first by referring to the Enforcement Authority, reasoning that the squatters might in fact have some legitimate claim to the site simply due to the fact that the owner had waited so long to take action on the matter. The chief operating officer, Mats Karlsson, went on record saying that 'now that the people have been there so long they have some form of occupancy right. It is complicated, but that is our interpretation' (quoted in Persson, 2015). Later the official story changed. When Mats Karlsson was asked the same question a few months later, he responded that it had simply been a matter of priorities; the police had been overburdened with other, more pressing issues, and half a year later when I interviewed Mats Karlsson he admitted that he and many others had felt 'uneasy about the case' and wary that any involvement would reflect negatively on them' (personal communication, 12 April 2016).

## Administrative attempts to circumvent the challenges of identification

When the Environmental Administration's initial injunction did not produce the intended outcome, and in recognition of the fact that it had proved difficult for the owner to have the squatters evicted, the administration attempted instead to impose a prohibition (Miljöförvaltningen & Malmö stad, 2015b) which specified that *no one* should be allowed to do any of the following things on the site:

1) Erect or store tents, buildings, trailers and other devices for accommodation
2) Live and stay overnight
3) Disperse and store garbage
4) Defecate on land and facilities
5) Burn solid fuels

It is interesting to note that the problem definition changed from the first injunction to this prohibition. Whereas the former was based on nuisance complaints and centred on the supposed interests of 'those that live and work nearby', the latter, instead, foregrounded a language of humanitarianism and cast the residents of the settlement as sufferers of unsanitary conditions and poor housing standards.

The prohibition was addressed, in the first instance, to the owner. Shortly thereafter the Environmental Administration also issued a prohibition addressed collectively to the residents of the settlement (Miljöförvaltningen & Malmö stad, 2015c). After positing these prohibitions, the environmental administration announced that they would seek the assistance of the police to expel the residents and demolish the settlement.

With few alternative places to go, some of the squatters, along with allies and supporters, decided to appeal the decision. Members of the legal activism group Centre for Social Rights (*Centrum för Sociala Rättigheter*) drafted an appeal that challenged the prohibition on a number of different grounds. One of its main arguments was that the Environmental Administration's intended actions would only make the residents' health and sanitary situation worse. The County Administrative Board, which was the court of first instance, did not test this or any other substantive issue but overturned the case on procedural grounds. Specifically, the County Administrative Board ruled that since the prohibition failed to name its subjects, it would not be practically possible to enact it. Furthermore, the court stressed that the particular sections of the Environmental Code that served as the basis for the prohibition had to be explicitly addressed to individual persons in line with principles of legal certainty. The Environmental Administration appealed the judgement to the Land and Environment Court, which upheld it, and then again to the Land and Environment Court of Appeal.

Altogether this significantly delayed the Environmental Administration's efforts to do away with the settlement, and the ruling allowed the squatters time to organise opposition to the actions of the Environmental Administration and put together a call for an alternative site. Over the spring and summer and into the fall of 2015, they organised a number of protests, all calling on the municipality to provide some form of alternative shelter. According to some, this was the largest display of Roma rights activism in recent Swedish history (Lauffs, 2015).

Meanwhile, the public pressure on the authorities to expel the squatters and demolish the settlement was increasing. For instance, in September of 2015, the popular investigative TV show *Uppdrag Gransking* ran a feature story on the settlement, which depicted the squatters in an unfavourable light and called into question why the authorities would not simply evict them.

In late October 2015, the Environmental Council of the City of Malmö (the political counterpart to the Environmental Administration) made a decision to invoke what is called a ‘correction' (26 ch. § 18 Miljöbalken) in order to move the squatters along and demolish the settlement (Miljönämnden & Malmö stad, 2015). A correction is a special legal mechanism that allows the authorities to step in to correct a violation of environmental law when the responsible parties cannot be identified or when it is otherwise deemed necessary to do so. It is premised on the sovereign power of the state to instate what is essentially a state of exception in order to safeguard that which it deems to be the public interest. As such, a correction is effective even when it is appealed.

What is noteworthy about the decision is the extent to which it foregrounded a language of care and compassion for the squatters. It stressed the urgency of the situation and emphasised that the residents were in immediate danger of harm, that the sanitary conditions would only get worse over time and that the pending winter was likely to exacerbate the already difficult conditions in the camp. At a press conference, Carina Svensson, the chairperson of the Environmental Council, defended the decision to empty and demolish the settlement with the following words:

> We cannot let it be acceptable that people live in huts, in tents where there is no access to water, to sanitation, to hygiene, and so on. We have in Sweden a law which says that everyone should get to live in a dignified and good way, and it is not dignified to live [as they do in the settlement].
>
> (Field notes, 27 October 2015)

The Environmental Council based its decision on the first injunction, which identified the owner as being liable for the littering on the site, as well as on the prohibition that barred the owner from allowing anyone to live on the property. The correction, in other words, identified the owner as being liable for the situation on the site. At the same time, it reduced the residents to the legal status of a third party: a group of people that simply had to be removed from the site in order for the authorities to enact the decision. As a result of this, the residents were legally side-lined in a way that allowed the Environmental Council to circumvent the complicated issue of identification entirely and which ultimately left the residents with few opportunities for legal recourse. Meanwhile, the correction negated any claim they might have had to the property and reduced their dwellings and private possessions to the legal status of litter.

## Discussion and conclusion

Given that the presence and situation of homeless and otherwise marginalised Roma across Europe is frequently translated into 'a space problem' (Pusca, 2010) and framed around the materialities of their daily lives (Aradau, 2015), it is important to pay close attention to the specificities of the kinds of spatial tactics that characterise the governance of these persons and their whereabouts. In this chapter I have attempted to do so by tracing the administrative and legal processes that resulted in the demolition of the settlement in Norra Sorgenfri, Malmö, Sweden. As I have explained, the demolition undid the squatters' claims to the site and placed many of them in a situation in which they had, and still more than a year later have, minimal access to shelter. However, it was not a straightforward eviction or a simple case of exclusion. Rather, the Norra Sorgenfri case is an example of the often messy entanglements of property relations – and the technical details of property regulation – in urban social conflicts. In addition, it is an example that challenges the hegemonic conception of private property as an area over which a solitary owner exercises absolute and exclusionary rights.

The conflict over the settlement was never primarily about property in the conventional sense; the property owner, for one, did not attempt to evict the squatters except as a response to the actions of the Environmental Administration. Likewise, the various authorities, including the police, did not seem too concerned with the apparent breach of private property rights. Rather, the Environmental Administration's numerous attempts to do away with the settlement were a response to nuisance complaints and concerns about the sanitary situation in and around the settlement – and they centred heavily on a language of humanitarian concern for the health, safety and well-being of the squatters and nearby residents.

Furthermore, the administrative and legal action of the Environmental Administration mobilised property regulations in some rather convoluted ways. While demolition had the effect of restoring the exclusive and exclusionary rights to the private property owner, the Environmental Administration initially targeted the property owner for failing to uphold certain standards of order and cleanliness. In other words, the process involved the mobilisation of a negative instance of property rights, a kind of *proprietary duty*. This seems to lend support to Jennifer Nedelsky's assertion that '[if] property [is a] boundary to government power, [it is a] boundary government itself draws' (Nedelsky, 1990, p. 248). At the same time, the case blurs the distinction between the hegemonic and the proprietarian conception of private property (cf. Blomley, 2007b). The Environmental Administration accused the private property owner of failing to exercise their proprietary duties to maintain order and cleanliness. Their prescription for how the property owner should enact these duties, however, was steeped in a language of privacy that reflected the hegemonic conception of private property and property rights: 'erect a fence, lock the gates'. As in the case of the contested compulsory purchase order on the site of the Glasgow 2014 Commonwealth Games Athletes' Village that Neil Gray and Libby Porter discuss in their contribution to this volume, the authorities used their power to supersede private property rights in order to maintain the regime of private property.

Throughout this chapter I have attempted to highlight how some of the legal mechanisms that were mobilised to do away with the settlement actually had the opposite effect. The procedural technicalities, as well as the general confusion related to the issue of identification, influenced how the process unfolded and were consequential in determining its outcome, not least because they enabled the squatters to stay in the settlement for more than six months after the Environmental Administration first attempted to remove them. In fact, some of the legal activists who worked on the case were explicit (in conversation) about the fact that they had mobilised this procedural hurdle to allow people more time to organise and to find alternative accommodation. Of course, ultimately a different legal mechanism – a so-called 'correction' – allowed the Environmental Administration to circumvent the requirement to identify the squatters altogether. This correction, as I have attempted to show, effectively deprived the squatters not just of their access to the site and their dwellings but also of their legal standing in a way that left them with few opportunities for legal recourse and which effectively negated their claims to the site and to various other rights. This suggests that law, far from being a simple tool of domination, is full of internal contradictions and faults and highlights the importance of paying close attention to the workings and effects of particular forms of legal governance.

I want to stress that my emphasis on the administrative and legal details of the case is not meant to minimise its ideological dimensions or its social and political underpinnings. Rather, my hope is that this analysis might complement the existing literature on the governance of homeless and otherwise marginalised Roma in Sweden and elsewhere in Europe. For one thing, I hope that it might serve as an example of how the spatial governance of the Roma squatter communities both reflects and reinforces certain ethnic stereotypes, including metonymic associations between Roma and various objects of dirt and disorder (cf. Aradau, 2009, 2015). As I have shown, the administrative and legal process in question worked to translate subjective and frequently prejudiced complaints over the conditions in and around the Norra Sorgenfri settlement into a nuisance and an environmental health risk, thus elevating what were essentially private grievances into a public interest priority (cf. Ghertner, 2012).

It is worth noting that the discourse of health, safety and sanitation frequently overlapped with arguments about legal equality. Carina Svensson's assertion that the authorities 'cannot let it be acceptable that people live in huts' because there is 'a law which says that everyone should get to live in a dignified and good way' is a case in point. Such statements seem to ignore the reality that most of the squatters ended up on the street following the demolition. Indeed, the mobilisation of environmental law to resolve the conflict over the settlement in Norra Sorgenfri framed it, from the point of view of the authorities, as being about a particular type of issue – an environmental, health and nuisance problem – while simultaneously precluding other possible framings. At the same time, it located and localised the problem to the site of the settlement, and in doing so it identified the object of the settlement as risk to the squatters: a *cause* of their hardship as opposed to an *effect* of their active marginalisation and disenfranchisement. This worked to depoliticise the conflict and served in important ways to obscure the economic, political and social inequalities that produce extreme poverty and homelessness among European Roma. By attempting, legally speaking, to govern space (i.e. the property the settlement was located on) as opposed to people (the squatters), the Environmental Administration were able to circumvent the complicated issue of identification, thus effectively undoing the squatters' legal standing in a way that left them with few opportunities for any sort of legal recourse and which served to deflect their claims to the site and to more far-reaching rights and protections.

## Notes

1 The legal owner of the site is Industrigatan i Malmö AB, a subsidiary to Granen Exploateringsfastigheter Holding I AB, which in turn is owned more or less entirely by a real estate developer and speculator named Per Arwidsson.

2 Flyvbjerg (2006, p. 229) argues that 'atypical or extreme cases often reveal more information because they activate more actors and more basic mechanisms in the situation studied'.

3 All translations by author.

4 The complaints were obtained through a public information request. They are available on file with the Environmental Administration of the City of Malmö (Miljöförvaltningen, Malmö stad) with the reference number drn 2014–01614.

5 In my understanding, this has been the case since 1992, when some of the procedural aspects of the laws were revised in order to streamline procedures and make it easier for property owners to have trespassers removed.

6 The Enforcement Authority reserves the term 'eviction' (*avhysning*) for situations when the person who is to be evicted has, at some point, held a formal lease on the property in question. In situations of trespassing, the procedure is instead called 'special assistance' (*särskild handräckning*).

7 There is evidence that the Enforcement Authority does not apply these principles consistently. For instance, in Umeå in Northern Sweden, they addressed an eviction order concerning a community of homeless EU citizens to the church that hosted them (Angerbjörn, 2015).

8 This has been an issue not just in Malmö but in cities and towns across Sweden. In 2015 the Swedish government initiated a process to revise a number of laws and regulations to make it easier to do away with unauthorised settlements. As part of this process, a government report (DS 2016, p. 17) was published which proposes that private property owners should be able to obtain the assistance of the Enforcement Authority without specifying the names of the persons who are to be evicted.

9 The name has been changed to protect the anonymity of the individual.

## References

Alexander, G. S. (1998). Property as propriety. *Nebraska Law Review*, *77*, 667–702.

Andersson, J. (2010). *Sorgenfri – ett studieobjekt* [Web log post]. Retrieved from http://norrasorgenfri.blogspot.ca/2010/04/sorgenfri-ett-studieobjekt.html

Angerbjörn, P. (2015, 3 December). Kronofogden bör tillämpa sina bestämmelser. *Dagens Samhälle*. Retrieved from www.dagenssamhalle.se

Aradau, C. (2009). The Roma in Italy: Racism as usual? *Radical Philosophy*, *153*(153), 2–7.

Aradau, C. (2015). Security as universality? The Roma contesting security in Europe. In T. Balzacq (Ed.), *Contesting security: Strategies and logics* (pp. 89–103). Abingdon: Routledge.

Blomley, N. (2004a). Un-real estate: Proprietary space and public gardening. *Antipode*, *36*(4), 614–641. Retrieved from https://doi.org/10.1111/j.1467-8330.2004.00440.x

Blomley, N. (2004b). *Unsettling the city: Urban land and the politics of property*. New York, NY & London: Routledge. Retrieved from https://doi.org/10.4324/9780203499801

Blomley, N. (2007a). How to turn a beggar into a bus stop: Law, traffic and the 'function of the place'. *Urban Studies*, *44*(9), 1697–1712. Retrieved from https://doi.org/10.1080/00420980701427507

Blomley, N. (2007b). The borrowed view: Privacy, propriety, and the entanglements of property. *Law & Social Inquiry*, *30*(4), 617–661. Retrieved from https://doi.org/10.1111/j.1747-4469.2005.tb01142.x

Blomley, N. (2010). The right to pass freely: Circulation, begging, and the bounded self. *Social & Legal Studies*, *19*(3), 331–350. Retrieved from https://doi.org/10.1177/0964663910372183

Blomley, N. (2011). *Rights of passage: Sidewalks and the regulation of public flow*. New York, NY: Routledge.

Bubenko, A. (2014, 29 January). Skärpt koll på bostäder i Malmö. *Sveriges Radio*. Retrieved from www.sr.se

Clough Marinaro, I., & Sigona, N. (2011). Introduction: Anti-Gypsyism and the politics of exclusion: Roma and Sinti in contemporary Italy. *Journal of Modern Italian Studies*, *16*(5), 583–589. Retrieved from https://doi.org/10.1080/1354571x.2011.622467

Doherty, J., Busch-Geertsema, V., Karpuskiene, V., Korhonen, J., O'Sullivan, E., Sahlin, I., . . . Wygnańska, J. (2008). Homelessness and exclusion: Regulating public space in European cities. *Surveillance Society*, *5*(3), 290–314. Retrieved from www.surveillance-and-society.org/articles5(3)/homelessness.pdf?q=the-peripheralisation-of-office-development-in-the-dublin.

DS. (2016:17). *Otillåtna bosättningar*. Retrieved from www.regeringen.se

Flyvbjerg, B. (2006). Five misunderstandings about case-study research. *Qualitative Inquiry*, *12*(2), 219–245. Retrieved from https://doi.org/10.1177/1077800405284363

Ghertner, D. A. (2012). Nuisance talk and the propriety of property: Middle class discourses of a slum-free Delhi. *Antipode*, *44*(4), 1161–1187. Retrieved from https://doi.org/10.1111/j.1467-8330.2011.00956.x

Häggström, B. (2015, 27 February). Kronofogden kan köra bort EU-migranterna. *Sydsvenskan*. Retrieved from www.sydsvenskan.se

Hansson, E. (2014). *Som att världen har kommit hit*, Master's thesis, Stockholm University. Retrieved from www.diva-portal.org/smash/get/diva2:721768/FULLTEXT01.pdf

Harding, V. (2002). Space, property, and propriety in urban England. *The Journal of Interdisciplinary History*, *32*(4), 549–569. Retrieved from https://doi.org/10.1162/002219502317345501

Honoré, A. M. (1961). Ownership. In A. G. Guest (Ed.), *Oxford Essays in Jurisprudence* (pp. 107–147). London: Oxford University Press.

Johansen, N. B. (2016). Controlling Roma in Norway: Governing through the administration of social distance. In A. Eriksson (Ed.), *Punishing the other: The social production of immorality revisited* (pp. 165–183). Abingdon: Routledge.

Karlsson, J. (2015, 3 December). Lägret i Sorgenfri – ödetomten som blev Sveriges största slum. *Expressen*. Retrieved from www.expressen.se

Kronofogdemyndigheten. (2015). *Handräckningar rörande otillåten bosättning: Statistik för 2015*. Retrieved from www.kronofogden.se

Krueckeberg, D. (1995). The difficult character of property: To whom do things belong? *Journal of the American Planning Association*, *61*(3), 301–309. Retrieved from https://doi.org/10.1080/01944369508975644

Länsstyrelsen Skåne. (2015, 17 June). *Överklagande av miljönämnds beslut om föreläggande avseende fastigheten Brännaren 19, Malmö kommun*. Retrieved from www.malmo.se

Lauffs, T. (2015, 3 November). Soraya Post: 'Jag skäms för Sverige'. *SVT Nyheter*. Retrieved from www.svt.se

Law Solution. (2015, 20 March). *Överklagan av Malmö stads miljöförvaltnings beslut den 27 februari 2015 i ärende 548:01614–02014*. Retrieved from www.malmo.se

Levy, J. (2016). *A right to the 'world-class city'? A case study on the spatial exclusions of Romanian Roma*, Master's thesis, Stockholm University.Magnusson, E. (2015, 4 November). Fullt av beröm i Carina Nilssons mejlbox. *Sydsvenskan*. Retrieved from www.sydsvenskan.se

Malm, V. (2015, 30 October). Vräkningen i Malmö beror på rasistisk logik. *Expressen*. Retrieved from www.expressen.se

Mendez, K. (2015, 29 October). Debattinlägg: 'En del av Sveriges rasistiska historia reproduceras nu'. *Sydsvenskan*. Retrieved from www.sydsvenskan.se

Miljöförvaltningen, Malmö stad. (2015a, 27 February). *Föreläggande vid vite avseende nedskräpning på fastigheten Brännaren 19. Delegationsbeslut*. Retrieved from www.malmo.se

Miljöförvaltningen, Malmö stad (2015b, 7 April). *Förbud mot boende och övernattning m.m. på fastigheten Brännaren 19*. Retrieved from www.malmo.se

Miljöförvaltningen, Malmö stad. (2015c, 23 April). *Förbud mot boende och övernattning m.m. på fastigheten Brännaren 19*. Retrieved from www.malmo.se

Miljönämnden, Malmö stad. (2015, 27 October). *Rättelse enligt 26 kap 18§ miljöbalken, Brännaren 19, rivning av läger städning av fastigheten*. Retrieved from www.malmo.se

Molina, I. (1997). *Stadens rasifiering: Etnisk boendesegregation i folkhemmet*, Doctoral dissertation. Retrieved from http://uu.diva-portal.org/smash/record.jsf?pid=diva2:161611

Nedelsky, J. (1990). *Private property and the limits of American constitutionalism: The Madisonian framework and its legacy*. Chicago, IL: University of Chicago Press.

Nilsson, A. (2010). Environmental law. In M. Bogdan (Ed.), *Swedish legal system* (pp. 466–489). Stockholm: Norstedts juridik.

Persson, A. (2015, 12 March). Ägare försöker tömma tomt på EU- migranter. *Sydsvenskan*. Retrieved from www.sydsvenskan.se

Picker, G., Greenfields, M., & Smith, D. (2015). Colonial refractions: The 'Gypsy camp' as a spatio-racial political technology. *City*, *19*(5), 741–752. Retrieved from https://doi.org/10.1080/13604813.2015.1071123

Pusca, A. (2010). The 'Roma problem' in the EU: Nomadism, (In)visible architectures and Violence. *Borderlands E-Journal*, *9*(2), 1–17.

Rose, C. M. (1994). *Property and persuasion: Essays on the history, theory, and rhetoric of ownership*. Boulder, CO: Westview Press.

Saarinen, M. (2015, 31 October). Valfridsson: Nolltolerans mot tiggares läger. *Sveriges Radio*. Retrieved from http://sverigesradio.se

Santos, B. de S. (1987). Law: A map of misreading: Toward a postmodern of conception of law. *Journal of Law and Society*, *14*(3), 279–302. Retrieved from https://doi.org/10.2307/1410186

Sigona, N. (2011). The governance of Romani people in Italy: Discourse, policy and practice. *Journal of Modern Italian Studies*, *16*(5), 590–606. Retrieved from https://doi.org/10.1080/1354571x.2011.622468

Singer, J. W. (2000). Property and social relations: From title to entitlement. In C. C. Geisler & G. Daneker (Eds.), *Property and values: Alternatives to public and private ownership* (pp. 3–20). Washington, DC: Island Press.

Smith, N. (1996). *The new urban frontier: Gentrification and the revanchist city*. New York, NY: Routledge.

SOU. (2016:6). *Framtid sökes – Slutredovisning från den nationella samordnaren för utsatta EU-medborgare*. Retrieved from www.regeringen.se

Sylvestre, M. E., Damon, W., Blomley, N., & Bellot, C. (2015). Spatial tactics in criminal courts and the politics of legal technicalities. *Antipode*, *47*(5), 1346–1366. Retrieved from https://doi.org/10.1111/anti.12161

Thörn, C. (2011). Soft policies of exclusion: Entrepreneurial strategies of ambience and control of public space in Gothenburg, Sweden. *Urban Geography*, *32*(7), 989–1008. Retrieved from https://doi.org/10.2747/0272-3638.32.7.989

Thornell, K. W. (2016, 10 October). Kanske kommer läsarna känna, med både hjärnan och hjärtat, hur mitt liv är. *Sydsvenskan*. Retrieved from www.sydsvenskan.se

UN-OHCHR. (2015, 30 October). *Joint urgent appeal from Special Procedures to her excellence Ms. Veronika Bard, permanent mission of Sweden to United Nations Office in Geneva*. Retrieved from blogg.socialrattigheter.se/wp-content/uploads/2015/11/Brev-från-socialrapportören-för-minoritetsfrågor151030.pdf.

Valverde, M. (2009). Jurisdiction and scale: Legal 'technicalities' as resources for theory. *Social & Legal Studies*, *18*(2), 139–157. Retrieved from https://doi.org/10.1177/0964663909103622

Valverde, M. (2011). Seeing like a city: The dialectic of modern and premodern ways of seeing in urban governance. *Law and Society Review*, *45*(2), 277–312. Retrieved from https://doi.org/10.1111/j.1540-5893.2011.00441.x

Wacquant, L. (2009). *Punishing the poor: The neoliberal government of social insecurity*. Durham, NC: Duke University Press.

Wacquant, L. (2014). Marginality, ethnicity and penality in the neo-liberal city: An analytic cartography. *Ethnic and Racial Studies*, *37*(10), 1687–1711. Retrieved from https://doi.org/10.1080/01419870.2014.931991

Chapter 4

# Urban emptiness, ghost owners and squatters' challenges to private property

*Miguel A. Martínez*

*This chapter explores the legitimation strategies that political squatters use to justify their occupation of property they do not own and how those strategies often 'soften' what could otherwise have been a more radical anti-capitalist stance. Taking a starting point in empirical work done on Spanish squatting and focusing in the latter half on the housing struggles after the financial crisis and the emergence of strong housing movements, the chapter discusses the ambivalences and strategies of squatters both needing a place to live and trying to translate that need into a broader political and economic critique not only of housing but of the capitalist system. The chapter contributes to the squatter literature and to the discussion of the legitimation strategies of peoples and groups challenging the prevailing property regimes.*

## Introduction

Squatters occupy vacant properties without asking for permission. This practice dates back to long before the inception of capitalism (Ward, 2002). Legal regulations regarding squatting vary from place to place, although they are usually set at the state level in each country. According to various legal codes, the acts of trespassing, breaking in and remaining in a previously owned or rented house and occupying empty premises may be determined and dealt with in different manners by the authorities. Nevertheless, policies on squatting seldom pay attention to the owners' behaviours. It is increasingly assumed that owners are legitimately managing their vacancy regardless of the context of social needs and urban dynamics. According to this prevailing policy narrative, the squatters are the main party at fault. Making a profit from vacant property is rarely criticised.

Vacancy is caused by abandonment, ruin, substandard conditions and owners' decisions to postpone any action aimed at the redevelopment or sale of their property. Most squatters claim that occupying empty properties is a legitimate action. This means, first, that they cannot afford to buy or rent an adequate space for living or organising collective activities. Second, they argue that the satisfaction of their needs is morally superior to the legal rights that enable private owners to keep their properties vacant. As previously stated, legislation differs from country to country, and the absolute principle of private property is usually constrained by minor rules (Persdotter, this volume). No owner can set his or her building on fire, for instance. Damage to other residents and the commission of crimes are also prosecuted. Unjustified delays with licensed renovations may be subject to sanctions if the norms are effectively enforced by the authorities. More importantly, the legal doctrine of 'adverse possession' that serves to grant property rights to squatters if specific conditions are met, such as continuous occupation for a certain number of years, was regarded in some countries as juridical grounds for countering the criminalisation of squatting (O'Mahony, O'Mahony & Hickey, 2015).

Not all squatters are outspoken about their claims and right to squat. I designate here those who take a public role as 'political squatters' – whether or not they speak on behalf of all squatters. In so doing, they often explicitly contest the liberal regulation of private property at large. An overall critique of the capitalist system may even be conveyed through squatters' movements (SqEK, 2013). According to Cobb (2015, p. 16), 'the squatter remains a symbol of [the high levels of] precariousness [in the housing market] and so constitutes an on-going challenge to neoliberal hegemony'. However, neither activists nor academics have investigated the deeper implications of such an anti-property statement. For example, major contributions to the analysis of squatting (Cattaneo & Martínez, 2014; Pruijt, 2013; Van Der Steen, Katzeef, & Van Hoogenhuijze, 2014) do not usually delve into the nuances of this question and the types of properties and proprietors involved. In the following sections, I argue that, over the past four decades, political squatters across Europe have challenged the capitalist notion of private property, albeit through very broad statements. In many cases, as I will show, it is not the abolition of private property that is demanded.

How can the 'urban voids' that are targeted by squatters be classified? Is the social identity of their 'ghost owners' a significant dimension of squatting? What are the roles of both buildings and owners in the legitimation of squatting? To answer these questions, I examine first how private property is dealt with given the class and classification struggles in which squatting is embedded. This section provides a full scope of the main arguments used to justify squatting as a limited intervention into the cracks opened up by capitalism in urban spaces. Second, I distinguish the types of squatted properties in a specific city (Madrid) to provide an understanding of the shifts in squatting practices and legitimation strategies in a specific historical context. I finally summarise my interpretations by arguing that (a) in practice, squatters question more the social functions, policies and effects of private property than its role as a founding tenet of capitalism and (b) squatting, when generalised, politicised or self-organised as an urban movement, defies the key dynamics of urban capitalism, such as real estate speculation, but rarely threatens capitalism as a whole because of its exclusive focus on vacant properties.

## Property and legitimation strategies

Political squatters who take an anti-capitalist and left-libertarian stance tend to justify squatting by expressing an idealistic appeal to the abolition of private property in all forms. However, there is little evidence that this claim is at the core of their legitimation strategies. Rather, squatters actually challenge the specific aspects of capitalism at work in cities, particularly the management of empty property. To clarify this point, I distinguish two main types of arguments: (a) those based on the criteria of necessity, affordability and nonprofitability and (b) those stressing the contribution of squatting to the common good (or, more precisely, to the *urban commons*). The first type of argument points to the various aspects of the social groups who may legitimately squat empty properties from an anti-capitalist perspective. The second type introduces three broader dimensions of urban life in capitalist cities that are affected by the squatting of urban vacancies, namely anti-fascist politics, interactions with neighbours and housing policies.

### *Necessity, affordability and nonprofitability*

Squatting empty properties is usually considered legitimate by political squatters, anti-capitalist activists and some scholars whenever it is practised according to a specific agenda. Squatting is widely accepted when it is practised by homeless people and anyone who cannot access social housing or affordable shelter (Reeve, 2011). To buy or rent an expensive dwelling may imply the serious erosion of other aspects of buyers' and tenants' well-being. Squatting can thus mitigate these undesirable effects. People with low or unstable income, such as unemployed people, students and the elderly, may resort to squatting as a solution to their urgent economic needs, especially in the absence of any state measures that suit them in terms of quality and timeliness. Hence, the abolition of private property is not the main goal underlying their claim to the empty property. They rather criticise their exclusion from the private property system. Even political squatters who are not necessarily subject to economic or resource scarcity refuse to pay high rents or selling prices that could undermine other aspects of their lives. This is especially justified when the targets of squatting are spaces left unused in convenient locations for collective gatherings and activities supplied by squatters at no or low cost. The more unaffordable rental or selling prices are compared with squatters' incomes, the more squatters claim rightful use of the occupied place.

Based on the rampant speculation of urban properties and the functional contribution of vacant state-owned properties to that dynamic, some municipal governments have even agreed to grant temporary lease contracts to activists who are former or potential squatters (Colomb, 2012; Martínez, 2014). By calling on the arguments of necessity, affordability and nonprofitability rather than challenging capitalism and private property regimes, squatters are mainly questioning the failures of that system to properly accommodate everyone. Many squatters who squat solely for housing purposes usually try to claim private ownership for themselves or, at least, to legally secure occupancy for as long as possible. Therefore, this demand of tenure does not entail a struggle against the private property regime either.

Nonetheless, some well-off political squatters (from the middle or well-paid working classes) may, remarkably, reject the argument of necessity in their own case by stating that wealthier owners cannot legitimately profit from their empty properties. The homeless population living in substandard dwellings or slums would eventually benefit from an overall legitimation of squatting. Regardless of the squatters' reasons for occupancy, to actively question the existence of empty properties is a direct attack on the real estate business. Market speculation involving land, houses and other urban assets is the main target of squatting because it deepens wealth gaps, which inevitably cause residential exclusion. A continuous reproduction of a 'reserve army' in demand of affordable urban space in the form of the homeless population is a basic condition for the competitive housing market. Therefore, the act of squatting, regardless of the needs of those involved, releases manufactured market pressure.

This reasoning leads to an additional question: what is illegitimate squatting with regard to the intersection of necessity, affordability and profitability? The more affluent individuals are, the less legitimate it may be perceived for them to occupy another's property. In particular, those who own one or more homes; possess available commercial, office, factory, leisure and land spaces; and, in general, those whose income and wealth enables them to either participate successfully in the real estate market or be eligible for (and effectively granted) public housing benefits are in a weak position to claim that their squatting is legitimate if they are the ones who enjoy the benefits of that action. Again, they improve their reputation if others in need are the main beneficiaries – which tends to occur, for example, in squatted social centres when they are open to the broader public and also in activists' provision and management of squatted shelters for undocumented migrants (Mudu & Chattopadhyay, 2016).

These arguments incite controversy because all parties engaged in a specific squat must demonstrate how individuals' assets match the conventionally accepted circumstances of necessity and affordability in a particular urban and economic context. From an anti-capitalist point of view, affluent people and for-profit businesses may practice extreme forms of illegitimate squatting. These for-profit businesses may take the form of mafia- or gang-like criminal organisations by violently harassing tenants and neighbours. In general, renting, subletting, or selling occupied property to others is viewed as illegitimate by anti-capitalist squatters. Other economic activities within squats that reproduce capitalist practices of labour exploitation and private accumulation of wealth are also subjected to anti-capitalist criticism. Selling food, beverages, books, clothes or handicrafts is deemed legitimate when it is not for profit and democratically managed among the squatters. Informal self-employment in the squats is more problematic because the satisfaction of spatial needs for housing and collective self-organisation must also accommodate the urgent need to make a living among the few self-employed.

As Ward (1980, p. 104) highlighted, capitalists and private owners were the first squatters – squatting is 'the oldest mode of tenure in the world'. Indeed, unlawful occupations are at the origins of the establishment of private property and thus of primitive capital accumulation. Along with land requisitions and legal dispossession in the forms of enclosures and privatisation (Harvey, 2006, pp. 90–115), far from questioning property as such, capitalists may effectively pursue their interests by occupying vacant properties. Therefore, real estate developers and agents, banks, or factory owners might participate in squatting. It is this extreme – though unusual – practice of squatting which is fully opposed from an anti-capitalist standpoint in a sort of Möbius strip. Anti-capitalist squatting thus claims legitimacy while opposing pro-capitalist squatting because this is seen as a source of private property and social inequality.

### Common good

The theory of the commons has been revived recently (Dardot & Laval, 2016; Stavrides, 2016) and forms a fundamental basis for squatting as a potential emancipatory movement (Cattaneo & Martínez, 2014). The urban commons, in particular, do not encompass only public spaces but comprehend every collectively self-managed practice, institution, good, infrastructure and struggle able to overcome the duality of state-owned and privately owned modes of tenure, government and judgement. However, there is little evidence of the social contributions of squatting to the urban commons (Martínez, 2013). To fill the gap of this line of analysis in urban studies, I suggest focusing on three key dimensions in which both legitimate and illegitimate squatting interacts with a political economy of the commons.

For the first dimension, the question to reflect upon is, what are anti-capitalist politics in the context of squatting? Consider, for instance, the phenomenon of neo-Nazi/neo-fascist squats in major European cities (such as Rome, Madrid and Frankfurt), which also define themselves as anti-capitalist groups (Birdwell, 2012). Should their anti-capitalist stance be articulated, it remains rather low on their political agenda. This calls for a more precise qualification of 'political squatting'. Far-right squatters systematically, and often violently, attack left-libertarian squatters as well as homeless people and many social groups viewed by them as 'inferior', including people with disabilities, migrants, ethnic minorities and gay and transgender people. Hence, no matter how much in need far-right squatters are, their politics against other people who are needy, oppressed, excluded, dispossessed and anti-capitalist takes priority over any squatting actions. Fascist squatters destroy the very basis of any democratic sphere of political dissent by explicitly aiming to suppress or expel people who take direct action to help themselves.

Furthermore, fascist squatters do not usually question private property as a pillar of capitalism. If so, it is questioned in a rhetorical fashion, without any mention of the class structures that capitalism created. For fascist squatters, the nationalistic – xenophobic *struggle* takes priority above all, and class struggle may be considered subsequently, if at all. Eventual self-management of fascist squats is also subordinate to strict authoritarian hierarchies intended to undermine any bottom-up democratic reconstruction of the urban commons.

Conversely, long-lasting anti-fascist and inclusive traditions characterise squatting across Europe (Cattaneo & Martínez, 2014; Mudu & Chattopadhyay, 2016). At best, the emergence of far-right squats helps designate a bottom line of what is not anti-capitalist squatting. Left-libertarian political squatters in turn may find it difficult to define in positive terms what true anti-capitalist politics is, given the diverse ideological and cultural milieu in which they are engaged and the internal contradictions they live with. By opposing or preventing fascism, anti-capitalist squatters contribute to the invigoration of local democracy as well. In addition to the denunciation of labour exploitation and class inequalities, Holloway noted that the creation of cracks and the struggle for dignity can help break the logic of a capitalist society. 'Dignity consists in setting our own agenda (. . .): we take the initiative, we make it clear that it is capitalism struggling against us, our lives, our projects, our humanity. Dignity is to refuse-and-create: to refuse to make capitalism and to create a new world' (Holloway, 2010, p. 50). As a corollary, fascism neglects human dignity in general and creative dignity as a breeding ground for anti-capitalist societies in particular. Therefore, fascist squats represent the most illegitimate form of squatting, one that erodes the potential of the urban commons.

The second dimension to consider is how open squatters are to cooperating with the dispossessed locals. A crucial aspect of squatting is the relationships between squatters, neighbouring residents and local–metropolitan social groups. Stereotypes about good and bad squatters play an important role when the groups approach each other to create potential bonds of cooperation. Squatting practices may either confirm or contradict the established stereotypes. When a squat is a source of trouble, noise or disturbance or involves the abusive occupation of public spaces, the surrounding community will not perceive the squat as beneficial in any sense. Squatters are often newcomers to the area, so they face inquiry and inspection by local residents if they are to be made welcome.

Furthermore, squats that include almost no working-class residents and are instead made up almost exclusively of middle-class native-born students and artists, tend to be the utmost expression of a *ghetto*. This stigma may also fall on working-class or *underclass* squatters if they are unable to cooperate with other social groups in the neighbourhood. Some so-called 'crusty' squatters who trash the buildings they occupy and maintain socially sealed-off groups reinforce this isolation from the local community and subsequent illegitimacy. The more the ghettoised image of the squat is spread, the harsher the rejection by other local residents. For example, the location of a squat next to newly built blocks can clash with other residents' fear of the market devaluation of their properties (Di Feliciantonio, 2016, p. 190). When strong processes of real estate speculation are involved, developers put more pressure on squatters to force them to leave (Seminario, 2015).

This is why developers and others with vested interests in a given territory attribute all the real and imagined evils of a neighbourhood (such as dirtiness, thefts, drug trafficking and loitering) to the squatters. By contrast, squatters may be highly resourceful and valuable to the local community when they disclose the speculative processes underway. It is this struggle that makes them essential echelons of the urban commons and accentuates their capacity of legitimation.

The third angle of this debate asks the following: what has squatting to do with housing policies? When squatters take over apartments in social housing estates, they are immediately accused of jumping the queue because other home seekers in need might be waiting for those apartments. Anti-capitalist squatters tend to argue that it is the inefficient state bureaucracy that should receive the blame – it is too slow to assign the available social housing and has not built sufficient social housing stock to accommodate all who are registered on the waiting list. In fact, many squatters do not jump the queue, because they never apply for social housing. They are reluctant to do so, either because they cannot meet the selection criteria set by the housing authorities or because they want to criticise how these departments operate.

Social housing policies run by the state (let alone those run independently by grassroots organisations, such as housing cooperatives or syndicates) may fill the void left by the failures of the market when they provide affordable, decent and well-located homes for all residentially excluded people. However, capitalist private developers are usually in charge of building the social housing stock. Furthermore, in urban development plans, this stock tends to be subordinate to non-social housing and designed and built in lower proportions. Social housing may also be granted either as private property or as a social rental, and social rental housing may be subject to further arbitrary privatisation by housing managers. This was the case, for instance, when the former conservative government of Madrid sold 1,860 units of social housing to the 'vulture fund' Blackstone.

Some social housing beneficiaries become squatters once the authorities threaten them with eviction because they have failed to pay their rent or bills on time as a result of impoverishment. In capitalist societies, people rely on social housing as a last resort when they cannot access the property market instead of being motivated by strong beliefs in state property as the preferred mode of tenure. In general, housing policies in liberal democracies protect and subsidise homeownership. Squatting in social housing may then entail a sort of war among the poor over the scant resources provided by the state. This type of squatting becomes legitimate only as a powerful source of criticism of the insufficient and inefficient welfare allocated by the state. In addition to the aforementioned critiques, some scholars indicate grievances such as long-term vacancies in the social housing stock and the unfair means employed by management agencies to prolong the suffering of applicants and deteriorate the living conditions of current residents (Reeve, 2011, p. 14).

In sum, anti-capitalist squatters legitimise each occupation according to certain conditions – who squats and what social benefits squatting entails. As previously argued, most of these conditions do not pose a direct challenge to private property as a basis of capitalism. Rather, they challenge the specific and perverse consequences of the uneven distribution of urban property and the management of vacancies. This discussion often omits a detailed analysis of the types of properties and owners targeted by squatters. The following section engages with this and presents an analysis of how effective these legitimation strategies are. Different sources of data and the examination of crucial historical shifts further illustrate the nuances of my argument.

## Urban voids, ghost owners and squatted social centres

When examining empirical information about squatting, one must acknowledge, above all, the blind spot in which most illegal occupations of buildings lie. I came across many activists and neighbours who were squatting but decided not to go public because of various concerns, their main conviction being that stealth squatting has greater long-term prospects. In particular, in Spain until 2011, the number of housing squatters might have been in the thousands, but reliable information about this phenomenon is lacking. The main source of trustworthy data is records on 'political squatting' (i.e. when squats are overtly claimed and publicised). This applies to squatted social centres (SSCs) and also to the recent wave of housing squats promoted by the Platform for People Affected by Mortgages (PAH) and other groups since 2011. My research on both in the city of Madrid unveils how squatters interfere in the capitalist dynamics of urban emptiness by distinguishing the patterns of occupied buildings, their ownership and the eventual legitimation of squatting practices in varying contexts.

The timeframe of data collection on SSCs was 1977 to 2015. Three main periods or cycles were distinguished according to the major events that influenced squatting before and after 1995–1996 when squatting became a criminal offence, and the cycle opened up in 2011 when the 15M/Indignados movement erupted and the number of squats increased substantially. The database comprises a total of 155 cases. Inspired by the Ateneos Libertarios, which the anarchist union National Confederation of Labour (CNT) established at many occupied venues in the late 1970s, and by the numerous examples of autonomist squats that have bloomed across Europe since the late 1960s, SSCs sprang up all over Spain, mainly after 1984. The geographical location of my analysis is the Autonomous Community of Madrid (6.5 million inhabitants in 2013), including the main municipality of Madrid (3.2 million residents in 2013). Quantitative data were collected from secondary sources (such as academic publications, mass media news, websites, blogs, activist leaflets and documents and mapping projects) and supplemented with my direct accounts as a participant and activist observer (occasionally since 1988 and on a more regular basis from 2007 and 2013), 23 in-depth interviews conducted between 2008 and 2016, and the organisation and facilitation of a series of 14 public debates held between 2008 and 2010, involving squatters active in different historical periods (Seminario, 2015).

More than one-third (36 per cent) of the squats took place in formerly inhabited buildings, suggesting that some SSCs also hosted squatters as residents, although they usually kept this activity secret. The SSCs mainly functioned as cultural and political venues, which obliged squatters to adapt some of their residential spaces. Because dozens or hundreds of visitors could gather for certain events, squatters were often compelled to perform some minor renovations in the building to accommodate them. This was the leading category of building use throughout the evolution of the movement, with no significant differences across the periods (28 per cent in the first period, 41 per cent in the second and 37 per cent in the third). A few of the buildings were never completed by developers and were not officially licensed to be used as dwellings. Most of the squatted buildings remained abandoned because they were old and required serious renovations; sometimes they were almost in ruins. According to my informants and my own observations, the owners were frequently waiting for a convenient deal that could bring them immediate and substantial profits after selling or for the legal right to build a newer or taller building instead (which would, in turn, also increase their revenue in the long run).

A simple correlation of residential category with property type shows that 33 buildings were privately owned, and only 13 cases were owned by different state agencies. When a correlation is made with urban location, we find that most were in the city centre (33 cases); an even distribution occurred in the city periphery (10 cases) and the metropolitan area beyond the municipality of Madrid (12 cases). This evidence corresponds with the general pattern of legal ownership of the premises upon which SSCs were established – namely, 61 per cent were privately owned and 24 per cent were state owned. The prevailing pattern of central location in almost half of the SSCs also roughly matches the predominance of residential buildings among the targets of squatting.

Industrial buildings were the second type subject to squatting (21 per cent). Variation across the periods of evolution was more significant in this category. In particular, during the final cycle, after 2011, the occupation of industrial buildings represented only 11 per cent of the total, which was slightly below the 13 per cent each for commercial buildings and schools (including an incomplete public library). Therefore, we can assume that the restructuring processes that shut down factories were more intense before the 2000s (Alguacil, De La Fuente, Martínez López, Ubrich, & Velasco, 2011, p. 114), with fewer buildings of this type remaining vacant in the final period. According to spatial correlation, this phenomenon is not dependent on an urban location because, again, centrally placed buildings (21) were the main targets of squatters, regardless of the number of opportunities available in the periphery (eight effective occupations) and metropolitan areas (only four squats of this type).

Although former factories suitable for use as SSCs are not only found in the city centre, squatters prefer central locations in order to attract local residents.

Although industrial buildings are being increasingly displaced to the urban and metropolitan periphery, and despite their higher rates of vacancy during periods of economic crisis (the early 1980s and after 2008), SSCs were rarely established there or were comparatively short lived. In addition, as expected, properties that include industrial buildings were almost always held by private owners (27 cases out of 33).

In terms of ownership, these cases might be closely associated with the 14 per cent that incorporated 'commercial buildings' and 'ground-floor businesses', among which only 4 buildings out of 22 were state owned. Thus, it can be inferred that squatters do not much alter the real estate market in the realm of small companies and buildings designated for commercial purposes despite their abundance. Either these vacant buildings are not abandoned for long, or squatters do not consider them suitably accommodating for activities involving large numbers of visitors.

By contrast, schools were more popular and politically significant for squatters in Madrid, especially in Cycles 1 (23 per cent of all SSCs of that period) and 3 (13 per cent). These buildings are usually well equipped and designed, which simplifies the renovations needed, if any, to convert them into SSCs. They may also be claimed as social facilities that neighbourhoods should preserve. In the 1980s and 1990s, many schools closed because of new legal requirements for size, safety and facilities. This primarily affected small private companies unable to further invest or who preferred to sell the land if it was centrally located, moving the school to the periphery if land was more affordable (Alguacil et al., 2011, p. 126).

In sum, the available records indicate that SSCs in Madrid were more often located on privately owned properties (61 per cent) than state-owned properties (24 per cent). Consequently, this form of squatting directly interfered with the real estate market. This might be interpreted as a straightforward challenge to urban capitalism, especially if we bear in mind that most private owners are companies (33 per cent) rather than individual proprietors (17 per cent). Notwithstanding, state-owned stock is also subject to a substantial amount of grassroots direct action through squatting. In particular, state-owned targets mainly include houses (13 cases), although other public assets such as wet markets, offices or factories (11 cases) and schools (7) provided spatial opportunities that squatters made effective use of.

According to these figures, squatting on private property is more likely to be interpreted as an action against capitalist dynamics of urban speculation, whereas squatting on state property is more of a protest against bureaucratic and inefficient methods of managing public resources. State inaction related to its own assets has varying effects on real estate speculation. For example, if these assets are scheduled for privatisation, squatters are directly addressing state involvement in urban speculation. Conversely, if state properties are abandoned and decaying, the area is less attractive for private investments but residents' discontent is increased, especially if the buildings are landmarks because of their large size or special significance for the urban commons. Examples include former schools, university buildings (when squatted in for the long term, not as a temporary protest), libraries, train stations and theatres.

An illustration of these trends is the *Squatters' Handbook*, written by anti-capitalist squatters in Madrid (Manual, 2014, p. 20). They do not prioritise a specific type of building or owner. Rather, they focus solely on the buildings' emptiness and the squatters' political projects. Vacant state-owned properties are also welcomed as a means of gaining legitimacy in the eyes of neighbours (Manual, 2014, p. 94). However, their principal aim is simply to make use of empty spaces to criticise urban injustice, housing unaffordability and the right to private property. Squatting is thus framed as a political tool to fight capitalism through direct action, community support and self-management, but not as a practice that can abolish private property or even satisfy all housing needs (Manual, 2014, p. 16). Even temporary stays are considered partial victories:

> An eviction is just part of the game. 'You squat, you are evicted' is the inevitable essence of this cycle and struggle. We should not fall down at this bump in the road – that would mean true defeat. Mutual aid and solidarity must not be empty slogans. Every blow makes us stronger, more experienced, and more professional. Thus, we can enhance our noble art and keep eroding the pillars of private property that hold up this system, a system that suffocates us and squeezes the sweet juice out of our lives.
>
> (Manual, 2014, p. 116)

## The politicisation of housing squatting

A different story emerged when two not-yet-mentioned conditions were met in a specific wave of occupations: (1) a strong, organised social movement began to practise squatting actively; and (2) politicised (publicly claimed) housing squatting was incorporated in SSCs. This happened after the upheavals of 2011, known as the 15M/Indignados movement. By then, the PAH had been already active for two years (slightly less in Madrid) and started opposing the evictions of people subject to foreclosures. This campaign was soon supplemented with another called Obra Social (literally, 'Social Work'; Martínez & Cattaneo, 2014; García, 2015; Di Feliciantonio, 2016). Thus, the PAH supported occupations of houses by those who had joined the organisation and had been evicted from their own dwellings (a similar politicisation is narrated by Kolling, this volume). Some of these occupations still followed the trend of secrecy and involved the selection of individual apartments instead of whole residential buildings. However, most of the PAH occupations were publicly presented, claimed and fought for – as opposed to most of the squatted houses, which remained hidden. Housing groups other than the PAH also imitated their procedures and political discourse.

What is significant here is the explicit targets of owners and types of buildings set by the PAH: banks and houses. Squatters that could potentially be helped by the PAH were those evicted from their own homes because of an inability to meet the deadlines for mortgage loan payments. Rather than using the term 'squatting', the PAH opted for 'recuperation' as a means of distinguishing themselves from other squatters with more diffuse or radically anti-capitalist stances. Furthermore, the intention of these takeovers was to obtain an affordable rent for the residents, not just to live for free for as long as possible. 'Usually we will search for newly constructed buildings that are owned by financial companies and are fully empty. We will prioritise the properties of bailed-out banks'. My interviewees in Madrid informed me, nonetheless, that they had also occupied individual apartments, and PAH groups had hosted people who were previously tenants rather than homeowners. A branch of PAH activists was even established to unite people evicted from social housing estates.

As for the ownership of residential squats, the rule of thumb was to focus on banks while assuming they must be held responsible for the home evictions, abuses and legal tricks that have harmed thousands since the global financial crisis. Yet many of the banks set up their own real estate agencies or development companies to manage their portfolios, which widened the scope of the targets. These included both new buildings unable to be sold at regular market prices and many scattered housing units resulting from foreclosures. Once again, the material opportunities within a particular context intersected with the urgent housing needs of an increasingly impoverished population. As a result of the PAH's public discourse, emptiness was not considered a mere market failure but instead the result of a massive fraud orchestrated by banks and the government (García, 2015, p. 161). Squatting thus was embraced and legitimised in order to support the victims of that fraud, which is far from a substantial critique of the capitalist system, let alone an examination of the principle of private property.

Across Spain, the PAH groups occupied 43 buildings and hosted 3,500 people. In Madrid, the PAH and other housing groups started the aforementioned Obra Social campaign in 2013, although a wide wave of occupations had already spread since 2011 (Martínez & García, 2015). The campaign had recovered 14 buildings by September 2016. One (Sierra de Llerena) had been previously squatted in 2012, but activists and residents adhered to the campaign once they learned the property had been transferred from the developer to a bank rescued by the government. In another case (La Leona), there was so much internal strife that housing activists eventually withdrew their support for the squatters. Notably, three of the buildings belonged to developers or estate agencies, whereas all the other cases were straightforward, involving bank-owned buildings. Interviewees told me that they followed the directions of the PAH but interpreted them in a broad sense. Large owners and developers in general could be singled out as potential speculators whose properties were legitimate to occupy.

PAH activists offered occasional support to those who occupied social housing estates when the cases quite obviously involved institutional abuse (for example, that of Lanjarón), although they never planned to occupy state-owned houses. Various housing groups in Madrid, especially before they became associated with the PAH, also launched campaigns to help people who already had squatted in their own houses, which were at risk of repossession for nonpayment of rent or bills or as a result of renovations (the *corralas* of Lavapiés, for instance). Every local group of activists had to assist in dozens of individual cases when a bank was designated as the main culprit, although some squatting actions remained silent. Despite the broad impact of the Obra Social campaign across Spain, in Madrid only two local branches were continuously active (Vallecas and Centro, responsible for 10 collective buildings), while other PAH groups were more reluctant to squat.

Compared with the established patterns of squatting followed by SSCs, the patterns of squats affiliated with the Obra Social campaign were not so different in practice – privately owned residential buildings were the primary targets. The striking difference between them lies in the PAH being more specific about the types of private owners (banks and wealthy developers above all) and the complete exclusion of other types of owners and buildings. The rationale behind this most explicit option was that squatting was now motivated by an exceptional housing crisis, the extraordinarily high number of empty dwellings and the massive numbers of unemployed and poor people who had become homeless or faced the threat of it. Squatting was then a tool to both obtain temporary accommodation and force owners to offer affordable tenancy contracts. Therefore, squatting was not seen necessarily as the most favoured means of struggle against emptiness, real estate speculation or private property.

This legitimation discourse was thus more easily accepted and digested by sympathetic journalists and a large part of society. In addition, it facilitated the legal defence of the housing squats, which were at risk of harsher sentences than those for SSCs once in court. Notwithstanding, in parallel to the political campaign, all forms of squatting are still performed by current practitioners, and the PAH's prevailing narrative is not uniformly embraced among activists and supporters. The main consequence of this strategy is that the combination of existing structural opportunities of vacancy, ghost owners (clearly identified with banks) and a conscious collective self-organisation that advocates civil disobedience to overcome the hardships of the economic crisis makes squatting appear as an effective interference in capital accumulation in cities.

The PAH's discursive strategy has enjoyed wider public backing than the hardcore justification of anti-capitalist squatting. The recent wave of housing occupations extends beyond the reach of the PAH, although this movement organisation has been highly influential in public debates and the policies aimed at squatters. SSCs have lasted for more than three decades. They have hosted various generations of activists, sympathisers and visitors. However, the much more limited number of that type of political squat means that their method has not been able to spread to broader social circles beyond anti-capitalist ones. Notwithstanding, in the city of Madrid, many former political squatters have merged with new PAH activists. The prevailing discourse of the Obra Social was also used as a tactic by anti-capitalist squatters in the context of a lingering economic crisis. In addition, identity symbols, experiences and arguments coming from the SSC tradition have occasionally drawn various newcomers to squatting, as I noticed in my interviews with members of the Obra Social–PAH committee and in some of the documents they have written.

Squatters guided by the PAH have arrived at a similar point to that of many SSCs – in a capitalist society, there are numerous marginalised people who are forced to resort to squatting to live a decent life. However, these groups have different rationales and political approaches. As discussed previously, this is reflected in the empirical manifestations of both types of squatting. Although residential buildings are preferred by all, SSCs are more often located in city centres, whereas housing squats tend to be located in peripheral working-class areas where some PAH groups are more active. Private owners, in addition to various types of private firms, are the main targets of SSCs, whereas housing activists mostly target financial corporations. Although most squatters might be willing to accept trade-offs with owners in order to be granted temporary but durable possession, only housing activists have sought from the beginning to forge agreements by which they manifest their will to pay rent to the owners (this was successfully achieved by three groups of squatters in Madrid: La Manuela, Argente and Lanjarón). This is seldom sought or accepted by most anti-capitalist squatters, although negotiations may be held occasionally.

## Conclusions

Here, I return to the initial research questions: How is private property contested by squatters? What are the roles of buildings and owners in the legitimacy of squatting?

The preceding analysis indicates that there are prevailing trends in the types of buildings and ownership subjects to take over and convert into SSCs, at least in the city of Madrid. In the interviews and discussions I attended, the squatters' agency was always at stake when a suitable building was being identified, investigated, preliminarily explored, and finally occupied. This meant that the history of the building, its former use and significance in the area, knowledge about the owner, the existence of private security or guards and the convenience of the space for the pursued activities were carefully assessed in advance by the squatters. As I verified in the squats in which I participated more actively, these decisions were also intended to unmask the speculative operations of some owners, although this was not the only motivation. Contrasting this with data collected over the past few decades, I conclude that squatters adjusted or limited their preferences to four major types of buildings (residential buildings, industrial buildings, schools and commercial offices), and mostly to privately owned properties located in central metropolitan areas. Remarkably, however, one-third of the cases were state-owned properties.

This does not suggest a mechanistic adjustment of the proportion of urban vacancies and the practice of squatting. More precisely, these patterns show that when running SSCs, squatters held their own deliberations regarding both the spatial opportunities at hand and their political projects. As mentioned, they also tended to choose large residential and industrial buildings belonging to private owners. On the one hand, the corruption or wealth of the owners was beneficial to the squatters' legitimation discourse and legal self-defence in anti-capitalist terms (see, for instance, the squats of Malaya and Casablanca: Martínez, 2014). On the other hand, when the owner was a state agency or semi–state-run company, squatting was presented as a legitimate action in terms of a response to the unmet collective needs of both squatters and the local community.

In general, whenever their choices meshed well with state-owned properties (either empty schools or buildings serving various functions), squatters did not hesitate to use these properties. This implies that there was no single ideological plan or scheme underlying such actions (i.e. an orchestrated operation against the major real estate holders in highly desirable urban areas where speculation occurs). Political squatters intend to change capitalism, but in each of their attempts, they occupy what is available, feasible and convenient. Squatters' agency in SSCs is significant, although it is also diverse and flexible in setting their targets. It thus plays a limited role, as we have seen, as a result of the specific sociospatial opportunities in each historical and urban context.

The advantage of anti-capitalist discourse is that the occupation of urban emptiness unveils the processes of urban speculation in which most vacant properties and private owners are involved. The catch-all strategy of squatters, which targets state-owned properties as well, suggests that they likewise contest the role of state authorities in the satisfaction of social needs at large during urban planning and management. Public housing policies are incorporated into this critique, although it has greater breadth concerning the many types of buildings with a past or potential capability to provide social services for the local community. Additionally, the great diversity of existing squatters means that they cannot all be defined as anti-capitalist activists; some squatters and many infrequent participants in SSCs do not adhere to such a radical agenda. The high numbers of stealth squatters and the occasional agreements between squatters and owners (see, for example, the legalisations of SSCs where anti-capitalism was not the leading discourse, such as Montamarta or Seco) are clear indicators that the goal of guaranteeing a durable stay overshadows systematic opposition to private property and the capitalist system at large.

These patterns are slightly different when embedded in a wider context of economic crisis, dramatic shortages of affordable housing and massive occupations of dwellings that eventually have taken the form of a politicised housing movement. In particular, the Obra Social campaign signalled a turning point in the long tradition of urban squatting. Most of the literature has not paid attention to this contextual shift when examining squatters' challenges to private property or has not compared the two forms of political squatting.

In comparison with SSCs, the legitimation discourse promoted by the PAH more explicitly targets owners (banks, preferably those that have been bailed out) and buildings (almost exclusively collective residential ones). This means that the traditional pattern of occupying privately owned residential buildings for SSCs is now exacerbated and polished by the purposive avoidance of state-owned properties and other types of buildings. The culprits of the housing crisis, evictions and rising homelessness are the financial corporations that manipulate markets, social needs and the legal terms of mortgages. Governments are also responsible for their collusion with banks' interests, for not overseeing their operations and, finally, for the transfer of massive amounts of public monies in order to prevent their collapse. The lack of a sufficient social housing stock supplements the critique by pointing to the heart of the shrinking welfare state and the neoliberal policies under way. Although state-owned properties are not directly threatened by the PAH, these activists also put pressure on local governments and the state by demanding specific policies to address the dire housing emergency.

Therefore, the Obra Social campaign is demonstrably more restricted in the acceptable types of ownership for vacancies that activists occupy. As confirmed by observations and interviewees, the range may be widened by the inclusion of some real estate developers and wealthy owners. Even squatters in social housing estates have enjoyed support from the PAH and other housing activists from 2011 onwards. A key difference is that the strategy adopted by the PAH to both gain public favour and efficiently house people in need is distanced from the anti-capitalist discourse of former political squatters. Instead of addressing the subject of private property, the PAH focuses on the violation of rights experienced by homeowners. Financial, labour and housing markets are blamed on that account, in addition to the neoliberal state swallowed by the ruling economic elites in former markets. Consequently, it is assumed that housing property rights would be acceptable in a context of increased social protection by the state. Otherwise, dispossessed people are entitled to disobey the very legal basis of private property when it is disused. Squatting is thus considered legitimate when the markets erode the basic living conditions for a large part of the population and when the state does not compensate for this situation with sufficient welfare.

In short, squatting practices and discourses question private property in a capitalist society in different fashions and with varying consequences. Rather than private property as such, it is usually vacant property, urban speculation and housing unaffordability that is confronted in conflict with the rights of specific private owners. Political squatters may adopt either a loose or a tight approach when deciding on the types of buildings and owners to target, and this determines their social influence and support. However, their legitimation discourse is constrained by the practical patterns of choices made, the availability of empty properties in specific urban contexts and the overall significance of the housing crisis for the surrounding society. As the evidence presented here shows, this unstable balance has proved sufficient to allow the transgressive action of squatting to continue over various decades in cities such as Madrid.

## References

Alguacil, J., De La Fuente, R., Martínez López, M., Ubrich, T., & Velasco, M. (2011). Madrid. In M. Iglesias et al. (Ed.), *Políticas urbanas en España. Grandes ciudades, actores y gobiernos locales* (pp. 105–141). Barcelona: Icaria.

Birdwell, J. (2012). *CasaPound: The new face of fascism?* Retrieved from www.opensocietyfoundations.org/voices/casapound-new-face-fascism

Cattaneo, C., & Martínez, M. (Eds.) (2014). *The squatters' movement in Europe: Commons and autonomy as alternatives to capitalism*. London: Pluto.

Cobb, N. (2015). The political economy of trespass: Revisiting Marxist analysis of the law's response to squatting. In L. F. O'Mahony, D. O'Mahony, & R. Hickey (Eds.), *Moral rhetoric and the criminalisation of squatting: Vulnerable demons?* (pp. 13–37). Oxon: Routledge.

Colomb, C. (2012). Pushing the urban frontier: Temporary uses of space, city marketing, and the creative city discourse in 2000s Berlin. *Journal of Urban Affairs*, *34*(2), 131–152.

Dardot, P., & Laval, C. (2016). *The common: An essay on the 21st-century revolution*. Retrieved from www.transform-network.net/publications/yearbook/yearbook-2016/news/detail/Journal/the-common-an-essay-on-the-21st-century-revolution.html

Di Feliciantonio, C. (2016). *Reversing neoliberal subjectification: The re-emergence of social movements around housing and real estate in the metropolitan areas of Rome and Barcelona*, Doctoral dissertation, Rome and Leuven: Sapienza University and KU Leuven.

García, O. (2015). *Sociology of discourse: From institutions to social change*. Amsterdam: John Benjamins.

Harvey, D. (2006). *Spaces of global capitalism: Towards a theory of uneven geographical development*. New York, NY: Verso.

Holloway, J. (2010). *Crack capitalism*. London: Pluto.

Manual de Okupación. (2014). *Manual de Okupación*. 2ª edición, revisada y ampliada. Retrieved from www.okupatutambien.net/wp-content/uploads/2014/05/M2.pdf

Martínez, M. A. (2013). The squatters' movement in Europe: A durable struggle for social autonomy in urban politics. *Antipode*, *45*(4), 866–887.

Martínez, M. A. (2014). How do squatters deal with the state? Legalization and anomalous institutionalization in Madrid. *International Journal of Urban and Regional Research*, *38*(2), 646–674.

Martínez, M. A., & Cattaneo, C. (2014). Squatting as a response to social needs, the housing question and the crisis of capitalism. In C. Cattaneo & M. A. Martínez (Eds.), *The squatters' movement in Europe: Commons and autonomy as alternatives to capitalism* (pp. 26–57). London: Pluto.

Martínez, M. A., & García, A. (2015). The occupation of squares and the squatting of buildings: Lessons from the convergence of two social movements. *ACME-An International E-Journal for Critical Geographies*. Retrieved from http://acmejournal.org/index.php/acme/article/view/1145/1107

Mudu, P., & Chattopadhyay, S. (Eds.) (2016). *Migration, squatting and radical autonomy*. Oxon: Routledge.

O'Mahony, L. F., O'Mahony, D., & Hickey, R. (Eds.) (2015). *Moral rhetoric and the criminalisation of squatting: Vulnerable demons?* Oxon: Routledge.

Pruijt, H. (2013). Squatting in Europe. In SqEK (Squatting Europe Kollective) (Ed.), *Squatting in Europe: Radical spaces, urban struggles* (pp. 17–60). Wivenhoe: Minor Compositions.

Reeve, K. (2011). *Squatting: A homelessness issue: An evidence review*. London: Crisis & CRESR-Sheffield Hallam University.

Seminario. (2015). *Okupa Madrid (1985–2011): Memoria, reflexión, debate y autogestión colectiva del conocimiento*. Madrid: Diagonal.

SqEK (Squatting Europe Kollective) (2013). *Squatting in Europe: Radical spaces, urban struggles*. Wivenhoe: Minor Compositions.

Stavrides, S. (2016). *Common space: The city as commons*. London: Zed.

Van Der Steen, B., Katzeef, A., & Van Hoogenhuijze, L. (Eds.) (2014). *The city is ours: Squatting and autonomous movements in Europe from the 1970s to the present*. Oakland: PM.

Ward, C. (1980). The early squatters. In W. Nick (Ed.), *Squatting: The real story* (pp. 104–109). London: Bay Leaves Books.

Ward, C. (2002). *Cotters and squatters: Housing's hidden history*. Nottingham: Five Leaves.

# Intermezzos

Chapter 5

# Landed (Freeman's Wood)

## An exploration of landownership through contemporary art

*John Angus and Storey G2*

*This artistic intervention narrates an art project developed in response to an enclosure of a plot of land used by generations of people on the edge of Lancaster, England. As the curator, the author explains the historical background of the land, the contemporary conflict between private investors and the community, and most importantly about three artistic commissions which take this conflict as their starting point to explore the topic of landownership. The project provides an example of the roles art can play to comment on and raise awareness of social and political issues, such as property conflicts.*

Freeman's Wood is a plot of land on the edge of Lancaster, where the interests of the local community have collided with those of global capital. This plot has been used by local people for decades, and they have regarded it as common land, but fencing was installed around it in 2012, resulting in public unrest and reports in the local press. The land belongs to a company registered in Bermuda. This contemporary art project, "Landed (Freeman's Wood)," takes the situation of conflict over this plot as an appropriate example through which to explore the topic of landownership and its effects on people's lives. It was undertaken by StoreyG2, which is a small art organisation based in Lancaster, in North West England. Our aim was not to be activists involved in the contest over this particular plot but simply to raise awareness and discussion of the topic.

Ownership of land is fundamental to all social and economic structures. The unequal ownership of land provides owners with social and economic power. It is estimated (Monbiot, 2012) that about 70% of the land in the UK is owned by 0.7% of the population. However, landownership is a hidden political topic in England. In the 1970s there was political discussion and academic research about it, but since then, landownership and the redistribution of land has largely disappeared from political debate. More recently, in his introduction to a lengthy review of a book about landownership, Ferdinand Mount (2014, p. 11), a former Conservative MP, wrote, "In this case, the elephant is the room. There can be few enormous subjects more often dodged than land ownership. It is the great ignored in politics today."

## Art and land

For several decades, many contemporary artists have been working outside galleries and museums in search of a more interactive context and a clearer social role. These artists are not primarily interested in exhibiting in galleries. They are conducting extended 'research' projects in which they engage community participants to address a range of current social, political, environmental, and economic issues. Art can provide a lateral approach to complex topics and can illuminate issues in creative ways which engage the imagination of an audience, which academic reports or newspaper articles might not.

Land has been a subject for artists for centuries. Landscape painting, the depiction or representation of natural scenery such as mountains, valleys, trees, rivers, and forests, has been widely practised. One of the earliest functions of the pure landscape picture seems to have been to provide evidence of ownership, like an entry in a land register. In the later twentieth century artists started to produce works by working directly in, and with land, a genre known as 'land art'. A few artists have engaged with political and economic issues about land, such as Maria Eichhorn (1997) in "Acquisition of a plot of land" in Munster; Amy Balkin (2003) in "This is the Public Domain" project in California; and Patrick Keiller (2010) in series of films about landscape, place, politics, and economic history in England.

StoreyG2 is a contemporary art organisation which has a long history of running gallery exhibitions. It has recently taken a radical shift away from exhibition delivery and is now commissioning artists to work with local people to explore features of the local area which illuminate global social issues. We believe that a key role of art is to imagine how things could be different and to communicate with a wide audience.

Identifying Freeman's Wood as a significant example of contest over land, StoreyG2 commissioned three sets of artists to produce artworks to stimulate thought about and raise awareness of the effects of landownership on people's lives.

Many people have an emotional attachment to a plot of land or to a broader landscape. An art project about landownership could address such emotions. Our curatorial approach, however, is to intellect rather than emotion, to effect rather than affect. We are interested in the effects which the gross inequality in landownership has on people's economic and social circumstances. The contest over property which we wish to address is that between the idea of owning land as property for the benefit of a few, as opposed to land as a communal resource for all. We selected Freeman's Wood because it is an example of this contest over land being property or not. The fence installed around this land, together with the gaps which have been created in it, symbolise that contest between private property and communal resource. Should land be owned at all? The treatment of land as property is so ingrained in our society that it can be difficult to imagine how it could be otherwise.

## The plot of land – Freeman's Wood

The plot of land known as Freeman's Wood is located on the edge of the city of Lancaster, in North West England.

It is bounded by an industrial estate, a cycle path, a public footpath, and a public recreation ground. It is close to residential housing and open farmland and near to the tidal estuary and salt marshes of the river Lune. It was a part of the site of the now defunct factory of the major employer in Lancaster in the late nineteenth and early twentieth centuries, Williamsons, which made linoleum. The owner, James Williamson, later Lord Ashton, became one of the richest men in the world at that time through this production.

The land was originally part of Lancaster Marsh, which by the late eighteenth century belonged to Lancaster Corporation. It was then common pasture on which the 80 oldest freemen of Lancaster had grazing rights. The Enclosure of the Commons Act of 1795 allowed Lancaster Corporation to 'enclose' the land, to divide it up into fields, and to rent it out to private tenants. Legislative Acts of 1864 and 1892 gave the Corporation power to sell parts of the Marsh.

Williamson's lino factory was created on land nearby in the mid-nineteenth century and, as it gradually expanded, Williamson bought additional plots of land on the Marsh. The area now known as Freeman's Wood was used as a factory tip, one area included a gravel pit, and part of it was a recreation ground for the factory workers. In its heyday, Williamson's was a huge factory, but it declined in the 1950s and 1960s. The factory continued to operate under new names and owners but ceased in 2001.

The Land Registry documents the current owner of the Freeman's Wood plot as Lune Industrial Estate Ltd and that it purchased this land in 1994. However,

*Figure 5.1* Freeman's Wood: aerial view

*Figures 5.2–5.5* Amended “Warning: Keep Out . . .” signs

The Property Trust Plc is generally recognised as being the real owner. This property development company is registered in Bermuda, and its directors are said to be based in Hong Kong.

The planning consultancy company acting for them, Satnam Investments Ltd, is based in Gloucestershire. Its director was born in the Punjab, moved to the UK in his youth, and is now a multi-millionaire. He has also been very socially successful and is chairman of the polo club at which members of the royal family play. He is a friend of Prince Charles and Camilla. His son plays polo with Prince Harry. So this scrubby patch of land on the edge of town has a rich history and now has direct links to national and global power structures and economic, social, and political networks.

Although industrial use of Freeman’s Wood diminished as the factory declined, recreational use continued. Local people regard it as common land and have apparently been using it since the 1950s for dog walking, biking, den building, tree climbing, bird watching, picnicking, playing football, and so on. It is home to a wide diversity of wildlife, including deer.

Spiked metal fencing was installed around it in early 2012, together with “Warning – Keep Out” signs. Various tree houses and a complex system of bike ramps which had been constructed by local people were destroyed. There was a public outcry and several reports in the local press. The signs were rapidly and creatively defaced (see pictures). Local people submitted applications to Lancashire County Council for Town Green status and for three designated public footpaths. Lancaster City Council imposed a Tree Protection Order on the site.

## Use of this land

The land has been used by local people for decades, some say as much as 60 years. The plot is close to a large area of terraced houses without gardens. Before the fencing was installed, three distinct footpaths, created by generations of local people, ran across the site. The woodland areas along the south and west had an extensive network of paths through them. The south-western corner had a BMX cycle track on it, with numerous ramps and obstacles constructed by local users. The open grassland in the middle was used as a football pitch and part as a cricket pitch. This site is a mixed mosaic of habitats, and locals had built hides to watch the varied wildlife.

The local community was outraged by the fencing of the land. The individuals who submitted evidence forms for the applications to Lancashire County Council (2012) for Town Green status and Designated Footpaths claimed to have been using this land for between 2 and 64 years, with an average of about 20 years. These people stated that they had used the land for a wide variety of activities including dog walking, walking, children playing, picking blackberries, picnicking, nature watching, BMX riding, running, and cycling. The majority of the evidence statements state that they had never seen any signage or other indications that crossing the land would be trespassing until the fence was erected in 2012.

The owners claim that use of the cricket and football pitches on this site in the 1960s to 1980s was not by the 'public' but by local clubs with permission from the landowners. A former manager at the factory has stated (Lancashire County Council, 2014) that part of the site was once the Sports Ground of Nairn Williamson Limited and Lancaster Cricket Club. This manager states that measures were put in place at various times over the years to stop travellers moving onto the site. On a number of occasions fencing was erected with signs stating that the land was private property and that public access was not permitted. On each occasion the fencing was vandalised and signs were destroyed. He remembers arranging for damage to the fencing around the site to be repaired in April 1998 and again in January 2004. Signs warning that the site was private land and that access was only permitted with permission were erected at the same time. He claims that while it has been used by dog walkers, efforts have continuously been made by the owners to prevent such unauthorised use of the site, but fences were regularly vandalised and damaged to allow continued unauthorised access onto the property.

## An art project?

This complex situation of contested property at Freeman's Wood offered an ideal illustrative example for an exploration of the subject of landownership. I had been aware of the site for many years and knew that it was thought of and used by local people as common land. I often commuted along a cycle track which went by this site. One day I found a group of men installing a high spiked metal fence along its edge by the cycle path. Their responses to my questions were not helpful. The public outcry soon followed, with reports in the local press.

I had been interested in landownership for some time and had read Kevin Cahill's (2002) book *Who Owns Britain* a decade before. I now undertook wider research about landownership and about the history of this particular plot. I considered artists who might be interested and who had a suitable track record. I made funding applications to Arts Council England, Lancaster City Council, and Lancashire County Council and succeeded in obtaining their financial support.

I appointed two Lancaster-based artists, Helen Hicks and Rachel-Ann Powers, as 'engagement artists' to assist with the project, particularly in contacting and interviewing local people about their memories of Freeman's Wood. We contacted the people who had made and supported the applications for Designated Footpaths and Town Green and followed up a variety of other contacts, including three academics at the Law School at Lancaster University. We talked to local people who have used this land – the dog walkers, footballers, cyclists, den-builders, nature watchers, and the like – and collected their memories of Freeman's Wood, and their wishes for its future.

We recorded interviews with over 30 individuals. Here are a few short quotes:

> *With a space like Freeman's Wood you can just make it up as you go along. It's a creative space for kids to do whatever their imagination tells them they can do.*
>
> *We used it as our playground. We used to swing in the trees and bike-ride along the paths. We would act out the film we had seen that week. We would be Tarzan in the trees one week, sword fencing the next.*
>
> *Local BMX fans had modified the footpaths in the wood to make a bike course. They had made artificial hillocks and ramps. They were wonderful, made out of pallets and tree stumps.*
>
> *The fence felt like an insult.*
>
> *It was almost like the Berlin Wall*

I commissioned three sets of artists to lead an investigation of the Freeman's Wood site, to research and explore land ownership and its social effects, and to produce new art works which would aim to raise awareness of and stimulate thought about these issues.

The artists Layla Curtis, Goldin+Senneby, and Sans Façon, who each have an international profile, were selected because they produce high-quality work, and their practice and approaches are appropriate for the topic. I wanted the project to have potential to reach a large audience, so I asked these artists to produce artworks in forms suitable for distribution on the internet rather than objects for display in a gallery. I sent the artists all the information I had collected, both as background and as a curatorial context for the kind of artwork I hoped they would produce.

## Layla Curtis

Curtis was the first to begin. She is a British artist who makes artworks about maps and mapping. Extensive travel has informed her work, which explores boundaries, both physical and metaphorical. She has undertaken projects in the Antarctic and the Borneo jungle. Her early cartographic work, developed during a residency in Japan, is in the Tate's collection. Layla's investigations often utilise digital technologies.

Curtis is based in London but visited Freeman's Wood several times. She found herself being drawn back to it, saying it would have been a wonderful place to play as a child. We talked a lot about the fence and its symbolic significance and its effect on the experience of being in this place.

She is interested in the ways in which digital technologies offer both new types of experience and understanding for the user and also opportunities for surveillance and tracking of users' behaviour for various organisations. She had not produced an app before, but it seemed to offer an appropriate technology for engaging an audience with this site. Curtis was keen to highlight the role of the fence in this situation, so the first step was to GPS map it.

Following our preparatory work, she then recorded conversations with local people about their memories of this site and their speculations on its future. She also included two academics from the Law School at Lancaster University.

The resulting audio tracks are compilations of these conversations. Memories and accounts of how this land has been used as a recreational space over recent decades are intertwined with discussions of wider issues of land ownership, trespass, territory, common land, and activism. The soundtracks are GPS mapped, so users of the app listen to the recordings while walking in the place where they were recorded and to which they refer and can follow their own movements on a map. Conversations were recorded both outside and inside the area enclosed by the fence. The conversations on 3 of the 13 audio tracks were recorded outside the boundary and are available to listeners anywhere in the world. However, to access those tracks which were recorded inside the boundary fence, the listener must cross into Freeman's Wood itself.

The app is entitled 'TRESPASS'. It tells the story of Freeman's Wood from the perspective of people who have used it. This app forms a lasting document of the local community's long relationship with this piece of land. Even if the land is developed in the future and is changed beyond all current recognition, this app will continue to map these stories onto it indefinitely.

Apple were initially reluctant to approve the app. They suggested that we were encouraging criminal activity, but we pointed out that trespass is not criminal in the UK. They then said that we were inciting 'reckless behaviour' in encouraging people to go onto private land, but we told them that the County Council had given approval in principle for three designated public footpaths across the site. At this stage, we decided that if Apple did not approve we would make the app available by another route and highlight Apple's refusal as part of the project and

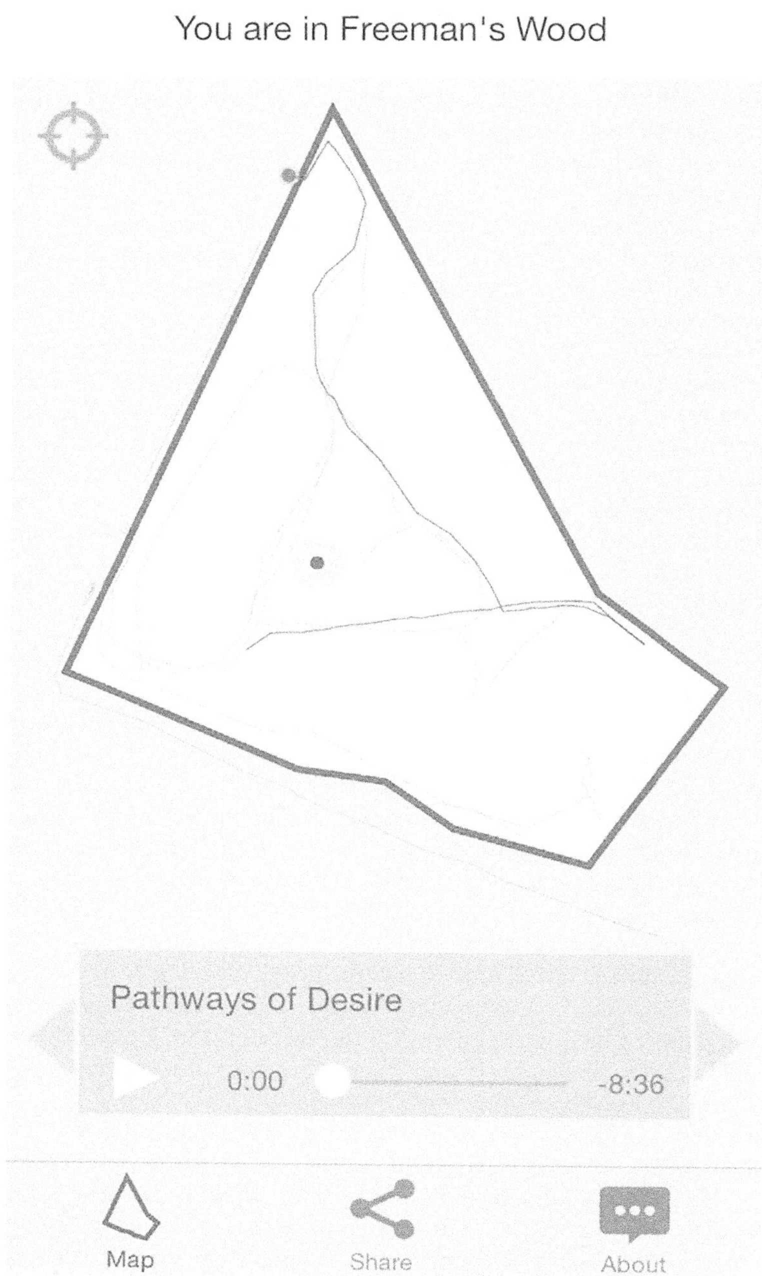


*Figure 5.6* Trespass app: sample screen view

an example of contests over real property rights and access to land transferring to digital space. However, fortunately, after further negotiation and explanation, we were pleased that Apple approved the app.

## Goldin+Senneby

Goldin+Senneby are a pair of artists based in Stockholm. Their work addresses bureaucratic and financial systems. Their projects create a complex structure in which multiple voices of actors and agents are presented, but the artists are absent, reflecting the public absence of the wielders, manipulators, and systems of social and economic power. I felt there was an appropriate similarity in their mode of operation to that of absentee landlords.

I first came across them through a small book documenting part of their ongoing project 'Headless'. They had commissioned a novelist to go to the Bahamas to investigate an offshore company called Headless and to write about it. They commissioned the writer by email, without ever meeting. I'm not sure if this company exists. In their work it is not always clear what is real and what is not.

They decided that buying a plot of land was to be a core component of their project. They said, "We need to become complicit in what we are investigating." My preference was for a plot of land near Lancaster, but the ones we found were too expensive, so we gradually spread the search more widely. Eventually, for pragmatic reasons, they decided on a plot in Kent, in South East England, whose previous owner was living (or at least registered) in Bahrain.

Goldin+Senneby have used this plot of land as a stage from which to present ideas about landownership. Their artwork, entitled 'A3 – A PLOT', presents fake estate agent's 'For Sale' details for "a stage measuring 130 metres by 40 metres". These sale particulars feature a photograph of a plot of land, directions to it from London, plus the text of a short conversation between two people who enter the stage and survey the site. This conversation is a prologue for a theatre play script to which there is an online link as a separate PDF document. The script, which Goldin+Senneby commissioned from playwright Pamela Carter, forms the apparent estate agent's sale description of the plot. It presents an imagined history of the continual contestation and transfer of ownership of this plot of land, using it as an example to narrate the history of landownership in England.

## Sans Façon

Sans Façon is a collaborative art practice between French architect Charles Blanc and British artist Tristan Surtees, based in the UK. Their work predominantly explores the complex relationship between people and place. They state that "We like to see the role of the artist and art as a catalyst in a process of raising questions and inviting one to look and think differently about a place, hoping to create an opportunity rather than an inanimate object."

*Figure 5.7* A3 – A PLOT

Sans Façon have been working on a long-term project entitled 'WATER-SHED+', a public art program in the city of Calgary, in Canada. It is hosted by the Utilities and Environment Protections department, which aims to embed artists and their creative process within the department's core activities.

When Charles and Tristan visited Freeman's Wood they were smartly dressed and wearing city shoes, so they were slithering around a bit on the muddy paths. A passing dog-walker asked if they were estate agents, much to their dismay but

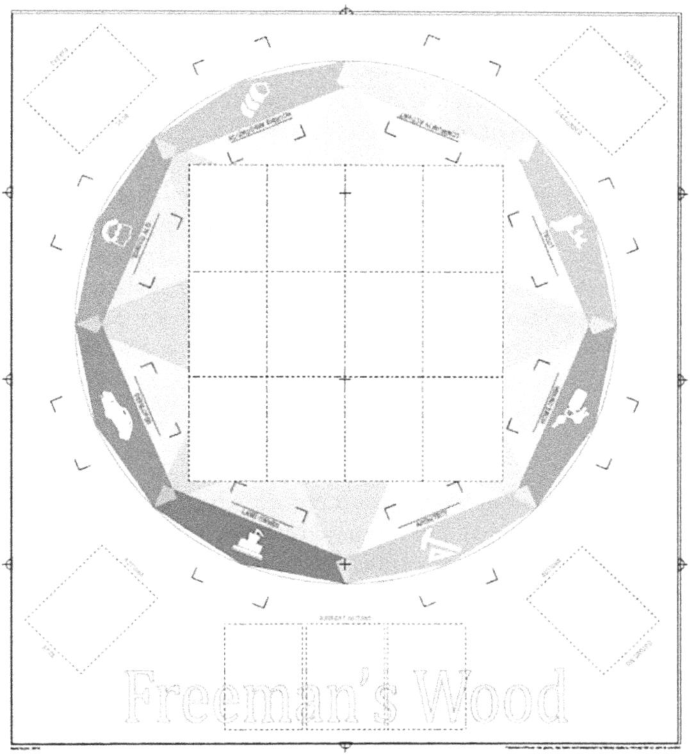


*Figure 5.8* FREEMAN'S WOOD – THE GAME board

also amusement. A few weeks later they proposed to create a board game about landownership. Over the next few months their ideas gradually evolved, and they sent a series of developmental stages.

'FREEMAN'S WOOD – THE GAME' involves verbal negotiation between the players. It is intended to encourage the players to consider the points of view of the various stakeholders with an interest in a plot of land. Individual players take on the role of a designated stakeholder, such as Developer, City Council, or Community Activist, and they have to inhabit the point of view and interests of this stakeholder, even if they do not personally share those views. 'Event' and 'Action' cards are presented which feature a wide variety of potential events and actions which might occur, from discovery of archaeological remains to changes in the composition of the local council. Players are required to react to these events and to discuss their potential effects. Each player role-plays their allocated stakeholder and tries to influence other players and gain their support for their favored response. A player may seek influence through discussion, by bartering influence chips, and by buying votes. It is a game of strategy, influence, and compromise. This game for three to eight players is available for download from the StoreyG2 website. The board, all the cards, and full instructions can be printed out on A4 sheets with a standard domestic colour printer. The board is easily assembled and the cards cut out.

The game is still in a testing or beta phase, but it is successful and effective in achieving its primary aim – to get people thinking and talking about landownership and related issues, particularly the social and legal power structures which provide support for private landowners and the obstacles which these present to any attempts at communal contestation. Players seem particularly amused by having to speak from political positions different to their own. Some are surprised by the ease with which they can adopt a position of power and others by the difficulties of being a protestor.

## Discussion

Local activists create a public outcry and protest when a tangible event such as erection of a fence takes place. But it is hard to maintain interest and activity over time, and the initial scarring of the landscape by the installation of a fence is gradually healed and softened as the plants and trees grow back and the fence becomes partially obscured and absorbed. Landowners presumably operate on a long time scale. They know that their investment will take time to accumulate value. They know that objections will diminish and dissipate. They simply sit and wait.

But in the Freeman's Wood case, the objectors have taken actions which are having long-term effects. The application for footpaths was approved by the County Council, then objected to by the landowners. Further hearings will have to be held, but no date has been suggested. The application for Town Green status appears to have made negligible progress. The landowners cannot proceed towards development until these issues have been resolved. The current austerity has led to massive cuts in the Council's budgets and operations, so these decisions may be interminably delayed.

Some individuals have told us that they have stopped going into Freeman's Wood since the fence went up. The fence obviously deters access, so the use of this land by members of the public diminished initially. But the fence is not continuous, and openings were created, so it is still easy to access the land. During this project, it has become well used by local people once more. Some of the previous paths have become overgrown, as access to them was difficult, but others are still well walked, and completely new ones have become established where new openings in the fence have been made.

It was not our intention to be activists or to take part in any campaign to fight for retention or acquisition of this land for common use and benefit. We intended simply to draw attention to it as an illustrative and juicy example, using the abilities of art to produce novel and imaginative perspectives.

We have not attempted to be objective in our approach. We have not tried to speak to the owners of the land or their agents. The people we have talked to are users of the land, who are objectors to the fence and the consequent restriction of use, or outsiders with particular expertise such as legal academics, the Council footpaths officer, and historians. At the same time, we have taken a detached stance and avoided an emotional response, as have the artists who we commissioned.

We wanted to examine landownership as an extreme example of economic inequality through property ownership in the UK. In the increase of economic inequality globally over the past decade or more, landownership is a prime example, but it is little discussed. Many of those who hold political power are and always have been landowners themselves. Landownership used to be a requisite to be a voter in the UK. Landowners are unlikely to raise ownership as a political issue for discussion and reform.

Many of the people we have spoken to about this project have commented that they had not previously thought about the effects of landownership and had not considered it as an example of gross inequality. I have been surprised in reading about the widespread discussions of landscape, environment, and sense of place that ownership of land is rarely mentioned. It seems that it is so well submerged that few people even think about it.

Many people seem to think that there is such a thing as 'common land', which is owned publicly. The knowledge of the objectors about the ownership of Freeman's Wood was sketchy and anecdotal, as was ours when we started. Most had some idea of this plot as being common land, by which they meant that it was publicly owned. What this meant was vague and included the understanding that it had been given to local people by James Williamson or that it is owned by the City Council. We learned from our legal academics that all land in the UK is owned by someone, and there is no such thing as common land in the sense of being in communal public possession. Our wider casual conversations about the project have indicated that these misconceptions about common land are widespread in the UK.

The aim of StoreyG2 is to stimulate thought. This project has been successful in raising awareness and discussion about landownership among a wide audience. It has been reported in a wide variety of publications, both printed and online, including an article in *The Guardian* national UK newspaper (Garrett, 2016), and presented at two local artists' seminars and four international academic conferences.

Kester (2004) states that this type of art practice creates "a space in which certain questions can be asked, certain critical analysis articulated, that would not be accepted or tolerated elsewhere." Edwards, Collins, & Goto (2016, p. 321) suggest that "By bringing an artist's aesthetic attention to the historical, cultural and institutional context of a topic or issue, and maintaining a critical distance from established agendas and forms of knowledge, the dialogue can lead to unexpected insights and outcomes, which more conventional approaches might fail to recognize or realize."

The art works produced in this project provide an example of how artists can contribute to the understanding and dissemination of ideas around complex social and political issues, and to shift perceptions and discourses.

## Access to the artworks

All three artworks are available on our website (www.storeyg2.org.uk). There is also a video which provides an overview of the site.

## References

Balkin, A. (2003). *This is the public domain.* Retrieved from www.thisisthepublicdomain.org/index.html

Cahill, K. (2002). *Who owns Britain?* Edinburgh: Canongate Books.

Edwards, D. M, Collins, T. M., & Goto, R. (2016). An arts-led dialogue to elicit shared, plural and cultural values of ecosystems. *Ecosystem Services, 21*, 319–328.

Eichhorn, M. (1997). *Acquisition of a plot: Tibusstrasse, corner of Breul.* Retrieved from www.skulptur-projekte.de/archiv/97/eichho/index.htm

Garrett, B. L. (2016, 10 February). What the battle for Freeman's Wood says about the future of our common land. *The Guardian.* Retrieved from www.theguardian.com/uk

Keiller, P. (2010). *Robinson in ruins.* Retrieved from www.bfi.org.uk/distribution/robinson_in_ruins

Kester, G. H. (2004). *Conversation pieces: Community and communication in modern art.* Berkeley and Los Angeles: University of California Press.

Lancashire County Council. (2012). *Application document for Town Green status for Freeman's Wood, Lancaster, plus supporting evidence forms.* Application documents for three Designated Footpaths across Freeman's Wood, Lancaster, plus supporting evidence forms, and objection letters. Supplied by Council Officer and lead applicant.

Lancashire County Council. (2014). Retrieved from www.lancashire.gov.uk Regulatory Committee, 17 December 2014, Item 7. Applications for the Addition to the Definitive Map and Statement of Three Public Footpaths across Coronation Field, Lancaster City. Application Nos. 804–541, 804–542, 804–543. (Note the name 'Coronation Field' seems to be an error).

Monbiot, G. (2012, 4 June). Our countryside has once again become a playground for the rich. *The Guardian.* Retrieved from www.theguardian.com/uk

Mount, F. (2014, 8 May). That disturbing devil. *London Review of Books, 36*(9), 11–14.

Chapter 6

# In the time of Trump

## Housing, whiteness, and abolition

*Manissa M. Maharawal and Erin McElroy*[1]

### The Anti-Eviction Mapping Project

*How is Trump the landlord connected to Trump the president? How can we think about the ascendancy of Trump's reign through a lens critical of racialized and colonial US histories of private property? How might Trump's presidency call for an abolitionist rather than simply reformist perspective on private property? As an 'activist-intervention' this piece focuses on the San Francisco Bay Area and the analysis produced through our work with the Anti-Eviction Mapping Project, theorizing that an abolitionist approach to private property is requisite in contextualizing data and in fuelling intersectional movement building.*

Upon the United States presidential victory of real estate mogul Donald Trump, we at the Anti-Eviction Mapping Project (AEMP) – an activist data visualization, data analysis, and storytelling collective documenting the dispossession and resistance of San Francisco Bay Area residents upon contemporary gentrifying landscapes – have been conceptualizing his victory as reflective of contemporary power, property, race, and displacement imbrications.[2] As an 'activist intervention' into studies of contested property, here we theorize what having a corporate real estate investor president indexes of San Francisco Bay Area and US housing justice struggles.

In 1950, Woodie Guthrie, the well-known American political folk musician, wrote a song about Frederick 'Fred' Christ Trump, Trump's landlord father, denouncing him for his racist housing policies. Fred Trump, who established million-dollar tax-sheltered trusts for each of his children and grandchildren, and who gave Donald hundreds of thousands a year, also left his son $40 million of his $250 million real estate empire – a literal passing down of white inheritance through private property (Stein, 2016). Not only has this inheritance fuelled Donald's own real estate industry, but it also financed his presidential campaign, one that capitalized upon historic racism while speculating upon racist futures.

Today, the US president has assembled a staff around him that is, among other things, determined to maintain the whiteness of private property. As of February 2017,[3] Trump has made the following appointments to key government positions: Steve Bannon to the position of Chief Strategist, an overt white supremacist who once suggested that only property owners should be able to vote (Shane, 2016); Ben Carson as the Department of Housing and Urban Development (HUD) Secretary who overtly opposes fair housing law (Resnick, 2016); Steve Mnunchin to Secretary of Treasury who is popularly known as the 'foreclosure king' of California (Anderson, 2016); and Trump's son-in-law Jared Kushner as official senior advisor, known for eviction and harassment of tenants in his Manhattan buildings (Wishnia, 2017).

How does one think about the ascendancy of Trump, along with his new appointees, through a lens critical of racialized and colonial US private property histories? How might this moment call for an abolitionist rather than simply reformist perspective on private property? Focused within the geographic scope of the San Francisco Bay Area and the analysis produced through the AEMP, we argue that an abolitionist approach to private property is requisite for fuelling intersectional movement building. Here we focus on the Bay Area not only because it is where the AEMP is based but also because it is the most expensive US region (Pereira, 2016). This wealth is constituted by imbrications of the US's oldest industry – real estate, with its leading one – technocapitalism (Chan, 2013; Haider, 2017; Harris, 1993; O'Mara, 2011). Written as an exploratory intervention, this piece presents a series of relationships among luxury development, public housing, Bay Area gentrification, and racialized dispossession.

In the first section, 'White Supremacist Political Grammars', we outline the loss of subsidized housing in the Bay Area as a racialized process that is in line with Trump's racist narratives about the 'inner city'. In the second section, 'Mapping White Supremacy and Bay Area Gentrification', we further trace these connections, looking at the whiteness of private property through the eviction of Black and immigrant communities in the Bay Area as well as through the history of racist housing laws. Finally, in the last section, 'Abolition', we connect carcarel landscapes to the call for prison abolition, advocating for an abolitionist approach to private property.

## White supremacist political grammars

It is important to note that first and foremost, Trump is not an anomaly. Rather he embodies, as the novelist Junot Díaz said, 'a tendency in U.S. politics that has always been with us: a tendency that is pugnaciously nativist, racist, xenophobic, reactionary and White supremacist' (Rao, 2016). This is a tendency that has always had power in the US political sphere and has been a core part of the neoliberal agenda that characterized the Democratic administrations of Clinton and Obama. In this sense, Trump's white supremacist stances represent a continuation and deepening of trends that groups like the AEMP have already been fighting against – trends that include increased forms of racialized displacement, police violence against communities of colour, and neoliberal urban policies that criminalize the poor. Thus, in this piece, we suggest that the very fact that Trump and his family have acquired capital through real estate investments is not an exception but integral to understanding the ideology that weaves private property, white nationalism and violent social policies together.

We begin by thinking about HUD, the agency in charge of federal public housing and rental assistance programs that serve millions of low-income families throughout the country. Aside from having no prior housing policy experience, its current director, Ben Carson, has criticized Section 8 – part of the Housing Act of 1937 authorizing the payment of rental housing assistance to landlords on behalf of low-income households. As Carson argued, 'This is what you see in communist countries, where they have so many regulations encircling every aspect of your life that if you don't agree with them, all they have to do is pull the noose' (cited in Resnick, 2016). Pursuant to this logic, the Trump administration has asked for more than $6 billion in cuts to HUD as of March 2017, cuts that could mean the loss of 200,000 subsidized housing vouchers in coming years (DelReal, 2017). The gutting of Section 8 housing vouchers for the whims of the free market has long aligned with the capitalist dream of further privatizing public space and resources. For instance, the conservative Washington, DC–based policy think tank the Heritage Foundation has for years proposed cutting HUD completely while time-limiting Section 8 vouchers (Gray, Michel, & Sargent, 2015).

As AEMP maps and analyses reveal, there has already been a massive loss of Section 8 housing in the Bay Area. In a 2016 report released detailing displacement and resistance in Alameda County, we found an enormous loss in Section 8 housing between 2010 and 2015, in cities from Oakland to Alameda to Fremont (Anti-Eviction Mapping Project, 2016a). Working with data obtained and analysed by Matthew Palm and Deb Neimeier of the National Center for Sustainable Transportation at University of California, Davis, units were matched with their respective HUD–defined Fair Market Rents to identify if someone with a voucher could afford to access (rent) them. This was then averaged by census tract block group to calculate voucher accessibility by neighbourhood. We found that because the voucher amounts are not competitive with the amount that landlords can get from non–voucher holders once a neighbourhood begins to experience investment, landlords stop accepting Section 8, thus forcing voucher holders to move. In Oakland accompanying this loss of Section 8 housing was a substantial 4 per cent loss of its Black population, along with an unprecedented number of unlawful detainer evictions (17,317 during this 2010–2015 timeframe).

The loss of Section 8 housing is clearly a racialized phenomenon, part of a discourse that blames poor people for their poverty. And so it is little surprise that Trump spews racist narratives of the perils of the 'inner city'. As he described in 2016, the 'inner cities of our country [. . .] are a disaster education-wise, job-wise, safety-wise, in every way possible' (cited in Baer, 2016). As anyone immersed in the urban well knows, the term 'inner city' itself is outmoded, not to mention imprecise and inaccurate. The descriptive swelled in the 1960s and 1970s within the context of white flight and the pathologisation of urban anti-capitalist organizing by people of colour (POC). As such, Trump's use of the 'inner city' indexes a white nostalgia predicated upon structural racism. As Drake Baer argues, 'In addition to drumming up his trademark nostalgia, this allows Trump to define the residents of the inner city as the other, clearing the way for "law and order" and "tough" policing to be the best policies to reduce crime' (2016).

By mobilizing the language of 'inner city' Trump not only advocates for structures of racialized surveillance via 'broken window theory', but further, he deliberately ignores the histories of segregation, redlining, and white flight that constitute its origins. By broken window theory, we refer to a method of policing in which 'quality-of-life infractions' are issued to maintain 'urban order' and in which it is presumed that poverty and social disorganization result from crime (rather than the inverse; Wilson & Kelling, 1982). This logic has been used to legitimate initiatives such as the war on drugs and zero-tolerance policing, as well as a massive expansion of the carceral state (Gilmore, 2007; Shabazz, 2009; Vitale, 2014). Informed by Michel Foucault's idea of the carceral as a network of discipline and surveillance (1995), we refer to the carceral state as that which encompasses more than just prisons or the criminal justice system but instead a wide set of social and political exclusions that are state led. As such, it has become a mechanism through which Black and Brown communities are increasingly criminalized, their everyday lives policed and regulated.

But Trump doesn't stop with his reliance on 'inner city' as a racially coded way of saying Black and thereby mobilizing racist policing, in fact throughout his campaign and even during his inaugural speech he described urban life in the United States as some sort of dystopian hell: 'African-Americans are living in hell in the inner cities. They are living – they are living in hell. You walk to the store for a loaf of bread you get shot' (cited in Smith, 2016). Such discursive tropes have almost always served to set the groundwork for gentrification as a racialized process of dispossession (Camp & Heatherton, 2016; Hamilton, 2017; Maharawal, forthcoming).

These political grammars unearth a confluence of support for racialized policing along with police support of Trump (he was endorsed by the national police union, the Fraternal Order of Police). These discourses also reveal his administration's pro–real estate interests, anti–affordable housing and Section 8 positions, positions that in sum constitute a white supremacist ideology. This tenor is far from new, and as Robin D. G. Kelley accurately describes, instead of Trump's victory pointing to the dawn of a new 'Trumpocalpytic era' in which white relationships to property and policing reign supreme, rather it was, as Kelley says,

> among other things, a referendum on whether the United States will be a straight, white nation reminiscent of the mythic 'old days' when armed white men ruled, owned their castle, boasted of unvanquished military power, and everyone else knew their place.
>
> (2016)

We argue that place, housing, property and displacement have everything to do with this referendum and that the racism of the Trump administration calls all the more urgently for anti-displacement analytic. In the next section we turn to this, using the case of the Bay Area in California.

## Mapping white supremacy and Bay Area gentrification

How can we think about Trump's ascendency through a lens critical of private property in the US? What do relationships between whiteness and property look like in the San Francisco Bay Area? We suggest that one cannot speculate upon the future of the US without paying critical attention to its past and to the whiteness of private property. This then necessitates a decolonial and antiracist approach to spatiality. As Sam Stein argues,

> Trump's fortune is triply stolen by wage theft from the workers who build and maintain his projects; tax theft from the state that enables him; and land theft from the common spaces he encloses. While he extolls the benefits of private enterprise, Trump really got rich off public resources.
>
> (2016)

In what follows, we highlight several of our maps to show how historical relationships to whiteness and property are connected to conditions of racialized dispossession in the Bay Area, conditions we believe will only continue to grow under Trump's administration.

In 2015, in alliance with more than 100 tenants facing eviction by the City of San Francisco on Yerba Buena Island (YBI), the small island anchoring the Bay Bridge that connects San Francisco and Oakland, the AEMP created a timeline to document the complex history of the impending eviction. Essentially, the City had decided to evict the 40 households from what had been public land to create 285 units of luxury housing to be built by the Lennar Corporation. As we began our timeline of YBI dispossession we realized that to tell the actual history of privatization on the island, we needed to start the narrative in 1775, when the island was first colonized by Spain, a process that decimated the social worlds of the Muwekma Ohlone who lived there. In periodizing displacement as beginning with this history (Figure 6.1), we connected contemporary urban land grabs to settler colonialism, thus putting forth a decolonial approach to private property while avoiding reliance on simple metaphorical approaches to decolonization (Tuck & Yang, 2012).

Based on this decolonial cartographic methodology, we argue that Lockian logics of enclosure, ownership, and freedom are constitutive of neo/liberalism and that it is only through decolonial approaches to space that they can be taken apart. In fact, for Locke, property itself was 'pre-political', in that its constitution was requisite to state formation (Blomley, 2005, p. 125). As such, ontologies of

*Figure 6.1* A brief history of displacement on Yerba Buena Island, AEMP, 2015

Retrieved from www.antievictionmap.com/ybi/

the property-owning subject informed colonial projects and the impositions of state regimes. A decolonial approach to property undoes such ownership logics, invoking decolonial spaces, counterpublics, and in Audra Simpson's words, 'cartographies of refusal' (2014, p. 33). By understanding both private property and the state formation as colonially imposed constructs, we can understand the anti-immigrant stances taken by Trump (but also by previous political regimes) as based upon fictive borders and notions of sovereignty. Here Muslim registries and bans, enhanced deportation policies, and a southern border wall are *material* threats but ones predicated upon colonial and Lockian figments.

In thinking through the horrific immigration policies that Trump imposes through an anti-displacement analytic, it is important to remember that immigrant communities are already disproportionately targeted by another form of forced ejection: eviction. As the AEMP found through collaborative research with tenant organizations in San Francisco and San Mateo counties, Black and Latino/a renter households have been evicted at rates far higher than white ones (Figure 6.2). In San Mateo in 2015, for instance, we found that Latino/a residents comprise 25 per cent of the county's population but 49 per cent of its evictees, 34 per cent of whom speak Spanish as their primary language (Anti-Eviction

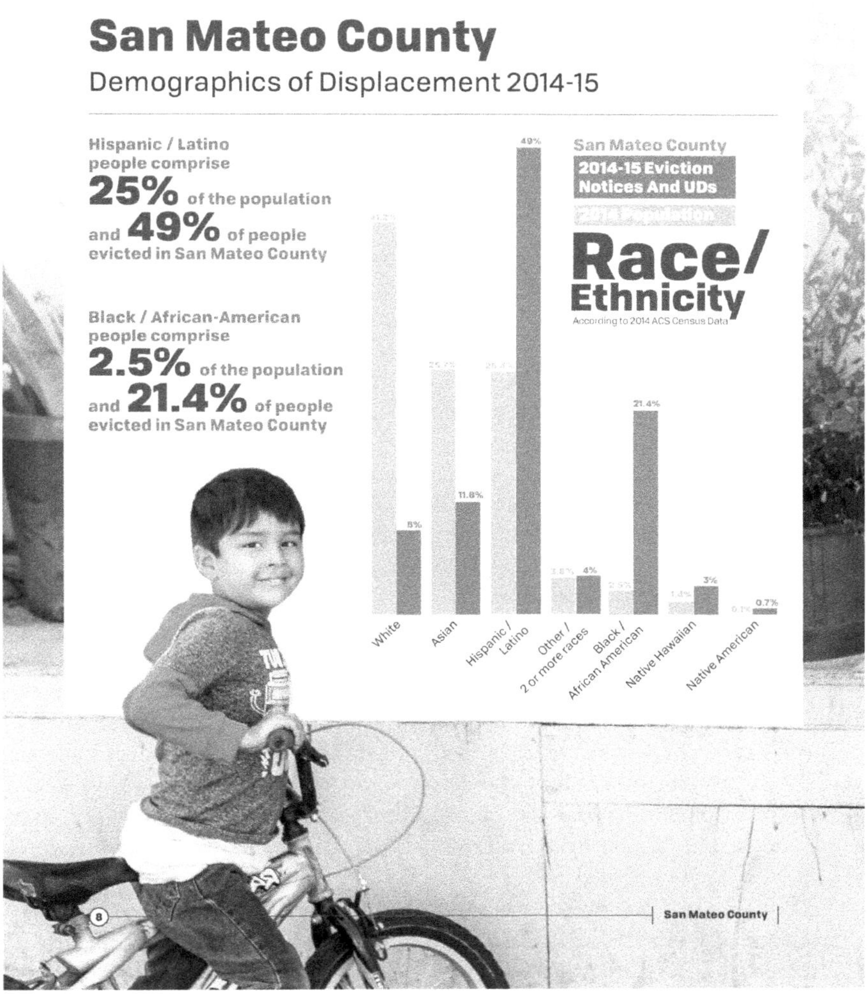


*Figure 6.2* San Mateo County demographics of displacement 2014–2015, AEMP et al., 2016

Retrieved from www.antievictionmappingproject.net/sanmateo.html

Mapping Project, San Mateo Legal Aid, & Community Services in East Palo Alto, 2016). As the housing organization Causa Justa has reported, there have been numerous accounts of non-English speaking tenants being threatened by landlords who make false eviction threats in English (Wong, 2014). Particularly vulnerable are those who are undocumented, as they are often harassed and unlawfully evicted by landlords who threaten to call Immigration Enforcement and Customs on them – a trend that has been reported as exacerbated post-Trump (Capps, 2017). There have been multiple cases in San Francisco's Mission District, for instance, in which landlords bolt tenants' doors shut and threaten to evict them unless they bring valid identification (Wong, 2014). This dirty tactic is used as a speculative real estate tool, in which post-eviction rental properties are converted into lucrative ownership units, amassing capital for speculator intermediaries. Such racialized technologies of eviction illuminate the dominance of white property ownership as it preys upon Latino/a residents, people who Trump has called 'criminals' and 'rapists' and who he has vowed to 'send back', to south of the border (Kopan, 2016).

The San Mateo eviction data reveals another important analytic to think through in correlation with Trump's impending presidency and processes of gentrification: gender. As we found, 63 per cent of residents in our dataset were from female-headed households, pointing to an analysis in which evictions are gendered as well as racialized. This is important to think through as Trump seems to view women as property, as exemplified by his now infamous comment that he would like to 'grab them by the pussy' (*New York Times*, 2016).

Our data has also indicated a dramatic disparity in evictions amongst Black tenants. For instance, in San Francisco in 2015, Black clientele seen by the Eviction Defense Collaborative was over 300 per cent overrepresented (18.5 per cent) compared to the city's population (5.5 per cent; Anti-Eviction Mapping Project & Eviction Defense Collaborative, 2016). Meanwhile, white clientele were inversely underrepresented (17 per cent) comparatively (41 per cent). But it is not only evictions that are racialized as anti-Black; landlords have long discriminated against Black tenants (Hanson & Hawley, 2011; Feagin, 1999). Similarly, when it comes to homeownership, Black buyers are disfavoured (Oh & Yinger, 2015). And this trend is far from new. As George Lipsitz contextualizes, not only are most Black residents not amongst the 46 million Americans today whose wealth is tethered to the Homestead Act of 1863 (because all that land was allocated to white people and specifically denied to Black people), but further, Black residents

> cannot include themselves among the major beneficiaries of the trillions of dollars of wealth accumulated through the appreciation of housing assets secured by federally insured loans between 1932 and 1962 because 98 per cent of FHA loans made during that era went to whites via the openly racist categories utilized in the agency's official manuals for appraisers.
>
> (2006, p. 107)

By these latter discriminatory loans, Lipsitz is referring to the post–New Deal 1930s-era federal practice of delineating city areas by their return on investment, often resulting in banks refusing loans and mortgages to residents of 'at-risk' neighbourhoods. These pathologised spaces were mapped by the government-sponsored Home Owner's Loan Corporation (HOLC), which mapped 239 cities, grading neighbourhoods based on racial and economic constitution. Due to 1930s-era racism, white neighbourhoods were given higher grades than POC ones. Once these maps were created, the FHA, the organization which took over HOLC, used the maps to determine who could apply for and receive mortgages or loans. As loans and investments were funnelled into the higher-grade areas, a wealth disparity grew between neighbourhoods, one that continues to impact lending and mortgage practices.

For instance, throughout California, twice as many Latino/a and Black homeowners reported prepayment penalty provisions on loans as white homeowners (Lipsitz, 2006, p. 109). These became the predatory loans used to decimate neighbourhoods throughout the foreclosure crisis. Thus, as research by Wyly *et al.* evidences, the foreclosure crisis has installed new racial meanings in the US (2012). Perhaps it should be little surprise then that just one hour after Trump was signed in as president, Carson indefinitely suspended a forthcoming rate cut for FHA–backed loan mortgage insurance, which had been popular amongst first-time home buyers and people with poor credit and which would have saved California FHA-backed borrowers roughly $860/year (Khouri, 2017).

In 2016, the AEMP created a set of comparative maps, studying correlations between 1939 redlining zones, foreclosure instances, and race in San Francisco and the East Bay (Anti-Eviction Mapping Project, 2016b, 2016c). As we found, areas given 'D' or red grades during the 1930s have experienced a disproportionate number of foreclosures in both regions. Further, these 'red' areas have higher Black populations than other areas, indexing contemporary spectres of New Deal segregation. Additionally, many of these evictions have been carried out by Wall Street investment companies, such as Waypoint, imparting what Lipsitz describes as a 'white spatial imaginary' (2008).

This sort of mass ownership and eviction practice is clearly supported by Trump, who appointed his son-in-law and fellow landlord Jared Kushner as an official senior advisor. Kushner, who over the last five years has spent more than $400 million on 50 New York City properties, primarily in the East Village, runs his Westminster Management investment company on a business model which Steven Wishnia describes as 'apex scavenger', working to empty 'rent-stabilized tenants through trumped-up eviction attempts, threats, and construction-as-harassment, and then flipping the buildings to new owners' (2017). The Cooper Square Committee and Fourth Arts Block, together organizing tenants in several of Kushner's East Village properties, issued a statement saying he has 'faced allegations of harassment and lack of essential services' (cited in Wishnia, 2017). These sorts of eviction efforts and displacement-by-harassment models are alive and well in the Bay Area, and we only expect them to balloon as Trump is advised by Kushner.

The Bay Area foreclosure and eviction crisis, which decimated and continues to deteriorate urban spaces, also has destroyed many surrounding suburban areas which have become increasingly POC with contemporary conditions of

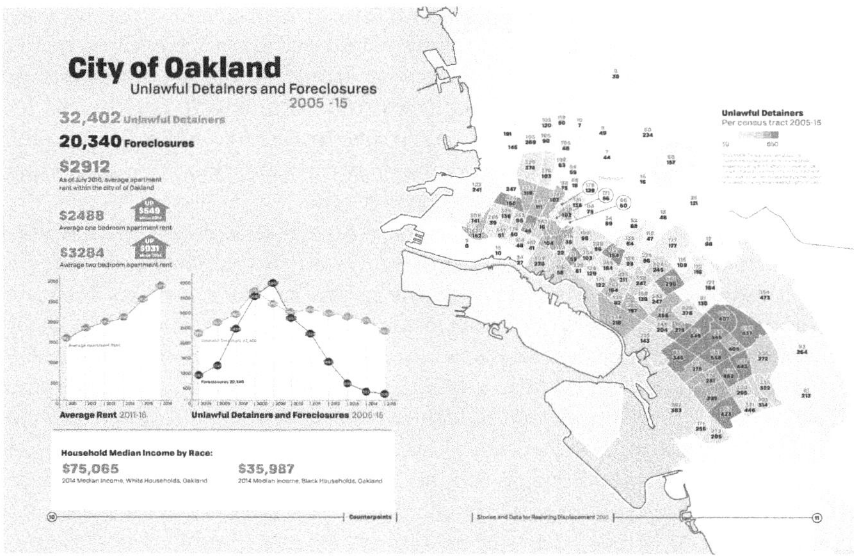


*Figure 6.3* Oakland evictions, foreclosures, rental increases, and income, AEMP, 2017
Retrieved from www.antievictionmappingproject.net/alamedareport.html

exurbanization (Schafran, 2013, p. 678). For instance, a 2007 study in Contra Costa County revealed that there were 20 per cent more African American and Latina/o residents in high-foreclosure areas than in low-foreclosure areas (Perkins, 2008). In the Bay Area, one of the main contemporary causes for racialized exurbanization is tech venture capital flowing into urban areas and Silicon Valley vis-à-vis the Dot Com Boom and now the 'Tech Boom 2.0'. In the 1990s, this capital incited the development of high-end lofts and then, in the 2000s, towers. Now, in the 2010s, as our research has shown, areas proximate to high-tech infrastructure are most valorised by the real estate industry and thus have the highest prices and eviction rates (McElroy, 2017). The unaffordability of urban cores has led to increased development in outer-fringe areas, which resultantly have become increasingly POC. And as hiring statistics have revealed, high-tech jobs in Silicon Valley – jobs that many newcomers to San Francisco and Oakland reverse-commute to – disproportionately hire young, white men. Here it is interesting to note that the tech industry itself is increasingly becoming pro-Trump. For example Peter Thiel, Facebook investor and PayPal co-founder, was part of Trump's transition team (Isenstadt, 2017), and Uber's CEO, Travis Kalanick, entered (and then dropped out of) Trump's advisory council, leading to protesters barricading Uber's San Francisco headquarters on Trump's January inauguration and causing the hashtag #DeleteUber to trend.

White predominance is not unique to tech, but as one of the most powerful local and global industries, its statistics are significant. As Black households typically earn 59 cents for every white household–earned dollar, and as white families come with much more inherited wealth than Black families ($33,500 versus $3,000), Lipsitz calculates that 'Whites who out-earn blacks by a 5:3 ratio out-own blacks by a 10:1 ratio' and that 'homeownership produces about $60,000 more wealth for whites than it does for blacks' (2006, p. 108), a figure that resonates with our map of Bay Area household income discrepancy between Black and white residents. For instance, in Oakland, the average white household makes $75,065 annually, whereas the average Black household only brings in $35,987 (Figure 6.3). These figures make clear that many of the cuts that the Trump administration plans to enact will disproportionately impact not only poor residents but also Black residents.

## Abolition

In September 2016, while campaigning, Trump proposed a nationwide expansion of stop-and-frisk policing – policing based upon the idea that police officers can and should stop people and 'frisk' them if they have reasonable suspicion that they can or will carry out a crime (Diamond & Wright, 2016). This sort of pre-emptive policing recently faced various constitutional challenges in New York City and has its origins in the previously mentioned doctrine of broken windows policing.

In New York City, as well as in Bay Area spaces, these racialized policing measures can be read as part of a security regime built to protect and facilitate urban redevelopment and gentrification. The relationship between police regimes and urban redevelopment is one in which processes such as homeless removal, the privatizing of public spaces, and the expansion of other practices that serve to police the poor redraws the social and political geographies of urban places (Camp, 2012; Davis, 2006; Low, 2006; Mitchell & Staeheli, 2006; Sorkin, 1992). In this strategy of capitalist development securitization attempts to solve what are in fact social and political crises (Camp, 2012; Gilmore, 2007). For instance, Ruth Wilson Gilmore argues that in the 1970s, California depended upon prisons to absorb post-industrial surplus populations, using Black and Brown people as fodder in its machinery. Rashad Shabazz suggests that this system has also penetrated Black household spaces, constituting a carceral network between the home and the prison as people rapidly move back and forth between the two, carrying carceral relationships of surveillance, masculinity, and resistance into the domestic sphere (2009).

In 2017, the AEMP mapped the connections between policing, gentrification and race in San Francisco (Figure 6.4). As we found, the Black neighbourhoods of Bayview Hunters Point and the Tenderloin are disproportionately policed, with the 'quality-of-life infractions' such as 'Danger of Leading an Immoral Life', graffiti, and 'suspicious behaviour' disproportionately issued. These quality-of-life infractions amount to what Simone Browne argues, are surveillance technologies employed by police and the white gaze, technologies that were 'first instituted during slavery to track blackness as property' (2012, p. 544), searching for what Rachel Hall describes as 'property out-of-place' (2006, p. 70). It is no coincidence that the spaces in which such technologies are deployed are also those undergoing the most rapid forms of gentrification (Anti-Eviction Mapping Project & Eviction Defense Collaborative, 2016). It is in the interest of private property regimes, rooted in notions of racialized people and all property being owned by white wealth, to remove racialized bodies from real estate geographies through policing, eviction, or other means. We can then understand policing, the expansion of the carceral state, and gentrification as co-constituted processes (Maharawal, forthcoming), enacting what Lacino Hamilton refers to as the 'gentrification-to-prison pipeline' (2017).

*Figure 6.4* Policing, race, and gentrification, AEMP, 2017

Retrieved from https://antievictionmap.com/policing-race-and-gentrification

The prison abolition movement has argued that the only answer to the prison–industrial complex, founded in the carceral state, is abolition. Here abolition is both a practical organizing tool and a long-term goal (Critical Resistance, n.d.). In fighting for abolition – rather than prison reform – a radical vision of society is articulated, one in which the underlying social and economic causes of harm are addressed. As the Critical Resistance website (n.d.) states,

> An abolitionist vision means that we must build models today that can represent how we want to live in the future. It means developing practical strategies for taking small steps that move us toward making our dreams real and that lead us all to believe that things really could be different. It means living this vision in our daily lives.

What can we in the housing movement learn from this demand for abolition rather than reform? If we agree that racial justice and economic justice are bound up in each other and that the history of private property in the United States is constituted by colonialism, racialized dispossession, and racialized surveillance regimes (Browne, 2012; Chakravartty & Da Silva, 2012; Harris, 1993; Lipsitz, 2006), if we understand the political moment in the United States as one in which a racist landlord has just taken power and empowered others like him, then we at the AEMP urge the housing movement to move beyond reformist arguments and to instead demand the abolition of private property.

Here we take inspiration from Gilmore, who writes, 'The struggle against group-differentiated vulnerability to premature death is waged in every milieu – environmental degradation, public-goods withdrawal, attacks on wages and unions, divide-and-conquer tactics among precarious workers, war, etc.' (2015). To this list of struggles against 'group-differentiated vulnerability', we add the lack of and people's dispossession from places to dwell.

Our demand for private property abolition is a demand that recognizes that neoliberal US housing reforms reproduce the status quo – one mired in historical racist and classist materialities. These reforms maintain policies, such as minimum affordable housing allowances in market-rate buildings, that lead to the deprioritization of more radical alternatives, such as community land trust funding. This reformist landscape leaves no room for eviction moratoriums or demands for 100 per cent affordable housing development. It is against this status quo that we argue for the abolition of private property, asserting that we cannot dismantle the racism and classism inherent to it without its abolition. This is a demand for public housing, collectively owned housing, eviction moratoriums, and land trusts. It is a demand that breaks down the exploitative relationship between landlord and tenant. It is a demand that our cities become and remain sanctuary cities. It is a demand that understands white supremacist ideologies as fundamental to relationships between people, race, and land. We argue that the times are too urgent for reformist measures and that, rather, now is the time to fight against the racist private property regime that the election of Trump has laid bare.

## Notes

1 Both authors contributed equally to this chapter, and are listed in alphabetical order. A previous version of this chapter was published 4 February 2017 in the *Abolition: Journal of Insurgent Politics* blog at https://abolitionjournal.org/in-the-time-of-trump-housing-whiteness-and-abolition/.

2 The Anti-Eviction Mapping Project (AEMP) emerged in 2013 in the wake of the Bay Area's latest wave of accelerated gentrification. Cofounded by McElroy, the project began by producing data visualizations and digital cartographies useful to anti-displacement eviction organizing, focusing on the abuses of real estate speculation and the material dispossession incited by the Silicon Valley Tech Boom. Then, in 2014, Maharawal and McElroy together cofounded its Narratives of Displacement and Resistance oral history component, collecting and embedding oral histories and video pieces into an interactive cartographic piece. The AEMP has continued to expand since then, with more than 25 active collective members working in San Francisco, Alameda, and San Mateo counties, having now produced more than 100 online interactive maps and more than 100 narrative pieces, along with several reports, murals, zines, and community events.

3 This piece was composed in December 2016–May 2017, shortly after Trump was elected and then took office. By the time of publication, there will be changes to the cabinet configuration that we reference, and most likely the violent effects of his presidency will grow tremendously.

## References

Anderson, S. (2016, 1 December). 'Foreclosure King' for Treasury. *Truthout*. Retrieved from www.truth-out.org/news/item/38579-foreclosure-king-for-treasury

Anti-Eviction Mapping Project (AEMP). (2015). *A brief history of displacement on Yerba Buena Island*. Retrieved from www.antievictionmap.com/ybi/

Anti-Eviction Mapping Project (AEMP). (2016a). *Counterpoints: Data and stories for resisting displacement*. Retrieved from www.antevictionmappingproject.net/alamedareport.html

Anti-Eviction Mapping Project. (2016b). *Redlining, foreclosures, and race, East Bay*. Retrieved from www.antievictionmap.com/alameda-county-foreclosures/

Anti-Eviction Mapping Project. (2016c). *San Francisco redlining, foreclosures, and race*. Retrieved from http:www.antievictionmappingproject.net/sfredlining.html

Anti-Eviction Mapping Project & Eviction Defense Collaborative. (2016). *San Francisco eviction report, 2015*. Retrieved from www.antievictionmappingproject.net/edc2015.html

Anti-Eviction Mapping Project (AEMP). (2017). *Policing, race, and gentrification*. Retrieved from https://antievictionmap.com/policing-race-and-gentrification

Anti-Eviction Mapping Project, San Mateo Legal Aid, & Community Services in East Palo Alto. (2016). *San Mateo eviction report, 2016*. Retrieved from www.antievictionmappingproject.net/sanmateo.html

Baer, D. (2016, 12 October). Trump's 'inner cities' fetish is nostalgic, messy racism. *New York Magazine*. Retrieved from http://nymag.com/scienceofus/2016/10/why-trump-saying-inner-cities-is-racist-and-wrong.html

Blomley, N. (2005). Remember property? *Progress in Human Geography*, *29*(2), 125–127. Retrieved from http://dx.doi.org/10.1191/0309132505ph535xx

Browne, S. (2012). Everybody's got a little light under the sun. *Cultural Studies, 26*(4), 542–564. Retrieved from http://dx.doi.org/10.1080/09502386.2011.644573

Camp, J. (2012). Blues geographies and the security turn: Interpreting the housing crisis in Los Angeles. *American Quarterly, 64*(3), 543–570. Retrieved from http://dx.doi.org/10.1353/aq.2012.0028

Camp, J., & Heatherton, C. (Eds.) (2016). *Policing the planet: Why the policing crisis led to Black Lives Matter*. New York, NY & London: Verso.

Capps, K. (2017, 5 April). In California, landlords threaten immigrant tenants with deportation. *City Lab*. Retrieved from www.citylab.com/equity/2017/04/landlords-are-threatening-immigrant-tenants-with-ice-deportations/521370/

Chakravartty, P., & Da Silva, D. F. (2012). Accumulation, dispossession, and debt: The racial logic of global capitalism – An introduction. *American Quarterly, 64*(3), 361–385. Retrieved from http://dx.doi.org/ 10.1353/aq.2012.0033

Chan, A. S. (2013). *Networking peripheries: Technological futures and the myth of digital universalism*. Cambridge, MA: MIT Press.

Critical Resistance. (n.d.). *What is the PIC? What is abolition?* Retrieved from http://criticalresistance.org/about/not-so-common-language/

Davis, M. (2006). *City of quartz: Excavating the future in Los Angeles* (New ed.). New York, NY & London: Verso.

DelReal, J. (2017, 16 March). Trump Budget asks for $6 billion in HUD cuts, drops development grants. *The Washington Post*. Retrieved from www.washingtonpost.com/politics/trump-budget-asks-for-6-billion-in-hud-cuts-drops-development-grants/2017/03/15/1b157338-157309a0-11e7-b77c-0047d15a24e0_story.html?utm_term=.9359ab1cecac

Diamond, J., & Wright, D. (2016, 22 September). Donald Trump touts stop and frisk practice amid Black outreach. *CNN Politics*. Retrieved from http://edition.cnn.com/2016/09/21/politics/donald-trump-stop-and-frisk/index.html

Feagin, J. (1999). Excluding blacks and others from housing: The foundation of White racism. *Cityscape: A Journal of Policy Development and Research, 4*(3), 79–91. Retrieved from www.huduser.gov/portal/Periodicals/CITYSCPE/VOL4NUM3/feagin.pdf

Foucault, M. (1995). *Discipline and punish: The birth of the prison*. New York, NY: Vintage.

Gilmore, R. W. (2007). *Golden gulag: Prisons, surplus, crisis, and opposition in globalizing California*. Los Angeles, CA: University of California Press.

Gilmore, R. W. (2015, 23 February). The worrying state of the anti-prison movement. *Social Justice*. Retrieved from www.socialjusticejournal.org/the-worrying-state-of-the-anti-prison-movement/

Goldenberg, S., & Cheney, B. (2016, 19 December). City officials brace for potential cuts to public housing under Trump. *Politico*. Retrieved from www.politico.com/states/new-york/city-hall/story/2016/12/city-officials-brace-for-potential-cuts-to-public-housing-under-trump-presidency-108179

Gray, J., Michel, N., & Sargent, M. (2015). *House transportation, housing and urban development appropriations: The highway to bankruptcy*. Issue brief 4414. Washington, DC: The Heritage Foundation. Retrieved from www.heritage.org/research/reports/2015/06/house-transportation-housing-and-urban-development-appropriations-the-highway-to-bankruptcy

Haider, S. (2017, 28 March). The darkness at the end of the tunnel: Artificial intelligence and neoreaction. *Viewpoint Magazine*. Retrieved from www.viewpointmag.com/2017/03/28/the-darkness-at-the-end-of-the-tunnel-artificial-intelligence-and-neoreaction/

Hall, R. (2006). Missing dolly, mourning slavery: The slave notice as keepsake. *Camera Obscura: Feminism, Culture and Media Studies*, *21*(1 61), 70–103. Retrieved from http://dx.doi.org/10.1215/02705346-2005-009

Hamilton, L. (2017, 30 April). The gentrification-to-prison pipeline. *Truthout*. Retrieved from www.truth-out.org/news/item/40413-the-gentrification-to-prison-pipeline#14948792174591

Hanson, A., & Hawley, Z. (2011). Do landlords discriminate in the rental housing market? Evidence from an internet field experiment in US cities. *Journal of Urban Economics*, *70*(2–3), 99–114. Retrieved from http://dx.doi.org/10.1016/j.jue.2011.02.003

Harris, C. (1993). Whiteness as property. *Harvard Law Review*, *106*(8), 1707–1791. Retrieved from www.jstor.org/stable/1341787

Isenstadt, A. (2017, 14 January). Peter Thiel considering bid for California governor. *Politico*. Retrieved from www.politico.com/story/2017/01/peter-thiel-california-governor-bid-233632

Kelley, R.D.G. (2016, 15 November). After Trump. *Boston Review*. Retrieved from http://bostonreview.net/forum/after-trump/robin-d-g-kelley-trump-says-go-back-we-say-fight-back

Khouri, A. (2017, 20 January). HUD suspends FHA mortgage insurance rate cut an hour after Trump takes office. *Los Angeles Times*. Retrieved from www.latimes.com/business/la-fi-trump-fha-cut-20170120-story.html

Kopan, T. (2016, 31 August). What Donald Trump has said about Mexico and vice versa. *CNN Politics*. Retrieved from http://edition.cnn.com/2016/08/31/politics/donald-trump-mexico-statements/

Lipsitz, G. (2006). *The possessive investment in whiteness: How white people profit from identity politics*. Philadelphia, PA: Temple University Press.

Lipsitz, G. (2008). *How racism takes place*. Philadelphia, PA: Temple University Press.

Low, S. (2006). The erosion of public space and the public realm: Paranoia, surveillance and privatization in New York City. *City & Society*, *18*(1), 43–49. Retrieved from http://dx.doi.org/10.1525/city.2006.18.1.43

Maharawal, M. M. (2017) Black Lives Matter, gentrification and the security state in the San Francisco Bay Area. *Anthropological Theory*, *17*(3), 338–364. Retrieved from http://dx.doi.org/10.1177/1463499617732501.

McElroy, E. (2017). Postsocialism and the Tech Boom 2.0: Techno-utopics of racial/spatial dispossession. *Social Identities*. Advance online publication, 1–16. Retrieved from http://dx.doi.org/10.1080/13504630.2017.1321718

Mitchell, D., & Staeheli, L. A. (2006). Clean and safe? Property redevelopment, public space, and homelessness in downtown San Diego. In S. Low & N. Smith (Eds.), *The politics of public space* (pp. 143–175). New York, NY & Abingdon: Routledge.

*New York Times*. (2016, 8 October). Transcript: Donald Trump's taped comments about women. Retrieved from www.nytimes.com/2016/10/08/us/donald-trump-tape-transcript.html

O'Mara, M. (2011, 16 June). Silicon Valleys. *Boom Magazine*. Retrieved from https://boomcalifornia.com/2011/06/16/silicon-valleys/

Oh, S., & Yinger, J. (2015). What have we learned from paired testing in housing markets? *Cityscape: A Journal of Policy Development and Research, 17*(3), 15–59. Retrieved from www.huduser.gov/portal/periodicals/cityscpe/vol17num3/article1.html

Pereira, A. (2016, 27 December). Over a third of the 100 most expensive U.S. zip codes are in the Bay Area. *San Francisco Chronicle.* Retrieved from www.sfgate.com/realestate/article/Over-a-third-of-the-100-most-expensive-zip-codes-10820663.php

Perkins, K. A. (2008). *The geography of foreclosure in Contra Costa County, California.* PhD Thesis, University of California, Berkeley.

Rao, S. (2016, 19 May). Junot Díaz talks gentrification, Trump and the power of theater in new Q&A. *Colorlines.* Retrieved from www.colorlines.com/articles/junot-d%C3%ADaz-talks-gentrification-trump-and-power-theater-new-qa

Resnick. G. (2016, 28 November). Ben Carson, Trump's HUD pick, once called fair housing 'Communism'. *The Daily Beast.* Retrieved from www.thedailybeast.com/articles/2016/11/28/ben-carson-trump-s-hud-pick-once-called-fair-housing-communism.html

Schafran, A. (2013). Origins of an urban crisis: The restructuring of the San Francisco Bay Area and the geography of foreclosure. *International Journal of Urban and Regional Research, 37*(2), 663–688. Retrieved from http://dx.doi.org/10.1111/j.1468-2427.2012.01150.x

Shabazz, R. (2009). 'So high you can't get over it, so low you can't get under it': Carceral spatiality and black masculinities in the United States and South Africa. *Souls, 11*(3), 276–294. Retrieved from http://dx.doi.org/10.1080/10999940903088309

Shane, S. (2016, 27 November). Combative, Populist Steve Bannon found his man in Donald Trump. *The New York Times.* Retrieved from www.nytimes.com/2016/11/27/us/politics/steve-bannon-white-house.html?_r=1

Simpson, A. (2014). *Mohawk interruptus: Life across the borders of settler states.* Durham, NC: Duke University Press.

Smith, C. (2016, 25 October). Trump warns of inner city 'hell' for Blacks where Trayvon Martin was shot. *ABC News.* Retrieved from http://abcnews.go.com/Politics/trump-warns-city-hell-blacks-trayvon-martin-shot/story?id=43057914

Sorkin, M. (Ed.) (1992). *Variations on a theme park: The new American city and the end of public space.* New York City, NY: Farrar, Straus and Giroux:

Stein, S. (2016, 4 August). How the Trumps got rich. *Jacobin.* Retrieved from www.jacobinmag.com/2016/08/trump-real-estate-theft-public-land-taxes/

Tuck, E., & Yang, K. W. (2012). Decolonization is not a metaphor. *Decolonization: Indigeneity, Education & Society, 1*(1), 1–40. Retrieved from http://decolonization.org/index.php/des/article/view/18630

Vitale, A. S. (2014, 1 August). The neoconservative roots of broken windows theory. *Gotham Gazette.* Retrieved from www.gothamgazette.com/index.php/opinion/5199-neoconservative-roots-broken-windows-policing-theory-nypd-bratton-vitale

Wishnia, S. (2017, 12 January). Jared Kushner's East Village tenants 'horrified' their landlord will be working in the White House. *Village Voice.* Retrieved from www.villagevoice.com/news/jared-kushners-east-village-tenants-horrified-their-landlord-will-be-working-in-the-white-house-9553850

Wong, J. (2014, 9 April). How to curb gentrification. *In These Times.* Retrieved from https://popularresistance.org/how-to-curb-gentrification/

Wyly, E., Ponder, C. S., Nettling, P., Ho, B, Fung, S. E., Liebowitz, Z., & Hammel, D. (2012). New racial meanings of housing in America. *American Quarterly, 64*(3), 571–604. Retrieved from http://dx.doi.org/10.1353/aq.2012.0036

# Part II

# Land rights and conflicting laws

Chapter 7

# The work of ownership

## Shaping contestation in Ontario's aggregate extraction disputes

*Estair Van Wagner*

*This chapter examines the ways in which law 'brackets' human relationships with land to produce and (re)enforce particular forms of land use. It examines the specific work that legal concepts of ownership perform in disputes about how private land can be used. Ownership shapes the relationship between private property and planning in order to expose opportunities for the creative rethinking of property relations. Further, ownership works through law to assert both the chronological power to control the sequencing of events and the substantive power to manage and control the messy complexity of relations engaged by decisions about how land can and should be used.*

### Introduction

Disagreements about property – what, where, and whose it is – take place in a range of forums and can take many different forms. Such contestation often engages with formal law at various stages. Therefore, while formal law may only be one aspect of contested property claims, 'law does matter' to property relations and to the ways in which they can be contested and transformed (Valverde, 2012, p. 6). This chapter examines the land use planning dispute as one particular space in which disagreements about property occur. While land use has been and continues to be treated as a presumptively neutral technical concept (Blomley, 2016), this chapter critically examines the role of legal ownership in land use law. It explores the ways in which law is used to 'bracket' human relationships with land to produce and (re)enforce particular forms of land use (Blomley, 2014) by examining the specific work that legal concepts of ownership perform in disputes about how private land can be used (Arnold, 2002; Blomley, 2016; Porter, 2012; Smit & Valiante, 2015; Valverde, 2012). The discussion that follows, like O'Donnell's work in this volume, explores the way that ownership shapes the relationship between private property and planning in order to expose opportunities for the creative rethinking of property relations. This chapter contributes to a small body of scholarship exploring this relationship in the Canadian context (Blomley, 2016; Smit & Valiante, 2015) through an examination of disputes about aggregate mineral mining in the province of Ontario.

Land use disputes about particular places and developments are often embedded in broader tensions about how private land can and should be used and in whose interest such decisions are made. Inherently involving a negotiation about the power of the state to place restrictions on private property rights in order to benefit particular conceptions of the 'public interest'(Smit & Valiante, 2015, p. 7), land use conflicts uniquely expose the relationship between private property and planning. Groves et al. argue that planning forums can provide critical opportunities to examine and rethink assumptions built into planning law and policy and to consider larger questions about social, economic and ecological relations: 'If a piece of infrastructure is a kind of solution to a problem, participatory governance may, by including more perspectives, enable the problem itself to be examined, along with the ways in which it has been framed *as* a problem' (Groves, Munday, & Yakovleva, 2013, p. 342). In this sense, planning disputes can be opportunities for creative rethinking about how we relate to each other and our environment despite being grounded in seemingly narrow or site-specific issues of infrastructure siting or zoning. Yet a resource-oriented and instrumental planning perspective can obscure non-instrumental relations with land while foregrounding instrumental relationships to land (Henwood & Pidgeon, 2001; Nash, Lewis, & Griffin, 2010). The ideological flexibility of planning makes it essential to identify how specific concepts and tools shape the boundaries of conversations we have in land use processes and, therefore, the outcomes.

British geographers Richard Cowell and Susan Owens point to the locally based resistance to aggregate extraction in rural England as having successfully 'reframed' both the problems and the solutions related to extraction (Cowell & Owens, 2006, pp. 405–406). As they argue,

> the importance of planning lies not simply in its instrumental capacity to deliver environmental sustainability, but in its relative openness to influence by environmental interests and concerned communities, which enable connections to be drawn between projects, plans and wider policies.
>
> (Cowell & Owens, 2006, p. 417)

They point to a key link between the successful use of participatory opportunities by environmental interests and concerned communities and the integration of environmental concerns into the formal land use decision-making framework (Cowell & Owens, 2006, p. 406; Owens & Cowell, 2002). This potential for creativity and reflection is largely dependent on the process – whether the broad policy goals are realized through genuinely deliberative processes and genuine opportunities to influence outcomes (Scotford & Walsh, 2013). One of the central functions of law in land use disputes is to structure the relations between the parties at all stages of the process. Law is used to order and manage relations between the parties and the decision makers but also the less visible relations between all of these actors and the land itself (Blomley, 2014; Nedelsky, 2012; Van Wagner, 2013, 2016a). As noted by both O'Donnell and Pasternak in this volume, the interests and agency of more-than-human actors are obscured by colonial property relations in settler states; however, this structure of legal relations is used to shape the extent to which and the ways in which all actors, human and more-than-human, engage with the particular decision making processes. Through this work, law is used to bound and define the nature of the contestation in procedural and substantive terms. In one sense this is a necessary exercise in organizing and scoping a particular dispute in order to find realistic and timely ways to resolve it. Nonetheless, the specific ways in which law is used to achieve this work have consequences beyond the outcome of a particular dispute as 'a set of relations specified as legally consequential are bracketed and detached from entanglements (ethical, practical, ecological, ontological) that are now placed outside the frame' (Blomley, 2014, p. 136). Layering on increasingly complex environmental regulatory regimes has done little to limit environmental degradation without attention to structural elements of the legal system that create rewards and incentives for particular forms of land use (Sax, 2008, pp. 9–10).

While the success of bracketing may be limited and partial, Blomley notes that the work of producing and upholding brackets is nonetheless deeply political: 'When and how they are constructed and who gets to bracket are deeply consequential questions. For not everyone has the opportunity or the power to successfully frame law in ways that stick'. It is, therefore, important to understand precisely how law is used to do this work and to trace its successes and failures (Blomley, 2014, p. 139). As Valverde's provocative work on spatiotemporalities in law suggests, we must do so in terms of the interrelations between space and time at work in particular contexts. She notes, 'for law to work smoothly, disputes about the substance and qualitative features of governance have to be turned into seemingly mundane and technical questions about who has control over a particular spacetime' (Valverde, 2015, p. 84). Both directly and indirectly, Valverde argues, the 'how of governance' is sidestepped by transforming political questions into purportedly technical questions about legal jurisdiction, and 'consumers of legal decisions are kept from asking: how should problem X or Y be governed in the first place' (Valverde, 2015, p. 86). Ownership, it is argued here, is one key category through which land use law is used to manage both the ordering of actors and events and to control the flows of knowledge and information that are included or excluded in the process. As such, ownership works through law in two key ways: It asserts the chronological power to control the sequencing of events, and it simultaneously upholds the substantive power to manage and control the messy complexity of relations engaged by decisions about how land can and should be used.

The disputes about aggregate mineral mining examined in what follows provide one example of how private ownership plays a critical role in bracketing the relationships between landowners, other parties, and the land itself through land use law. They demonstrate that despite explicit environmentally focused policy goals and opportunities for participation in planning law and policy, the enduring legal conception of property ownership as a 'thingless,' abstract bundle of rights is used to bracket the procedural and substantive nature of land use decision making in significant ways. The 'dephysicalized' formal legal concept of property deems human relationships *with* places legally irrelevant, and therefore attempts to assert limits on development or use based on other forms of relations with place are often not cognizable (Graham, 2010; Hohfeld, 1913). Dominant property relations successfully foreground the role of land as commodity – an object that can and indeed should be alienated and used for production and profit without regard to the specificity of location and relational spatial or temporal effects (Freyfogle, 2011; Sax, 2008). Other messy affective, social, and ecological relations with particular places are severed for the purposes of legal decision making, even where they have been invited (or perhaps tolerated) at consultative stages in the planning process or are acknowledged features of the natural systems at stake. As Blomley explains, this bracketing performs an 'attempt to stabilize and fix a boundary within which interactions take place more or less independently of their surrounding context' (Blomley, 2014, p. 135).

The centrality of the owner in aggregate extraction decisions is obscured by formal state control of the licensing process and structural opportunities for participation. However, the role of ownership in determining the sequence of events in the decision-making process not only results in the power to determine when a decision making process is initiated, it situates the private owner at the peak of a hierarchy of land use planning actors. As such, the owner is imbued with substantial power to shape spatial and temporal dimensions of how land use governance is enacted and who can meaningfully participate and influence the outcome. In Valverde's terms, ownership answers preliminary questions about the *who* of governance over the timespace of the application and the site and, in doing so, 'implicitly determines *how*' land use disputes should be governed (Valverde, 2015, pp. 84, 86). This 're-making of nature–society relations' through private property environmental governance mechanisms produces owners as 'efficient, profit-seeking, "rational" individuals' without regard to the nature of their relationship with the particular place at stake (Mansfield, 2007, p. 393) and without acknowledgment of the wider affective and more-than-human relations engaged (Murdoch, 2005; Whatmore, 2002, 2006).

These conflicts demonstrate that legal ownership remains a powerful determinant of when and how land is used. Ontario's land use planning framework formally upholds the public power to restrict private property rights (Smit & Valiante, 2015), yet private ownership remains a key category in shaping particular relationships to land as legally significant while others are deemed extra-legal or irrelevant. At the same time, these legal spaces of contestation about land use can provide important insights about challenging the boundaries set by dominant property relations. According to Carol Rose, moments of cultural and political recognition of alternative property relations have the potential to change our definition of property and property practices (Rose, 1998, p. 141). O'Donnell argues in this volume that land use contestation about the impacts of climate change can expose openings for alternative approaches to property relations. The Algonquin tenure system described by Pasternak, also in this volume, demonstrates the enduring jurisdiction of one Indigenous legal order over land use through relations of responsibility and care. As I have argued elsewhere, rural land use movements can play a role in redefining people-place relations if they resist a parochial politics of place and take on the difficult and unsettling work of meaningful engagement with Indigenous legal orders (Bartel & Graham, 2016; Van Wagner, 2016b, p. 323). The disputes about aggregate mineral mining examined in what follows reveal strategic opportunities to rethink property through land use planning law and to transform the ways in which law shapes and is shaped by people–place relations. In particular, this chapter argues that decentering ownership in land use disputes has the potential to transform power imbalances upheld by the hierarchical ordering of authority and the chronological ordering of key steps in planning processes.

## Aggregate extraction: the construction of a unique land use

Aggregate mineral resources – sand, gravel, rock, and stone – are widely acknowledged to be essential to the built environment as the foundation of infrastructure developments from roads to subways to housing and sewer mains. They are valuable natural resources with the potential to produce economic value when extracted and transformed into marketable commodities through industrial mining and production. At the same time, aggregate minerals are functioning and integrated parts of the physical environment in which they are embedded, with material, ecological, and social relations (Eyles & Eyles, 2002). These landscapes are often layered with other, potentially conflicting interests, such as agricultural production, housing development, recreational use, Indigenous land rights and jurisdiction, and ecological and amenity values (Van Wagner, 2013, 2016a).

While quarrying for aggregate minerals has long been practiced by many societies and in diverse locations, contemporary aggregate mines are large, industrial, open-pit mines. As such, they have significant, transformative, and enduring impacts on the land and the human and more-than-human communities in which they are located (Sandberg & Wallace, 2013; Sandberg, Wekerle, & Gilbert, 2013; Van Wagner, 2016a, 2016b). It is therefore not surprising that quarries have also long been a source of legal and political conflict about appropriate land use in the province (Binstock & Carter-Whitney, 2011, p. 1; Miller et al., 2009; Policy Division, Ministry of Natural Resources, 2010). Indeed, since 2005 aggregate extraction has become one of the most contentious land use issues (Sandberg & Wallace, 2013; Environmental Commissioner of Ontario, 2012; Patano & Sandberg, 2005). Disputes, including those examined for this research, often arise from disagreement about the nature and extent of these impacts on the local environment, human health, and social factors, such as traffic, noise, and employment. Aggregate extraction disputes therefore provide an important example of the material consequences of framing land use decisions through dominant property relations and instrumental relationships to land. In particular, aggregate extraction in Ontario primarily occurs on privately owned land. Therefore, the disputes that arise provide a unique case through which to explore how private ownership operates through law to shape procedural and substantive elements of disagreements about land use.

Land use is regulated by multiple complex and overlapping legal regimes in Ontario, including a range of land use planning statutes and policies, environmental regulation, and both the statutory registration framework and common law of property. While the development and oversight of aggregate mines have some similarities with other extractive activities and certain types of infrastructure, the majority of aggregate extraction is regulated through a distinctive interaction between the provincial planning policy, municipal plans and bylaws, and the *Aggregate Resources Act* (1990) [the 'Act'], a standalone statutory framework governing the process for aggregate licence and permit applications.[1] In this way, aggregate mines are structured as a legally unique land use, with decisions informed by general planning policy but set apart through distinct procedural and substantive considerations.

This chapter is focused on a subset of primary legal frameworks that have been the subject of disagreement and contestation through ongoing law reform and legislative review processes, the Act and the *Provincial Policy Statement*.[2] Formal oversight of aggregate extraction in Ontario was limited until the 1950s, when the scale of extraction and growth of suburban development led to increasing conflict (Sandberg & Wallace, 2013; Baker, Slam, & Summerville, 2001, p. 468; Cullingworth, 1987, p. 229). Since that time, aggregate regulation in Ontario has shifted to a provincially led and increasingly proponent-driven activity (Baker, Slam, & Summerville, 2001, p. 466) in which non-state actors are enrolled in flexible forms of regulation (Gunningham, 2009, p. 181; Neil Gunningham & Holley, 2010). This shift is consistent with the broader international 'shift from bureaucratic regulation to public entrepreneurialism' in planning, driven and shaped by inter-urban competition for global investment capital (Sager, 2011, p. 156).

Conflicts over large-scale quarry developments in the urban–rural fringe of Southwestern Ontario have resulted in major community mobilizations ("Mega quarry defeat is a lesson in activism," 2012), complex multi-year litigation (Bull, 2010), a foreign investment protection claim against the federal and provincial governments, (Halton Region, 2013; *St. Marys VCNA, LLC v. Government of Canada*, 2013), and a legislative review of the governing legislation (Ontario, Legislative Assembly, Standing Committee on General Government & Standing Committee on General Government, 2012).[3] With a fixed, non-renewable 'essential' resource situated in areas of overlapping and conflicting relationships with land and the potential for direct and cumulative social, health, and environmental impacts of extraction, aggregate mining exemplifies the 'wicked problems' that land use law and policy aim to resolve (Rittel & Webber, 1974). In this context, law works through ownership to simplify and sever this complexity and to uphold relations with land that support particular land uses and conceptions of economic development.[4]

## Extracting private profit in the public interest: the centrality of ownership in the aggregate licensing process

### *The legal structure of aggregate disputes*

In Canada, planning falls within provincial jurisdiction over municipal institutions and property and civil rights (*The Constitution Act, 1867*). Ontario provides broad provincial guidance and maintains considerable power to constrain local government action through both the *Planning Act* (1990) and the Provincial Policy Statement (Ministry of Municipal Affairs and Housing, 2014), a policy document that 'sets the policy foundation for regulating the development and use of land.'[5] The bulk of day-to-day planning powers and responsibilities are devolved to local municipalities who regulate land use through zoning in Official Plans and by-laws (Kong, 2010; Makuch, Craik, & Leisk Signe, 2004), though provincial planning regimes, such as the *Niagara Escarpment Development and Planning Act* (1990), retain significant centralized planning powers in particular parts of the province. While it is not the focus of this chapter, it is important to note that aggregate decisions directly engage the constitutional and/or treaty rights of First Nations and Metis communities and the applicable Indigenous legal orders. Indigenous communities in Ontario have long been asserting their right to consultation and accommodation and demanding more control over aggregate resource decisions (Ritchie, 2013); however, the duty to consult and accommodate such rights and interests was only formally acknowledged in the revised 2014 Policy Statement.

Adjudicative review of planning decisions in Ontario is divided between the Ontario Municipal Board (the 'Board'), which serves as the primary appeal body for planning and development decisions, and the Environmental Review Tribunal, ostensibly dividing 'land use' from 'environmental' decisions despite the environmentally focused nature of many objections to planning decisions (Sandberg et al., 2013; Van Wagner, 2013). One of the unique features of Ontario's planning system remains the powerful role of the Board in decisions with clear environmental implications such as amendments to Official Plans affecting public space, protected green space, and agricultural lands, as well as the often-contentious applications for aggregate development considered here. It has jurisdiction to deal with issues and disputes under more than 100 statutes, including the Act.[6]

As noted, aggregate decisions engage both the general land use planning process through municipal zoning and land use governance and the specific licensing process managed by the Ministry of Natural Resources and Forestry (the 'Ministry'). The current Act is an operational statute for the management of aggregate mining proposals. It is not a framework for broader planning inquiries dealt with under the *Planning Act* process and the resulting Official Plans. Section 2 sets out four purposes:

(a) to provide for the management of the aggregate resources of Ontario;
(b) to control and regulate aggregate operations on Crown and private lands;

(c) to require the rehabilitation of land from which aggregate has been excavated; and
(d) to minimize adverse impact on the environment in respect of aggregate operations.

'Management' is defined in the Act as the 'identification, orderly development and protection of the aggregate resources of Ontario,' clearly establishing the development focus of the Act (s 1(1)). No license can be issued if extraction is prohibited by an applicable zoning by-law (s 12.1.(1)); therefore, if the land for which a quarry is proposed is not currently designated as a 'mineral aggregate extraction area' under the applicable municipal Official Plan, the proponent will need to apply to local authorities for appropriate amendments under the *Planning Act* (s 22). Some applications will also involve special provincial planning regimes, such as the *Niagara Escarpment Development and Planning Act*, or urban growth plans (*Places to Grow Act*, 2005) and associated policy (Ministry of Public Infrastructure Renewal, 2006). This may mean additional planning authority approvals or the application of additional standards in certain areas. Therefore, the general planning question of whether extraction is an appropriate land use in a particular place should be the initial inquiry in siting aggregate development in accordance with planning documents of the local authority.

However, this order of decisions and jurisdiction is restructured by law in two key ways. First, s 66(1) of the Act expressly limits municipal powers to regulate aggregate extraction. Second, the *Planning Act* stipulates that all policy and decisions of municipal governments and land use tribunals *shall* be consistent with the Policy Statement (s 3). The hierarchical structure of interests in land set out in the Policy Statement expressly prioritizes aggregate development, restricts the power of local land use decision makers, and shifts the focus to the mechanics of operation to be presumptively approved. Indeed, it limits the municipal ability to impose higher standards where they would conflict with any of its policies (s 4.7). Official plans are required to identify and protect provincial interests in their land use designations and policies, particularly by directing development to 'suitable areas' (s 4.7).

The effect is to limit the ability of local authorities to regulate exploration, extraction, and operation, including the potential to prohibit extraction, to impose a needs-based analysis into the assessment of applications, or to impose protection on features not deemed provincially 'significant' (Bull & Estrela, 2012). The jurisdiction of local authorities over extraction is rendered hollow by this shift from an inquiry about land use governance throughout the area to one about the protection and development of one resource and the management of one site. This inversion of the land use versus operational decisions is compounded by the procedural practice of having the planning and licensing inquiries run parallel or even jointly once it reaches an appeal or adjudicative stage. While this may have important efficiency and clarity implications for all parties in an already complex and time-consuming process, the effect of compressing these distinct inquiries is that land use questions often end up secondary to the technical and managerial licensing inquiry about a specific site (*Re Walker Aggregates Inc.*, 2012). In this way, the messier and more difficult aspects of decisions about extractive and transformative land uses are severed and shifted outside of the legal decision-making space.

Within this spatial and temporal frame created by the intersection of general planning law and the aggregate extraction regime, private land ownership plays a particular role in upholding the ordering of interests in Ontario's aggregate mineral law and policy. In particular, legal ownership is used to perform two key boundary-setting functions in this process, which have both spatial and temporal dimensions. First, the owner becomes the planner by proposing a specific land use in a particular location and initiating a decision-making process. This may be accompanied by physical changes to the landscape that shape the material conditions of the site in advance of a decision or even an application, thus changing the baseline for social, physical, and ecological impacts. Second, in a proponent-driven process, ownership includes the power to shape the story and establish the factual record on which decisions are made. This exclusive spatial access and chronological power has consequences for the procedural and substantive outcomes of aggregate applications. Ownership, as a legal category, is used to both shape the sequencing of events and decisions within the process and to centre the landowner as the decision maker within a hierarchy of actors and interests. In doing so, ownership powerfully influences the outcomes for a complex network of social, material, and ecological interests and actors.

## The owner as planner: site selection and the (re)shaping of the landscapes of extraction

Aggregate minerals are fixed resources. As with other minerals, the rock is where it is, and that is where extraction must take place. As one large aggregate producer noted in their submissions to the 2012 legislative review, '[a]ggregate are fixed location non-renewable natural resources which can only be mined where Mother Nature deposited them'. The fixed nature of aggregate minerals also means that extraction is concentrated in particular areas, for example, the area around Orangeville, north of Toronto, has a high concentration of mine sites. This raises the potential for effects to be cumulative, both geospatially and temporally, rather than simply site and project specific and for contestation to cross jurisdictional, legal, temporal, and ownership boundaries.

But extraction is not only fixed by geological formations. According to the submissions of the Ministry of Natural Resources to the Legislative Review, more than 90% of aggregate production in Ontario is on private land (Aggregate Resources Act Review, 2012, p. G145). In Ontario, surface and sub-surface rights may be unified or separated, with mineral rights reserved to the Crown. However, the majority of private land includes both mineral and surface rights, and recent statutory reforms have further unified land rights, particularly in Southern

Ontario, where the majority of aggregate extraction disputes take place (Pardy & Stoehr, 2011, p. 6). Site selection is therefore inextricably linked to land ownership as it layers onto the fixed location of the resource. The rock is where it is, but it must be extracted where it is owned. In this way, land ownership and the rights associated with private ownership are central to the nature of the disagreements and contestations that arise in relation to aggregate disputes.

### Site selection and private planning

An aggregate licence application is based on the proponent's site selection. While some proponents lease private land for aggregate development from other landholders, selection is largely grounded in ownership of the land in question. In noting the preponderance of private land in aggregate resource development the Ministry of Natural Resources representative at the 2012 legislative review hearing observed, '[O]wnership of the land is very important' (Aggregate Resources Act Review, 2012). The link between private ownership and site selection raises concerns about whose interests are being served in the siting of transformative extractive development.

Because of the dual physical fix of an in situ resource extracted from privately owned land aggregate mineral extraction is not dealt with through public planning or environmental assessment processes. As noted, this distinguishes aggregate proposals from applications that go through processes such as environmental assessment and 'willing host' searches in which a number of alternative sites are considered. While these are subject to criticism in their own right, they do theoretically involve a broader type of deliberative public planning exercise than a process driven by private land ownership.[7] In the aggregate context, it is unlikely that a proponent would seriously consider alternative sites that they do not own and do not have access to for required testing and preparation when putting an expensive and time-consuming application together. Without such consideration of alternatives, there is a danger that site selection will be linked to an owner's ability to assemble land and to their economic assumptions and interests rather than to specific knowledge about local social and ecological relations of a particular place or to a notion of the 'public interest' in extractive land uses.

Some participants in the study expressed concerns about aggregate developers targeting areas with small populations and struggling economies with promises of jobs and economic development for land acquisition and future development (Participant 1, 2014; Participants 16–20, 2014). In the case of one large-scale proposal, an internal company communication obtained by a group opposing the quarry revealed that the site location had been selected because the area has one of the smallest populations in the province and the least regulatory governance controlling extraction in North America (Participant 1, 2014). The aggregate industry and government decision makers routinely characterize overlapping interests in land recognized in law and policy, such as the environmental protections in the Niagara Escarpment, as 'constraints' on the development of the resource. Extraction is both legally and politically constructed as a presumptively appropriate land use but for the intrusion of other values and relations on the land that limit or restrict development.

Other participants noted concerns about the transparency of a process driven by private land acquisition. The selection and assembly of land can potentially start years or decades in advance of an application. In this sense, the sequence of events is initiated long before the formal statutory process begins. One participant described the process: 'We found out later that they had been acquiring lands for 20 years, additional to what they already had. But under a numbered company, so it was not apparent that they were buying it. Some people sold it under a different understanding' (Participant 4, 2014). Another described the impact on sellers who sold under the pretence that the land would continue to be used for agricultural purposes (Participant 1, 2014): '[F]or some of the farmers who sold to see those houses be burned and lost was like us going to a year long funeral'.

Another participant recalled that the site owner went back to neighbouring land owners who had not sold prior to the Application and said, 'you can't sell your house now because there is going to be a quarry on it, nobody is going to buy it, we will take it off your hands' (Participants 13–14, 2014). This chronological power not only advantages the land owner by providing a head start in the process but also through the potential to affect the property relations of neighbouring lands in ways that facilitate particular forms of future land use.

A number of participants reflected on the need for a broader public form of aggregate resource planning between local and provincial governments that could separate the private ownership of lands from decisions about where extractive land uses are appropriate within the province (Participant 15, 2014; Participant 1, 2014; Participants 2, 3, 2014; Participant 4, 2014; Participants 13–14, 2014). Indeed, some groups intentionally shifted from site-specific opposition to demanding broader changes in the land use planning process in Ontario, calling for a different balance between different values and interests in land to be embedded within the legal and policy frameworks. Implicit within these reflections was a desire to engage directly with the 'how' of land use governance, the messy political elements of planning that were excluded as irrelevant in deliberations about specific applications (Valverde, 2015, p. 86).

### *Making spaces of extraction: the transformation of private land*

In a proponent-driven system, land ownership determines the physical location of the site and initiates the process of development. However, it also provides the owner with a more subtle chronological privilege: the power to determine the condition of the site at the time of application. Anglo-Canadian property conceptualizes ownership as a bundle of rights with respect to a particular piece of land or resource (Blomley, 2005; Davies, 2007; Mossman & Girard, 2014). This includes extensive rights to alter and transform the physical and material environment and therefore the material and temporal networks of relation embedded within or connected to that particular place – social, political, economic, ecological, geological, hydrological, and other forms of relation. Thus, ownership can be used to bracket what is considered by decision makers by determining what exists at the critical moment in which the licensing process applies to the site. Through an owner's right to transform their land and to exclude the relevant features of the site, such as endangered species, forests, or wetlands, from consideration they can determine what exists for the purposes of the law. This pre-application control has important consequences for the ability of parties seeking to assert competing values and overlapping interests in the land and for the potential for decision makers to assess such claims. Heritage and environmental features that could potentially 'constrain' development can legally be destroyed, removed, minimized, or transformed long before an application is made by virtue of the extensive rights to transform private property as of right. As a result, relevant features, relations, and interests are excluded from consideration in any subsequent planning process. In particular, and as noted by Pasternak in this volume, more-than-human beings and systems may be most profoundly impacted by these purportedly private decisions. Indeed, entire ecosystems and populations may be managed out of existence prior to the legal process being triggered. One participant expressed concerns about the impact of such transformation on the planning process (Participant 4, 2014): 'That is what is happening now with some developments. Yes, some developers buy the property, they clear it out, destroy value and then what is your argument? You have a woodland? I don't see a woodland'.

One dispute over a large-scale quarry began with concerns about violations of the local tree-cutting by-law. A participant in that process observed that the by-law had been put in place in the context of agricultural land use to facilitate farming activities, and large-scale woodlot removal would never have been contemplated (Participant 1, 2014). They later became concerned that the removal of hectares of trees was motivated by the desire to 'lessen the chances of wild life conduits and other conservation thought to stand in the way of their coming application' (Participant 1, 2014). Another participant involved in the same quarry dispute described the subsequent destruction of the homes and farm buildings on the land acquired for the proposed quarry site (Participants 13–14, 2014):

> There is a big house down the road . . . It is a huge, big house and they took all the windows out of the top part about November, December, let the wind and the snow and everything blow through and then they finally took it down. When that house went down, people started to believe that something was wrong.

These unanticipated changes not only impacted the physical landscape, but also initiated a sequence of events that transformed the social networks within the local community (Participant 13–14, 2014):

> Nobody really blamed the sale but it left such a hole of connections. It is like [you] lay out a thousand piece puzzle and take 30-pieces out. It is not the same. As much as your people might suggest that losing a couple hundred or 300 people out of the community, people come and go, this wasn't it. This was forced, violent, burned, blown up, dug under. Farmsteads that had been cared for 100 years by people disappeared from the landscape . . . dark and not a light of life anywhere at night. It left a profound emotional drain on the people.

In another case within the provincially protected Niagara Escarpment Plan Area, participants described the owner's attempt to destroy wetlands after the endangered Jefferson salamander was discovered on neighbouring property and the group opposing applied for provincial wetland designation over the area (Participant 15, 2014; Participant 4, 2014). The owner in that case was ultimately charged at the urging of local residents and opponents of the quarry and pled guilty. However, the success of this enforcement was due to the informal research and access of a neighbouring land owner to the habitat sites rather than any systemic legal safeguard.

Beyond the physical and ecological changes in advance of applications, participants reflected on the ways aggregate mining approvals in a particular place can facilitate a long-term and wider transformation of the landscape by fixing industrial extraction as an appropriate land use for future applications for expansion or new mines in the local area (Participant 22, 2014; Participants 2, 3, 2014; Participant 7, 2014; Participants 16–20, 2014; Participant 21, 2014). The Policy Statement imposes mandatory protection of aggregate resources for long-term use, including the protection of areas with known deposits, areas adjacent to known deposits, and/or current operations, from development or activities that would 'preclude or hinder' extraction (ss. 2.5.2.4, 2.5.2.5). In fact, this protection continues even where an operation or a license 'ceases to exist' (s. 2.5.2.4), resulting in a licensing regime with no possibility of expiration regardless of the length of time an area has remained undeveloped and the changes to surrounding land and land uses.

Several participants expressed concerns that once approved, expansion in size or below the water table was much easier to attain or that other proposals would be more likely to be approved once the area was seen as an extractive zone by decision makers (Participant 22, 2014; Participants 2,3, 2014; Participant 7, 2014; Participant 16–20, 2014; Participant 21, 2014). In the words of one participant: '[T]he only way to control it is to stop it' (Participant 16–20, 2014). However, as described in what follows, ownership also plays a strong role in shaping the process and substance of attempts to control or stop a particular application at both the planning and adjudicative stages. As I have demonstrated elsewhere, the overwhelming majority of applications are approved, by either the Minister or the Board, pointing to a structural imbalance in the process (Van Wagner, 2016a, pp. 45–46).

### *Controlling the facts, controlling the space: knowledge and power in land use decisions*

Citing public frustration with aggregate approvals and other types of land use decisions, the Environmental Commissioner has noted the importance of *meaningful* consultation:

> First, consultation is not simply telling people what you intend to do and, then, listening to their comments.
>
> . . .
>
> To be legitimate, an approval process must be able to reach a decision not to proceed. I'm not saying that this should be a common outcome . . . But, in a valid and meaningful consultation process, we would expect that sometimes rational arguments or contrasting societal value systems would and should lead to a 'No'. Without that possibility, there is no value in consultation.
>
> (Environmental Commissioner of Ontario, 2008, p. 5)

Participants in this study expressed concerns that despite opportunities for public participation, the process was structured to presumptively support development. Indeed, several noted that land owners proposing aggregate mines assumed that proposals would go forward despite the need for consultation and Ministerial or Board approval. One participant paraphrased a representative of the company at a community meeting: 'It doesn't matter what you people do, we are going to go forward with this' (Participant 16–20, 2014). Another described the 'arrogance' of the proponent: 'They had done the political legwork and under the Aggregate Resources Act and knew they could muscle this thing through. Couldn't care less what the community wanted' (Participant 1, 2014). A planner from one provincial planning agency reflected on the political pressure to move applications forward to approval (Planner 2, 2014, p. 2):

> If, say, the municipality or the agencies have made a decision and it is not a favourable one, the operator may express its concern to Queen's Park. In response, we have had calls from the MPP and Minister's office requesting to understand what is going on and why it is taking so long to bring the application to a final decision. Then we need a briefing note explaining the process, the stakeholders involved, and what are the key issues?

For many participants, this entitlement to approval was fuelled by a process driven by the proponent, who provides the majority of the information and expertise to decision makers for the express purpose of having the application approved. The *Aggregate Resources Provincial Standards* and the *Aggregate Resources Policy and Internal Procedures Manual* specify the technical information and reports the applicant is required to provide, including expert hydrogeologic report(s), natural environment report(s), and cultural heritage report(s), which must be prepared by a 'qualified' professional as defined in the Act (s 8). Licensing and planning approval processes and any subsequent litigation are based on this factual and technical record, subject to any independent technical or legal expertise and documentation that may be provided by Indigenous governments, municipal actors or planning authorities, and other groups or individuals at their own expense. The chronological power of site selection and modification, as well as initiation of the process, is thus compounded by the power to frame the questions and issues to be considered. By controlling the knowledge base on which the decision will be made, owners powerfully shape the narrative of what is at stake.

Independent expert evidence and review of the Applicant's documentation is both logistically and financially onerous for Indigenous and small local governments and community groups, particularly given they may or may not be accepted by the Board at a hearing and access to the proponent's land may not be granted for direct investigation and data review (*Re Town of Richmond Hill*, PL990303, r'vd by *Ontario (Ministry of Municipal Affairs and Housing) v Ontario (Municipal Board)* 2001). As one lawyer noted, 'It is phenomenally expensive to really mount a legal challenge to an application for aggregate licence' (Lawyer, 2014). Many participants explained that they had scoped down their appeal to one or two issues because of the cost or the accessibility of experts (Participant 22, 2014; Participants 8–12, 2014; Participants 16–20, 2014; Participant 21, 2014). Two experts who have worked with parties opposing quarries noted that the Board tends to accept proponent expert opinions and shared experiences of being challenged as 'advocates,' unable to be objective (Consultant, 2014; Planner, 2014). Further, proponents are under no obligation to allow other parties and their experts onto the site, making review of the data limited and potentially impossible, particularly with complex hydrological or ecological data that require in-season and regular onsite observation. Even government agencies have limited access to verify data and collect independent data to challenge proponent claims.

This evidentiary and narrative power is compounded by what an applicant is not required to establish. Until 2005 the Policy Statement maintained 'mineral resource needs' should be considered, providing a policy basis for supply-and-demand analysis as central to aggregate licensing decisions (2.2.3.1, 1996). Opposing parties and governments used this version of the policy to argue that the material to be extracted was not currently required and therefore that sites should not be approved (Bull & Estrela, 2012, p. 24). In 2005, the *Provincial Policy Statement* was revised to explicitly eliminate consideration of need in Policy 2.5.2.1:

> Demonstration of need for mineral aggregate resources, including any type of supply/demand analysis, shall not be required, notwithstanding the availability, designation or licensing for extraction of mineral aggregate resources locally or elsewhere.

One environmental lawyer characterized this lack of a needs analysis as the 'biggest stumbling block' in the aggregate planning decision framework (Lawyer, 2014). This was also raised by a number of deputants at the all-party review of the Act before the Standing Committee on General Government described in what follows and by commentators during the PPS review ("Review of the Aggregate Resources Act," n.d.; "Review of the Aggregate Resources Act," n.d.).[8] While the Board has concluded that a needs analysis is not required, it has nonetheless also been a live issue in several cases as parties continue to press for the opportunity to contest the underlying assumptions in the framework (*Jennison Construction Ltd. v. Ashfield-Colborne-Wawanosh (Town)*, 2011; *James Dick Construction*, 2010; *Re Walker Aggregates Inc. (Re)*, 2012). In one case the Board itself noted, '[a]ggregate extraction is the only use in the wide ranging PPS where need is not required' (*Capital Paving Inc v. Wellington (County)*, 2010, 16)

Planning and urban studies scholars have drawn attention to the operation and control of specific discursive frames that influence land use and environmental governance. Patano and Sandberg specifically note the 'need' or 'demand' narrative as a frame used by the aggregate industry to appeal to decision makers, including provincial and local governments and adjudicators (Patano & Sandberg, 2005; Young & Keil, 2005). Such 'narratives of necessity' place conceptual limits on the terms of debate about specific land use decisions (Cowell & Owens, 2006). Here the presumption of need embedded in the statute fixes the conception of the public interest as one of perpetual economic growth and expanding (sub)urbanism directly in law, foreclosing debate about the shape of the present and future built environment and the urban–rural relationship.

## Defining the landscape: the role of ownership in land use decision making

Ontario's planning law and policy does not expressly protect private property ownership. Nor does it expressly situate private owners as planners. Indeed, aggregate decisions engage many of the forward-looking, participatory, and consultative aspects of the province's public planning regime. Nonetheless, this chapter demonstrates how ownership endures as key legal category in land use law. Ownership is used to order actors in a hierarchy of interests in which aggregate development is prioritized over other relations with land and simultaneously to structure the sequence of events to produce specific spatiotemporal relations. The successful bracketing work done through ownership is reflected in the overwhelming success of aggregate applications in the province (Van Wagner, 2016a). However, the ongoing contestation about extraction points to the unsettled nature of the spatiotemporal boundaries law attempts to uphold. Understanding the specific work that ownership does through site selection, modification, and control of the factual record can serve to reveal strategic opportunities for intervention and the transformation of property relations into more just and complex people–place relations.

Transforming the aggregate planning process requires the decoupling of site selection from private ownership and the implementation of meaningful and inclusive consultation from pre-application throughout the life of a project. Decentring ownership, both temporally and spatially, could create opportunities for parties to introduce the material and spatial particularity of the human and ecological communities at stake and to expose the wider substantive and political aspects of the decisions. A better balance of power in the decision-making process would make visible what is really at stake (Nedelsky, 2012): how we make decisions about the extraction of important resources from their material and social context while attending to the transformative impacts of doing so for the human and ecological communities and networks of social and material relations. For example, aggregate development sites could be determined through a broad, policy-driven public planning process rather than purely site-specific private applications. Such a shift raises other concerns, particularly about the nature of participation in such a process, the power of private interests to determine 'the public interest', and the relationships between municipal and provincial actors and Indigenous governments; however, these are issues that land use governance must urgently and meaningfully address in planning more broadly. Perhaps transforming the way we make aggregate extraction decisions could be a starting point for this important work, including the recognition of Indigenous jurisdiction (Pasternak, this volume).

Would the legal decision-making process be transformed if the technical data was provided through an independent third party rather than by the proponent? Public funding for independent technical expertise and legal advice required by participating parties would be a first step towards a more balanced evidentiary record. However, to be meaningful this must include access to privately owned sites and oversight of pre-application site changes, and this requires a shift from property as the realm of fixed, exclusive individual rights towards 'more fragile, contextual, and limited use rights' (Davies, 2012, pp. 15–16). Certainly a first step in rebalancing the power between the parties would be to re-establish the requirement that the proponent demonstrate need such that the costs and benefits of the proposal can be explicitly weighed by decision makers and openly contested by participants. Decentering ownership could affect these sequencing and evidentiary transformations in aggregate licensing decisions and effectively reframe the question from *how* we will manage the extraction of this resource to *whether* we should be extracting this rock here, in this place, and in whose interests. Such a reorientation of decision making away from ownership as the chronological and spatial starting point for land use decisions certainly has the potential to change the outcome in individual disputes; but perhaps more importantly, it could strategically create space within the process of land use governance for urgently needed meaningful dialogue about how we should govern the messy complexity of our environmental relations.

## Notes

1 While the majority of aggregate production is covered by the Act, it should be noted that it has a limited geographic application, which excludes private land in most of Northern Ontario. Portions of the north have been progressively added as disputes arise with respect to specific applications, see *Citizens Concerned for Michipicoten Bay v Municipality of Wawa* (2009), PL040025.
2 In May 2012, an all-party review of the *Aggregate Resources Act* was initiated (Legislative Assembly of Ontario, Orders and Notice Paper, 1st session, 40th Parliament, March 22, 2012).
3 At the time of writing, a Bill to amend the Act had been introduced as a result of the review process: Bill 39 Aggregate Resources and Mining Modernization Act 2017: www.ontla.on.ca/web/bills/bills_detail.do?locale=en&BillID=4213. The Bill, which came into force in May 2017 retains key features of the existing regime discussed in this chapter. Notable changes are largely left to proposed future regulations.
4 This chapter is based on a larger qualitative research project examining aggregate mineral mining disputes in between 2001 and 2014. Specific cases for detailed documentary analysis and in-depth interviews were selected through a review of key documents. Eighteen unstructured in-person interviews were conducted with 25 participants. Participants were largely activists in local or regionally-based organizations formed to respond to a specific application or pre-existing organizations who chose to become involved with a particular quarry application based on a particular set of environmental or social concerns.
5 In April 2014 the Ministry of Municipal Affairs and Housing released the 2014 Policy Statement, which took effect on April 30, 2014 [the '2014 PPS'], however, the cases discussed in this chapter were considered under the former 2005 Provincial Policy Statement, www.mah.gov.on.ca/Page215.aspx [the '2005 PPS']. The key aggregate mineral provisions discussed in what follows remain largely unchanged in the new version.
6 For certain appeals, including some aggregate disputes where hearings may be required from both tribunals, a joint-board is formed under the *Consolidated Hearings Act* (1990). See, for example, *Nelson Aggregate Co., Re*, 2012 CLB 29642, [Nelson], *Re Walker Aggregates Inc. (Re)*, 2012 CLB 16274 [Walker].
7 The provincial and federal environmental assessment regimes applicable in Ontario have both been subject to critique (Auditor General, 2016; Environmental Commissioner of Ontario, 2008; Lindgren & Dunn, 2010). Notably, the regimes are also proponent driven and therefore share some of the issues outlined in what follows.
8 111 of 166 comments on the Provincial Policy Statement Review can be accessed on the Environmental Registry, Registry Number 011–7070.

## References

### Statutes

*Aggregate Resources Act*, R.S.O. 1990, c. A. 8.
*Consolidated Hearings Act*, RSO 1990. c C.29.
*The Constitution Act, 1867* (UK), 30 & 31 Victoria, C 3.
Greenbelt *Act*, 2005, SO 2005, c 1.
Niagara *Escarpment Development and Planning Act, RSO 1990 c N.2.*
Oak *Ridges Moraine Conservation Act, 2001, SO 2001, c 31.*

*Planning Act*, R.S.O. 1990, c. P. 13, s.22.
*Places to Grow Act*, 2005, SO 2005, c 13.

## Cases

*Capital Paving Inc v Wellington (County)*, 2010 CarswellOnt 697.
*Citizens Concerned for Michipicoten Bay v Municipality of Wawa (2009)*, PL040025.
*James Dick Construction Ltd. v Caledon (Town)*, (2010) 66 OMBR 263.
*Jennison Construction Ltd. V Ashfield-Colborne-Wawanosh (Town)*, 2011 CarswellOnt 14192.
*Nelson Aggregate Co., Re, 2012 CLB 29642*
*Ontario (Ministry of Municipal Affairs & Housing) v Ontario (Municipal Board)*, (2001), 20 MPLR (3d) 93, 41 OMBR 257.
*Re Walker Aggregates Inc. (Re)*, 2012 CLB 16274, aff'd Niagara Escarpment Commission v Ontario (Joint Board), 2013 ONSC 2496, 12 MPLR (5th) 51.
*Re Town of Richmond Hill*, PL990303, r'vd by *Ontario (Ministry of Municipal Affairs and Housing) v Ontario (Municipal Board)* 2001, 41 OMBR 257, 20 MPLR (3d) 93

## Other Sources

Aggregate Resources Act Review, Ontario, Committee on General Government, (7 May 2012)
Anders Sandberg, L., & Wallace, L. (2013). Leave the sand in the land, let the stone alone: Pits, quarries and climate change. *ACME: An International E-Journal for Critical Geographies*, *12*(1), 41–57.
Arnold, C. A. (2002). Land use justice. *Projections: The Massachusetts Institute of Technology Journal of Planning*, *3*(2), 32.
Auditor General. (2016). *Annual report 2016* (pp. 1–807). Toronto, ON: Office of the Auditor General of Ontario. Retrieved from www.auditor.on.ca/en/content/annualreports/arreports/en16/2016AR_v1_en_web.pdf
Baker, D., Slam, C., & Summerville, T. (2001). An evolving policy network in action: The case of construction aggregate policy in Ontario. *Canadian Public Administration*, *44*(4), 463–483.
Bartel, R., & Graham, N. (2016). Property and place attachment: A legal geographical analysis of biodiversity law reform in New South Wales. *Geographical Research*, *54*(3), 267–284.
Binstock, M., & Carter-Whitney, M. (2011). *Aggregate extraction in Ontario: A strategy for the future*. Toronto, ON: Canadian Institute for Environmental Law and Policy. Retrieved from http://cielap.org/pdf/AggregatesStrategyOntario.pdf
Blomley, N. (2005). Remember property? *Progress in Human Geography*, *29*(2), 125–127. Retrieved from https://doi.org/10.1191/0309132505ph535xx
Blomley, N. (2014). Disentangling law: The practice of bracketing. *Annual Review of Law and Social Science*, *10*(1), 133–148.
Blomley, N. (2016). Land use, planning, and the "difficult character of property". *Planning Theory & Practice*, *18*(3), 1–14.
Bull, J. (2010, 17 November). *Nelson aggregate hearing explained*. Retrieved from www.waterkeeper.ca/2010/11/17/nelson-aggregates-hearing-explained/

Bull, M., & Estrela, C. (2012). *Recent trends and issues in aggregate approvals*. Presented at the Ontario Bar Association Institute, Toronto, Ontario: Wood Bull LLP. Retrieved from www.woodbull.ca/docs/default-source/publications/recent-trends-and-issues-in-aggregate-applications-%28oba-institute%29

Consultant. (2014, June).

Cowell, R., & Owens, S. (2006). Governing space: Planning reform and the politics of sustainability. *Environment and Planning C*, *24*, 403–421.

Cullingworth, J. B. (1987). *Urban and regional planning in Canada*. Piscataway, NJ: Transaction Publishers.

Davies, M. (2007). *Property: Meanings, histories, theories*. London: Routledge Cavendish.

Davies, M. (2012). Persons and property. *Feminists@ Law*, *2*(1).

Environmental Commissioner of Ontario. (2008). *Annual report 2007/2008 – Getting to k(no)w*. Toronto, ON: Environmental Commission of Ontario. Retrieved from www.eco.on.ca/uploads/Reports-Annual/2007_08/ECO-Annual-Report-2007-2008.pdf

Environmental Commissioner of Ontario. (2012). *Land use planning in Ontario: A primer and summary of recommendations of the environmental commissioner of Ontario*. Toronto, ON: Environmental Commissioner of Ontario. Retrieved from www.eco.on.ca/uploads/Reports-Staff%20Reports-and-Publications/Land-Use-Planning-in-Ontario.pdf

Eyles, N., & Eyles, N. (2002). *Ontario rocks: Three billion years of environmental change*. Markham, ON: Fitzhenry & Whiteside.

Freyfogle, E. T. (2011). Private rights in nature: Two paradigms. In P. Burdon (Ed.), *Exploring wild law [electronic resource]: The philosophy of earth jurisprudence* (p. 270). Adelaide: Wakefield Press.

Graham, N. (2010). *Lawscape: Property, environment, law*. New York: Taylor & Francis.

Groves, C., Munday, M., & Yakovleva, N. (2013). Fighting the pipe: Neoliberal governance and barriers to effective community participation in energy infrastructure planning. *Environment and Planning C: Government and Policy*, *31*(2), 340–356.

Gunningham, N. (2009). Environment law, regulation and governance: Shifting architectures. *Journal of Environmental Law*, *21*(2), 179–212.

Gunningham, N., & Holley, C. (2010). *Bringing the 'R' Word back: Regulation, environment protection and NRM*. Academy of Social Sciences in Australia 3/2010.

Halton Region. (2013). *St. Mary's cement group – Update January 2013*. Retrieved from www.halton.ca/cms/one.aspx?portalId=8310&pageId=10296

Henwood, K., & Pidgeon, N. (2001). Talk about woods and trees: Threat of urbanization, stability, and biodiversity. *Journal of Environmental Psychology*, *21*(2), 125–147.

Hohfeld, W. N. (1913). Some fundamental legal conceptions as applied in judicial reasoning. *The Yale Law Journal*, *23*(1), 16–59.

Kong, H. (2010). Something to talk about: Regulation and justification in Canadian municipal law. *Osgoode Hall LJ*, *48*, 499.

Lawyer. (2014, 27 July).

Lindgren, R. D., & Dunn, B. (2010). Environmental assessment in Ontario: Rhetoric vs. reality. *Journal of Environmental Law and Practice*, *21*, 279.

Makuch, S. M., Craik, N., & Leisk Signe, B. (2004). *Canadian Municipal and Planning Law*. Toronto: Thomson Carswell.

Mansfield, B. (2007). Privatization: Property and the remaking of nature – Society relations introduction to the special issue. *Antipode, 39*(3), 393–405.
Mega quarry defeat is a lesson in activism. (2012, 25 November). *Toronto star.* Retrieved from www.thestar.com/opinion/editorialopinion/2012/11/25/mega_quarry_defeat_is_a_lesson_in_activism.html
Miller, G. R., Gilmour, B., Myrans, I., Nicolescu, E., Suska, D., Tilden, C., . . . Filip, M. (2009). *Between a rock and a hard place: Understanding the foundations of Ontario's Built Future.* Toronto, ON: Canadian Urban Institute. Retrieved from www.canurb.com/cui-publications/between-rock-and-a-hard-place-understanding-the-foundations-of-ontarios-built-future.html
Ontario, Ministry of Municipal Affairs and Housing, *Provincial Policy Statement.* Toronto, ON: Queen's Printer: 2014.
Ministry of Public Infrastructure Renewal. (2006). *Places to grow: Growth plan for the greater golden Horseshoe.* Toronto, ON: Ontario, Ministry of Public Infrastructure Renewal. Retrieved from www.placestogrow.ca/content/ggh/GPGGH_2006_ENG.pdf
Mossman, M. J., & Girard, P. (2014). *Property law: Cases and commentary.* Toronto: Edmond Montgomery Publications.
Murdoch, J. (2005). *Post-structuralist geography: A guide to relational space.* Thousand Oaks, CA: Sage.
Nash, N., Lewis, A., & Griffin, C. (2010). Not in our front garden: Land use conflict, spatial meaning and the politics of naming place. *Journal of Community & Applied Social Psychology, 20*(1), 44–56.
Nedelsky, J. (2012). *Law's relations: A relational theory of self, autonomy, and law.* Oxford: Oxford University Press.
Ontario, Legislative Assembly, Standing Committee on General Government, *Aggregate Resources Act Review* (7 May 2012), Ministry of Natural Resources.
Ontario, Legislative Assembly, Standing Committee on General Government. Report on the Review of the Aggregate Resources Act, 2nd Session, 40th Parliament (2013). Retrieved from www.ontla.on.ca/committee-proceedings/committee-reports/files_pdf/Legislative%20Assembly%20Aggregate%20English%20Readable.pdf
Owens, S., & Cowell, R. (2002). *Land and limits: Interpreting sustainability in the planning process.* New York: Routledge.
Pardy, B., & Stoehr, A. (2012). The failed reform of Ontario's mining laws. *Journal of Environmental Law and Practice, 23*(1), 1–15.
Participant 1. (2014, 12 March).
Participant 15. (2014, 11 August).
Participant 21. (2014, 28 August).
Participant 22. (2014, 9 September).
Participant 4. (2014, 7 May).
Participant 7. (2014, 18 July).
Participants 13–14. (2014, 8 August).
Participants 16–20. (2014, 23 August).
Participants 2,3. (2014, 23 April).
Participants 8–12. (2014, 8 August).
Patano, S., & Sandberg, L. A. (2005). Winning back more than words? Power, discourse and quarrying on the Niagara escarpment. *The Canadian Geographer/Le Géographe Canadien, 49*(1), 25–41.

Planner 1. (2014, 7 March).

Planner 2. (2014, 3 September).

Policy Division, Ministry of Natural Resources. (2010). *State of the aggregate resource in Ontario study: Consolidated report.* Ontario: Ontario Government, Ministry of Natural Resources. Retrieved from www.mnr.gov.on.ca/en/Business/Aggregates/Publication/287375.html

Porter, L. (2012). *Unlearning the colonial cultures of planning.* Farnham, MD: Ashgate Publishing, Ltd.

Ritchie, K. (2013). Issues associated with the implementation of the duty to consult and accommodate aboriginal peoples: Threatening the goals of reconciliation and meaningful consultation. *U.B.C. Law Review, 46,* 397.

Rittel, H.W.J., & Webber, M. M. (1974). Wicked problems. *Man-Made Futures, 26*(1), 272–280.

Rose, C. M. (1998). The several futures of property: Of cyberspace and folk tales, emission trades and ecosystems. *Minnesota Law Review, 83,* 129.

Sager, T. (2011). Neo-liberal urban planning policies: A literature survey 1990–2010. *Progress in Planning, 76*(1), 147–199.

Sandberg, L. A., Wekerle, G. R., & Gilbert, L. (2013). *The Oak ridges Moraine battles: Development, sprawl, and nature conservation in the Toronto region.* Toronto: University of Toronto Press.

Sax, J. L. (2008). Environmental law forty years later: Looking back and looking ahead. In M. Jeffery (Ed.), *Biodiversity conservation law + livelihoods: Bridging the North-South divide.* Cambridge: Cambridge University Press.

Scotford, E., & Walsh, R. (2013). The symbiosis of property and English environmental law – Property rights in a public law context. *The Modern Law Review, 76*(6), 1010–1045.

Smit, A., & Valiante, M. (2015). *Public interest, private property: Law and planning policy in Canada.* Vancouver: UBC Press.

St. Marys VCNA, LLC v. Government of Canada. (2013). Retrieved from www.international.gc.ca/trade-agreements-accords-commerciaux/topics-domaines/disp-diff/st_marys_vcna.aspx?lang=eng

Valverde, M. (2012). *Everyday law on the street: City governance in an age of diversity.* Chicago: University of Chicago Press.

Valverde, M. (2015). *Chronotopes of law: Jurisdiction, scale and governance.* New York: Routledge.

Van Wagner, E. (2013). Putting property in its place: Relational theory, environmental rights and land use planning. *Revue Générale de Droit, 43,* 275.

Van Wagner, E. (2016a). Law's ecological relations: The legal structure of people-place relations in Ontario's aggregate extraction conflicts. *The MIT Journal of Planning, 12,* 35.

Van Wagner, E. (2016b). Law's rurality: Land use law and the shaping of people-place relations in rural Ontario. *Journal of Rural Studies, 47*(A), 311–325.

Whatmore, S. (2002). *Hybrid geographies: Natures cultures spaces.* Thousand Oaks, CA: Sage.

Whatmore, S. (2006). Materialist returns: Practising cultural geography in and for a more-than-human world. *Cultural Geographies, 13*(4), 600–609.

Young, D., & Keil, R. (2005). Urinetown or Morainetown? Debates on the reregulation of the urban water regime in Toronto*. *Capitalism Nature Socialism, 16*(2), 61–84.

Chapter 8

# Climate adaptation on the Australian east coast

*Tayanah O'Donnell*

*This chapter explores tensions between property and land use planning law on the Australian coast as climate change disrupts relations between actors and between actors and their sense of place. Particular attention is paid in this chapter to legalities pertaining to coastal management and administrative law review litigation in which the relevant decision-maker has failed to properly consider climate change in their assessment of the development application. The chapter argues that climate change is a protagonist for a repositioning of place in law's responses to land use disputes.*

Relationality between space and time is magnified by climate change, the impacts of which manifest in short- and longer-term temporalities. The response of law to these impacts is often vested in past practices. Despite this, recent Australian case law demonstrates how courts are considering both present-day occurrences and future imaginings of climate change impacts. While broader categories of climate adaptation litigation are gaining momentum around the world, to date a significant proportion of this litigation has occurred due to contestations between property rights and land use planning. As litigation is central to "truth-claims in legal discourse" (Graham & Bartel, 2016, p. 231), legal disputes about land use planning and climate change impacts to property also illustrate the mutual relationships between people, place and time.

Twenty-six years ago, Nicholas Blomley argued that the material and relational landscapes in which socio-spatial outcomes occur were significant for understanding "socialised property relations" (2001, p. 120). Foundational to time-space scales in legal geography is an underlying and ever-present co-constitutive relationship between law and space. This co-constitution has been referred to as a 'splice' or 'nomosphere' (Blomley, 2003; Delaney, 2010). By encouraging the bounding of property into spaces and centralising the everyday enactment of property (Blomley, 2004, 2005a), Blomley has challenged us over the years to consider other "modalities of property", including diverse landscapes (Blomley, 2008) as a way of accounting for the intricate layers of the propert*ied* – the categorisation of our collective material parts. To balance this, immaterial ways of knowing property can be evidenced through localised enactment of place-specific behaviours and outcomes (Latour, 2005, p. 136); a perspective that relies in part on the importance of landscape as an embodiment of "particular logics of order and authority that represent places and spaces in which people live" (Darian-Smith, 1999, p. 13). This philosophy of place builds also on the relationship between such lived experiences and spatiality (Bennett, 2016; Amin, 2002). Blomley (2004). Layard and Milling (2015) argue that the ways in which dynamic places are constructed is largely relational. Following Braverman, Blomley, and Kedar's (2014, p. 1) contention that new advances in legal geography scholarship evidence "braided lines of enquiry", the door is opened for a fresh analysis of law and place networks. Thus, Blomley's early works have built and enabled a pathway by which we see reflections on placelessness (especially the placelessness of law), leading to works that emphasise not just interconnections between matter and meaning but their intra-connections as critical to relationships with place (see, most recently, Davies, 2017, pp. 58–61).

Recent legal geography scholarship that centralises place (see Delaney, 2016b) sees scholars concerning themselves with both the visible and invisible elements of geo-legality. Empirical contexts range from safe injecting rooms (Prior & Crofts, 2016) and rights to the city and public space (Blomley, 2004, 2011) to biodiversity laws and farmers' vernacular knowledges about place and property (Bartel & Graham, 2016), as well as land use planning and place making (Layard & Milling, 2015). Further analysis of place specificity in exploring legal-spatial co-constitutivities by Australian scholars includes Australian coal seal gas mining (Turton, 2015; Sherval & Hardiman, 2014), property tenure in non-Western settings and fishing rights in Cambodia (Gillespie, 2016a & 2016b, respectively), biopiracy of Indigenous Australian plants (Robinson & Raven, 2017) and coastal climate change adaptation (O'Donnell, 2016). Together, these works contribute to a deeper understanding of "place-based knowledge [that forms] law's basis" (Bartel et al., 2013, p. 349; Delaney, 2016b).

## A coastal lawscape

Viewed as a "single multiplicity", the concept of lawscape frames the flowing together of legal and spatial spheres (Philippopuolos-Mahalopoulos, 2007, p. 1). Lawscape can also draw attention to the physical and material landscape, and to the importance of localised qualities in specific physical places. In drawing attention to the materiality of property and to the linking of property (law) to its physical and material surrounds, the concept of lawscape (following Graham, 2011) offers a useful lens through which contested property claims on the Australian East Coast can be explored. Awareness of this materiality makes real both the law and the places in which the law operates. Paying close attention to this enlivens competing and complimentary relationalities – relationalities that give efficacy to the multiple layers of geo-legal co-constitutivities. This geo-legal lens offers a

> route to explicate the grounded, embodied effects of law in the constitution of the world and to challenge the impression that law aspires to

> dematerialisation, that it seeks to marginalise specificity (i.e. local distinctiveness) and that law seeks to erase spatiality, or indeed, ever could.
> (Bennett & Layard, 2015, p. 419)

In light of this argument, the discussion that follows explores two specific threads relating to an Australian coastal lawscape. First, it explores historical ways in which the common law has attempted to balance contested property interests in a dynamic landscape. Physical changes to coastlines can often occur slowly, building gradually over long periods of time. Conversely, physical changes to a coastline can occur suddenly, such as during a storm or flood event. In either scenario, where property boundaries change, specific common law legal doctrines have in the past been deployed to reposition the abstract legal boundary and the property rights that flow therefrom. Current and future social tensions pertaining to the wide variety of uses attached to the Australian coast further problematise the transient nature of access to and control of this dynamic landscape.

Following Layard and Milling's framing of place as relational, legally made and continually re-made (2015; see also Braverman et al., 2014), the second thread raises issues about current property rights, future development and place-specific impacts of climate change. Analysis of court decisions concerned to resolve land use conflicts, where climate change is a key protagonist, is provided. Key legal cases demonstrate ways of knowing and valuing place, and in so doing provide not only a window into the law's interactions with Australian coastal climate change adaptation but also serve to drape these conflicts and disputes with an acute awareness of local specificity. It is therefore argued that such litigation is building, piece by piece, a lens for understanding land use laws' bracketing and entanglements with private property interests (Blomley, 2014; Bennett & Layard, 2015).

## The Australian coast

The Australian East Coast is highly developed and commoditised. Simultaneously prized as a cultural signifier to which free public access is a valued right, and as an ideal place to live, the coast is a playground for Australians and those who visit and a favoured locality for the placement of settlements and infrastructure (Drew, 1994). The ongoing development of the Australian coast has resulted in more than 85% of the Australian population residing within 50 kilometres of the coastline (Department of Climate Change, 2009), for which law can provide value to coastal property relations through the exercise of exclusionary property rights. Legal frameworks governing permissible land uses attempt to manage these property relations. Together, these legalities have, over time, co-constructed spatial, legal and temporal levers that at once seek to both influence and shape the coastline, to varying degrees of success.

Unpacking this "everyday enactment" of property (Blomley, 2016, p. 224) is fraught with struggles over spatial power. Difficulties arise from the law's attempt to protect private property rights of coastal property owners as against public expectations of rights of free access to a coastline that continually shifts and moves. Climate change and increasingly severe storm impacts are disrupting these often already-tenuous relationships. Formal legal systems continue to prioritise abstract and dephysicalised legal rights attached to private property during major storm events. Attempts to achieve a better balance for coastal management in light of climate change adaptation requirements are fraught with difficulty, especially where land use planning governance arrangements are perceived to curtail private property rights. Despite this, it has been argued by scholars such as Thom (2004) that Australian coastal management strategies ought to be accompanied by a consistent regulatory approach for the wider benefit of the coast. Thom (2012) argues that such consistency is made more urgent by the exacerbating factors of coastal climate change, such as sea level rise, with consequentially more severe coastal storms and more severe coastal erosion events. Regulatory consistency for benefits wider than private property interests will require more thought to and the careful consideration of coastal property. Such consideration may be achieved not only by examining the mechanisms and impacts of property ownership and how climate change will in future influence this but by also drawing attention to the "much more interesting and complicated realities of property" (Blomley, 2005, p. 127). The current 'complicated realities' of Australian coastal property are such that climate risks are not consistently embedded into land use planning, and the adaptive capacity of coastal communities varies greatly (Serrao-Neumann et al., 2014). There is therefore an opportunity for new, imaginative thinking to realign the law's approach to coastal climate change adaptation.

In linking law and place, Bartel et al., (2013, p. 359) observe, "law is a powerful influence on people and place. Law both creates and is created by the relationships between people and place, though it rarely acknowledges this." Renewed consideration of previous place-based habitualities requires appropriate appreciation of the consequences associated with dephysicalised ways of knowing property (Castree, 2014). The idea of strict legal boundaries, prevalent in property law, is infringed upon by a planning law system that aims to regulate how one exercises those property rights, creating a 'complicated reality' of property. Graham argues,

> the question is not whether property relations are 'natural' or 'cultural' or if alternative property relations are more 'natural' . . . rather that property relations are lived through traditions or paradigms that are at once natural and cultural and that are particular to the times and the places in which they take root. In this way, thinking about property law in terms of adaptation links it to land use and creates a different relationship between people and place.
>
> (2011, p. 19)

In encouraging recognition of the material limits of places, Graham's approach is particularly important in light of the multiple facets of climate change risks and impacts, paving the way to giving more thought on "unsustainable people-place relations" (Graham, 2011, p. 5). In the process she provides opportunities for considering contestations arising in a dynamic landscape.

## Historical tensions: common law boundaries

Traditionally, the law's treatment of property rights is associated with a "rightful individual control over things to the exclusion of all non-owners," (Davies, 2007, p. 115), and in order to give effect to this exclusionary control, the common law relies on property boundaries to envelop land in order to delineate the exclusionary border. Where these boundaries were characterised by a meeting of water and land, there sometime arose legal questions on how to best determine the perimeter of legal property when the land (or water) scape naturally changed, causing the legal boundary to also change. The common law attached rights to this imagined border, and where land abutted water, the imagined boundary follows the course of this natural feature, marked at the 'in between point' (Moore, 1888). To address changes in the landscape, the common law developed the doctrine of accretion for situations where 'naturally occurring' weather events added land to one's private title. Examples include naturally occurring deposits of sand or soil sediments within waterways that result in an expansion of private land. Where it could be proved that land had accreted naturally, the owner could, if the type of property title permitted, apply to exercise exclusive rights over that additional land. *Gifford v Lord Yarborough* (1828) 4 ER 1087 developed the rights of the owner in possession rather than those of the Crown in recognising registrable land interests, and later cases *Re Hull and Selby Railway Co* (1839) 5 M&W 327, 151 ER 139 and *Attorney General Ireland v McCarthy* (1911) 2 IR 260 refined this doctrine. More recently, *Southern Centre of Theosophy Inc v South Australia* (1982) AC 706 recognised that the accretion of sediments of land may occur via wind as well as via water movements, and that the doctrine of accretion applied to lakes as well as to coastal lands. Lord Wilberforce summarised the basis of the doctrine of accretion, at par [287] as

> a doctrine which gives recognition to the fact that where land is bounded by water, the forces of nature are likely to cause changes in the boundary between the land and the water. When these changes are gradual and imperceptible, the law considers the title to the land as applicable to the land as it may be changed from time to time. This may be said to be on the grounds of convenience and fairness. Except in cases where a substantial and recognisable change in boundary has suddenly taken place (to which the doctrine does not apply), it is manifestly convenient to continue to regard the boundary between land and water as being where it is from day to day or year to year. To do so is also fair.

This doctrine responds to the addition of land to private title. While coastal climate change impacts such as sea level rise may be categorised as gradual, it may result in an eventual loss of land due to gradual inundation. However, erosion events that often accompany Australian coastal storms are sudden events and are expected to increase in frequency and severity due to climate change. Lord Wilberforce in *Southern Centre* treated this type of the loss of land and thus title quite differently, where at par [287] he opined,

> If a part of an owner's land is taken from him by erosion, or diluvion (ie advance of the water) it would be manifestly inconvenient to regard the boundary as extending into the water; the landowner is treated as losing a portion of his land. So if an addition is made to the land from what was previously water, it is only fair that the landowner's title should extend to it. The doctrine of accretion, in other words, is one which arises from the nature of land ownership from, in fact, the long-term ownership of property inherently subject to gradual processes of change.

Wilberforce thus rejected a fixed location of property title in favour of a moveable boundary where land is lost. The factual circumstances of the *Southern Centre* litigation argued that the legal obligation that the property be fenced was unreasonable in the circumstances. A requirement to maintain a fence in a body of lake water was categorised by the court as "absurd" (par [289]).

As coastal management increasingly seeks to include adaptive measures to accommodate climate change impacts, including sea level rise (Moser, 2010), ambulatory boundaries may potentially mean that, eventually, private property rights will be lost to the sea (Corkill, 2013; Coleman, 2010). Despite the prevalence of treating rights associated with property as abstract or removed from the physical landscape, these common law doctrines have imbricated a process by which the law has attempted to respond to a changing material landscape, forcing law to think about property in material terms (Blomley, 1998, p. 572; Graham, 2011). 'Sudden' coastal events are likely to occur more frequently and with more severity in their impact as climate change impacts continue to manifest. The pliability of common law property boundaries seems to indicate that there is flexibility of formal law in adjusting to dynamic, contested spaces. However, the increase of land use disputes that protest the curtailing of private property rights due to a variable climate and long climate risk horizons shows otherwise.

## Current tensions: public and private coastal property interests

In May 2009, a particularly severe coastal storm hit the East Coast of Australia, causing significant damage to the coastline and to a number of coastal properties. On Belongil Beach in Byron Bay, New South Wales, a sandbag wall that had been erected in 2001 failed. Prior to its failure it had been situated between private residential property and a public beach and was installed to protect against coastal erosion. Its failure in 2009 resulted in extensive damage and losses of public and private property. The Vaughans, residential property owners residing adjacent to Belongil Beach, lost several metres of their private property to the sea. The Vaughans have long been vocal residents in Byron Bay on private property rights protections and not averse to resorting to litigation to advance their property interests. Following this 2009 storm and loss of their private title that resulted, the Vaughans commenced legal proceedings in the New South Wales Land and Environment Court against the local authority that had given development consent for the construction of the sandbag wall.

As discussed in O'Donnell (2016), and following initial proceedings reported in *Vaughan v Byron Shire Council* [2009] NSWLEC 88, the 2009 Vaughan litigation with respect to this failed sandbag wall centred on two questions. The first was whether the local authority was acting legally in issuing the development consent to itself in 2001 to construct the sandbag wall. The second was whether the council, in issuing the development consent to itself, had an obligation to "monitor, maintain and repair" the sandbag wall, and if so, did it discharge this duty. In answering the first question, technicalities in the process of issuing the development consent, as well as the construction of the terms of the consent, were raised during the litigation. Evidence was given in court as to the structure of the sandbag wall and its engineering specifications. Was the building of the wall contrary to the council's policy of planned retreat, and if so, what was the consequence? Was the wall built correctly? Did the council have an obligation to maintain the wall? Was it built to the correct height? Was it built to withstand the wave run-up action of the sea? Photographs, maps, expert reports and a number of sworn affidavits were tendered to the court as evidence. Witnesses were called and cross-examined. On day three, during the cross-examination of an engineer on the capacity of the wall to withstand wave-run up during coastal storms, an unknown person seated in the court stood up and said "this is not about climate change!" This was true – the *Vaughan* litigation was about the construction of a development consent that Byron Shore Council issued to itself in 2001, which in turn detailed the perimeters of the construction of a sandbag wall designed to protect both the beach and the Vaughan property from coastal erosion. However, this statement made in a court case about interpreting the terms of a development consent highlighted a much bigger issue – that climate change impacts will be a significant disruptor to private property rights in an already contested coastal space.

The case settled between the parties in early 2010, and the case provides no legal precedent, though the subsequent discourse about the case framed it in terms of coastal climate change adaptation (ABC, 2010; Hawkes, 2015). The impacts of a changing climate on the Australian coast will exacerbate challenges such as these for municipalities that are required to make the day-to-day decisions governing land use in and the overall management of the coastal zone. It is in these circumstances that the complexities of materiality, relationality and temporality come together; linked by climate risk, new ways of thinking about the law's role in continually remaking places are now needed.

Additional court cases in Australia that illustrate the tensions between public and private interests on the coast include Victorian Civil and Administrative Tribunal (VCAT) cases. Climate change considerations under Victorian statutory frameworks have been incorporated via section 60(1)(e) of the *Planning and Environment Act 1987* (Vic), which states that, before deciding an application, the responsible authority must consider "any significant effects which the responsible authority considers the use or development may have on the environment or which . . . the environment may have on the use or development." In *Gippsland Coastal Board v South Gippsland Shire Council (No 2)* [2008] VCAT 1545, it was held that the requirements of section 60(1)(e) were "sufficiently broad to include the influence that climate change and coastal processes may have on the proposed developments," and so the risk of impacts of sea level rise to the proposed residential development in that litigation were deemed unacceptable by the Tribunal. This decision is significant in that it was the first Australian merits review decision to use climate change impacts as grounds for the refusal of development consent. Moreover, the practical effect of this remaking of the Gippsland Coast by refusing this development demonstrated not only an everyday enactment of legality but also a willingness of the law to consider temporality (see Valverde, 2015), even where the risks may be uncertain as to time horizons of the various expected impacts.

In the New South Wales Land and Environment Court, judicial review litigation resulted in a finding at first instance that the State Government Minister for Planning failed to consider climate change, despite being required to do so, in deciding to approve the building of a major aged care facility on flood-prone land on the New South Wales coast. His Honour Justice Biscoe said in *Minister for Planning v Walker & Ors* (2007) 157 LGERA 124 at par [161],

> Climate change presents a risk to the survival of the human race and other species. Consequently, it is a deadly serious issue. It has been increasingly under public scrutiny for some years. . . . Climate change flood risk is, prima facie, a risk that is potentially relevant to a flood constrained, coastal plain development such as the subject project.

Though this case was overturned on appeal, the appellate court in their judgment confirmed that there was little doubt that climate change impacts in high-risk locations were a relevant consideration in decision-making processes. As principles of ecologically sustainable development, enshrined in legislation, have been utilised by the courts to incorporate considerations of climate change, it was noted by Justice Bell in the New South Wales Court of Appeal that such principles are

> likely to come to be seen as so plainly an element of the public interest in relation to most if not all decisions [by the Minister] that failure to consider them will become strong evidence of failure to consider the public interest and/or to act bona fide.
>
> (*Walker & Ors v Minister for Planning* (2008) 161 LGERA 423, at par [56])

Climate litigation is increasing in a number of jurisdictions (Peel & Osofsky, 2015). The decisions discussed here demonstrate reciprocities between legal analysis and spatial justice (Harm-Benson, 2014; Delaney, 2016a) in an Australian context and offer insights into how litigation reinforces the importance of place in imbricating legal geographies. They also show the ways in which formal law can make inroads into breaking down the piousness of private property rights via land use planning mechanisms. This highlights the problematic nature of property rights in a contested and dynamic space.

## Future tensions: land use and climate change

In light of this, a question remains as to what role there is for land use planning as a tool by which competing interests in the coast can be 'managed' or if this is even possible. Between 2009 and 2015, several state jurisdictions in Australia enacted and then modified or repealed planning benchmarks by which current and future land use would be governed. The role of these benchmarks was to provide consistency for land use and minimise risk for new developments in locations to be impacted by future sea level rise as well as ensuring that the types of development permitted on the Australian coast could withstand future extreme weather events. These benchmarks sought, for example, minimum floor height requirements under future sea level rise scenarios. However, they were strongly opposed by property owners who considered the benchmarks to devalue their property (Cronshaw, 2013; Edwards, 2013). The contestability of various interests in the Australian coast remain strong.

The dynamic nature of the Australian coastline is well known (Chapman & Coastal Council of New South Wales, 1982; Department of Climate Change, 2009; Thom, 2012), and five years after Thom's (2004) observations, the Commonwealth of Australia tasked the House of Representatives Standing Committee on Climate Change, Water, Environment, and the Arts to "inquire into and report on issues related to climate change and environmental pressures experienced by Australian coastal areas, particularly in the context of coastal population growth" (Commonwealth of Australia, 2009, p xii). This inquiry led to 'the *George Report*' and had specific regard to a number of issues deemed pertinent for coastal zone management, including examining "the impact of climate change on coastal areas and strategies to deal with climate change adaptation, particularly in response to sea level rise" (Commonwealth of Australia, 2009, p. xii). In addition to this Parliamentary enquiry, spatial analysis carried out by the federal government (Department of Climate Change, 2009) detailed the 2008 replacement cost of damage to or loss of coastal residential property in Australia resulting from inundation due to climate change–induced sea level rise of 1.1 metres by year 2100 to be between $41 billion and $63 billion dollars, representing some 157,000 to 247,600 properties identified as exposed to coastal weather event damage (Department of Climate Change, 2009, p. 71). This is a significant proportion of coastal property in Australia. Despite the efforts of policy makers and land use planning guidelines and the in-roads made by courts and legal decisions concerned with climate change impacts and compatible land use planning permissions, there remains considerable growth of development and human population on the Australian East Coast.

The relationship between humans and the environment in the Anthropocene has come to detail the impact of human civilisation since the Industrial Revolution (Steffen, Grinevald, Crutzen, & McNeill, 2011; Castree, 2014; Lewis & Maslin, 2015), and it follows that the relationship between law and place is increasingly relevant in the Anthropocene epoch in order to understand how planetary boundaries will likely reshape social relationships. Such endeavours "require searching self-examination about the habits of social thought and action" (Castree, 2014, p. 464; Adger, 2016). These habits include the ways in which we think about property, how and why societies elevate (most) property rights, and to what end. "Property law insists that place is irrelevant to property" (Graham, 2011, p. 7), and yet climate change impacts will see that place(s), as they change, will demand changes of law, and of societies. Graham frames the centrality of "property to law" as a rationale for why many other laws, including, as I argue, those relevant to both coastal management and climate change adaptation, are "defined from the perspective of private proprietors" (Graham, 2011, p. 173). Because of the way the law treats place primarily as nature, people as culture and property law as rights, it follows that the dualisms created by property law and planning law are often incompatible, or at the very least "deny[ing] the necessary connection between them" (Graham, 2011, p. 175). As Graham observes, "because place is irrelevant to property law, the physical capabilities and limits of the specific places in dispute are merely meaningless spaces or sites of contest" (2011, p. 75). Climate change impacts will inevitably centre the uniqueness of specific places, as these places respond in their own distinctive ways.

Coastal management in Australia has often been reduced to a simplistic public–private dichotomy, wherein the rights of the coastal private property owners are pitted against the rights of the general public to attend and enjoy the beach without fear that an owner may have had legal recourse to privatise it (Godden, Rochford, Peel, Caripis, & Carter, 2013). While some argue that prioritising private property rights is an affront to the broader public interest of beach amenity and access (Lipman & Stokes, 2003; Bonyhady, 2010; Cohen, 2009; Burke, 2016), cases like the *Vaughan* litigation discussed earlier evidence the complexities of governing a dynamic landscape (Braverman, 2011) in which many competing and contested interests lie, and in which private property rights continue to be elevated. Land use planning frameworks struggle to balance these interests (McDonald, 2011; O'Donnell & Gates, 2013). Climate risk and its future impacts will eventually demand that the required localised responses (Adger, 2016) no longer treat property as dephysicalised. The ability of planning law to disrupt deeply entrenched attachments to private property rights may be limited, though eventually, legal liability concerns may force change. As McDonald observes,

> like the tail effect of greenhouse gas emissions, legal claims may be slow to gestate. But the law has a long memory, so courts of the future will reflect

> on the state of knowledge currently at hand to determine whether decision-makers of today did enough to avoid or minimise the worst exposures of climate change.
>
> (2007, p. 406)

## Placing climate

The disrupting forces of climate change as a protagonist on the Australian East Coast demonstrate the contestability between land use planning, which aims to balance competing interests in places, and the pre-eminence with which both the law and contemporary society afford private property rights that are attached to coastal development. The coast is a place that is not only an important and dynamic landscape but also holds multiple connotations about its best "use" (Harvey & Caton, 2010, pp. 32–37). At some point social justice considerations will inevitably flow where up to 85% of a population face significant climate change impacts (Burke, 2016). The cost of real estate has increased exponentially along the coast over time (Hoskins, 2013, p. 3), but it has not deterred settlement and infrastructure growth or attachments to coastal amenity. As Huntsman observes, "it seems to me that the place of the beach in Australian life is too prominent, our attachment to it too deep, for its history to remain unrecorded and its deeper significance to be ignored and unexamined" (2001, p. 5). Fiske, Hodge, and Turner (1987, p. 54) observe that the Australian beach could be categorised as "our great national playground." What then of the largely unfettered private property interests that line the coast and the ways in which climate change will disrupt these interests?

If the prioritisation of the individualism of property (Davies, 2007) is rejected in favour of a relational underpinning on the coast, the importance of the material environment will receive elevated status in its treatment by the law, resulting in new socio-spatial theorisations and outcomes. Watson argues for "different ways of knowing what is law" that focus on the importance of the relationships (to people, with country) that property may signify, which are infinitely "more complex than owning and controlling" a parcel of land (2005, p. 256). That is, by breaking down the artificial boundaries put in place by property law, a renewed sense of belonging and "relations of belonging" can be achieved (Keenan, 2015, p. 122; Keenan, 2013). Such change would likely only occur incrementally. Given the current policy landscape with respect to emissions reductions in Australia, a far more likely scenario will see significant coastal lands lost during a coastal storm event, prompting forced relocation.

One way to bridge these disparate future outcomes could be to use legal tools such as rolling easements. A rolling easement is a mechanism that can provide a platform for public recognition that the land being developed is at risk of change due to sea level rise or by some other predetermined trigger point. Once this predetermined trigger point is reached, the use of the land reverts to the use as specified in the easement (Titus, 2011). Popular in the United States (McLaughlin, 2010), and despite tensions existing in Australian law (Verschuuren &

McDonald, 2012), rolling easements are worth consideration because their usefulness and practicality allow for valuable coastal land to be used at its highest value at particular points in time. By balancing current competing interests on the coast for the benefit of both current and future generations, rolling easements offer a cost-effective option for coastal management in an increasingly risky future. They are also an example of a creative way in which statutory law can embody a place-based response to climate change. While Australian courts are playing an important role in linking law and place, the convergence of the legal and the spatial worlds as climate change impacts increase will produce further contestation between property, property rights and place. Climate change will continue to eschew material and immaterial boundaries as it reorients us toward a relational and temporal geo-legality.

## References

Adger, N. W. (2016). Place, well-being, and fairness shape priorities for adaptation to climate change. *Global Environmental Change*, *38*, A1–A3.

Amin, A. (2002). Spatialities of globalisation. *Environment and Planning A: Society and Space*, *34*, 385–399.

*Attorney General Ireland v McCarthy* (1911) 2 IR 260.

Bartel, R., Graham, N., Jackson, S., Prior, J. H., Robinson, D. F., Sherval, M., & Williams, S. (2013). Legal geography: An Australian perspective. *Geographical Research*, *51*(4), 339–353.

Bartel, R., & Graham, N. (2016). Property and place attachment: A legal geographical analysis of biodiversity law reform in New South Wales. *Geographical Research*, *54*(3), 267–284.

Bennett, L., & Layard, A. (2015). Legal geography: Becoming spatial detectives. *Geography Compass*, *9*, 406–419.

Bennett, L. (2016). How does law make place? Localisation, translocalisation and thing-law at the world's first factory. *Geoforum*, *74*, 182–191.

Blomley, N. (1998). Landscapes of property. *Law and Society Review*, *32*(3), 567–612.

Blomley, N. (2001). Landscapes of property. In N. Blomley, D. Delaney, & R. Ford (Eds.), *The legal geographies reader* (pp. 118–128). Oxford: Wiley-Blackwell.

Blomley, N. (2003). From 'what' to 'so what'? Law and geography in retrospect. In J. Holder & C. Harrison (Eds.), *Law and geography* (pp. 17–34). Oxford: Oxford University Press.

Blomley, N. (2004). *Unsettling the city*. New York, NY & London: Routledge.

Blomley, N. (2005). Remember property? *Progress in Human Geography*, *29*(2), 125–127.

Blomley, N. (2008). Simplification is complicated: Property, nature, and the rivers of law. *Environment and Planning A*, *40*, 1825–1842.

Blomley, N. (2011). *Rights of passage: Sidewalks and the regularion of public flow*. Oxfordshire, UK: Routledge.

Blomley, N. (2014). Disentangling law: The practice of bracketing. *Annual Review of Law and Social Science*, *10*(1), 133–148.

Blomley, N. (2016). The boundaries of property: Complexity, relationality, and spatiality. *Law and Society*, *50*(1), 224–255.

Bonyhady, T. (2010). Swimming in the streets: The beginnings of planning for sea level rise. In T. Bonyhady, A. Macintosh & J. McDonald (Eds.), *Adaptation to climate change: Law and policy* (pp. 80–97). Sydney: The Federation Press.

Braverman, I. (2011). Hidden in plain view: Legal geography from a visual perspective. *Law, Culture and the Humanities, 7*, 173–186.

Braverman, I., Blomley, N., & Kedar, A. (Eds.) (2014). *The expanding spaces of law: A timely legal geography*. Stanford, CA: Stanford Law Books.

Burke, L. (2016). *Havoc still to come as Collaroy residents brace for more damaging tides*. 7 June. Retrieved 14 October 2016 from www.news.com.au/technology/environment/havoc-still-to-come-as-collaroy-residents-brace-for-more-damaging-tides/news-story/1b0327d36ed9a74ffca6f9951122c532

Castree, N. (2014). The anthropocene and geography III. *Geographical Compass, 8*, 464–476.

Chapman, D. M., & Coastal Council of New South Wales. (1982). *Coastal evolution and coastal erosion in New South Wales*. Sydney: Coastal Council of New South Wales.

Cohen, I. (2009). Byron bay planning. *Parliament of New South Wales Hansard, 9*(September), 17553.

Coleman, K. (2010). Conveyancing and property: Coastal protection and climate change. *Australian Law Journal, 84*, 421–422.

Commonwealth of Australia. (2009). *Managing our coastal zone in a changing climate: The time to act is now*. House of Representatives Standing Committee on Climate Change, Water, Environment and the Arts.

Corkill, J. (2013). Ambulatory boundaries in New South Wales: Real lines in the Sand. *Property Law Review, 3*(2), 67–84.

Cronshaw, D. (2013). Fears sea-level policy may slash $1bn off property values. *Newcastle Herald*, 31 May 2013.

Darian-Smith, E. (1999). *Bridging divides: The channel tunnel and English legal identity in the new Europe*. Oakland, CA: University of California Press.

Davies, M. (2007). *Property: Meanings, histories, theories*. Oxford: Routledge-Cavendish.

Davies, M. (2017). *Law unlimited: Materialism, pluralism, and legal theory*. New York, NY & London: Routledge.

Delaney, D. (2010). *The spatial, the legal and the pragmatics of world-making: Nomospheric investigations*. New York, NY & London: Routledge.

Delaney, D. (2016a). Legal geography II: Discerning injustice. *Progress in Human Geography, 40*(2), 267–274.

Delaney, D. (2016b). Legal geography III: New worlds, new convergences. *Progress in Human Geography*, 1–9, doi:10.1177/0309132516650354

Department of Climate Change. (2009). *Climate change risks to Australia's coast: A first pass national assessment*. Canberra: Australian Government.

Drew, P. (1994). *The coast dwellers: A radical reappraisal of Australian identity*. Sydney: Penguin.

Edwards, G. (2013). *Parliamentary debates*, New South Wales, Legislative Assembly, 21 August 2013, 22579.

Fiske, J., Hodge, B., & Turner, G. (1987). *Myths of Oz: Reading Australian popular culture*. Crows Nest, NSW: Allen & Unwin.

Gillespie, J. (2016a). A legal geography of property, tenure, exclusion, and rights in Cambodia: Exposing an incongruous property narrative for non-Western settings. *Geographical Research, 54*(3), 256–266.

Gillespie, J. (2016b). Catch 22: Wetlands protection and fishing for survival. *Geographical Research*, *54*(3), 336–347.

*Gifford v Lord Yarborough* (1828) 4 ER 1087.

*Gippsland Coastal Board v South Gippsland Shire Council (No 2)* (2008) VCAT 1545.

Godden, L., Rochford, F., Peel, J., Caripis, L., & Carter, R. (2013). Law, governance and risk: Deconstructing the public-private divide in climate change adaptation. *University of New South Wales Law Journal*, *36*(1), 224–255.

Graham, N. (2011). *Lawscape: Property, environment, law*. Oxfordshire, UK: Routledge.

Graham, N., & Bartel, R. (2016). Special issue: Legal geography/ies. *Geographical Research*, *54*(3), 231–232.

Harm-Benson, M. (2014). Rules of engagement: The spatiality of judicial review. In I. Braverman, N. Blomley, D. Delaney, & A. Kedar (Eds.), *The expanding spaces of law: A timely legal geography* (pp. 215–238). Stanford, CA: Stanford Law Books.

Harvey, N., & Caton, B. (2010). *Coastal management in Australia*. Adelaide: University of Adelaide Press.

Hawkes, H. (2015, May 2015). Shoes fly as Byron Shire Council meeting gets ugly. *The Northern Star*. Retrieved 16 June 2015, from www.northernstar.com.au/news/shoes-fly-byron-shire-council-meeting-gets-ugly/2646288/

Hoskins, I. (2013). *Coast: A history of the New South Wales edge*. Sydney: University of New South Wales Press.

Huntsman, L. (2001). *Sand in our souls: The beach in Australian history*. Melbourne: Melbourne University Press.

Keenan, S. (2013). Property as governance: Time, space and belonging in Australia's Northern Territory Intervention. *Modern Law Review*, *76*(3), 464–493.

Keenan, S. (2015). *Subversive property: Law and the production of spaces of belonging*. New York, NY & London: Routledge.

Latour, B. (2005). *Reassembling the social: An introduction to actor-network theory*. Oxford: Oxford University Press.

Layard, A., & Milling, J. (2015). "Creative place-making": Where legal geography meets legal consciousness. In Saskia Warren & Phil Jones (Eds.), *Creative economies, creative communities* (pp. 79–102). United Kingdom: Ashgate.

Lewis, S. L., & Maslin, M. A. (2015). Defining the anthropocene. *Nature*, *519*, 171–180.

Lipman, Z., & Stokes, R. (2003). Shifting sands: Coastal processes and climate change: implications for owners and regulators of land. *Environmental and Planning Law Journal*, *1*, 1–17.

McDonald, J. (2007). A risky climate for decision-making: The liability of development authorities for climate change impacts. *Environmental and Planning Law Journal*, *24*(6), 405–417.

McDonald, J. (2011). The role of law in adapting to climate change. *Wiley Interdisciplinary Reviews: Climate Change*, *2*(March/April), 283–295.

McLaughlin, R. J. (2010). Rolling easements as a response to sea level rise in coastal Texas: Current status of the law after Severance v. Patterson. *Journal of Land Use & Environmental Law*, *26*, 365–394.

*Minister for Planning v Walker & Ors* (2007) 157 LGERA 124.

Moore, S. (1888). *A history of the foreshore and the law relating thereto*. London: Stevens & Haynes.

Moser, S. C. (2010). Now more than ever: The need for more socially relevant research on vulnerability and adaptation to climate change. *Applied Geography*, *30*, 464–474.

O'Donnell, T., & Gates, L. (2013). Getting the balance right: A renewed need for the public interest test in addressing coastal climate change and sea level rise. *Environmental and Planning Law Journal*, *30*, 220–235.
O'Donnell, T. (2016). Legal geography and coastal climate change adaptation: The Vaughan litigation. *Geographical Research*, *54*(3), 301–312.
Peel, J., & Osofsky, H. (2015). *Climate change litigation*. Cambridge: Cambridge University Press.
Philippopuolos-Mahalopoulos, A. (2007). Introduction. In A. Philippopuolos-Mahalopoulos (Ed.), *Law and the city* (pp. 1–20). London & New York, NY: Routledge.
Prior, J., & Crofts, P. (2016). Shooting up illicit drugs with God and the State: the legal-spatial constitution of Sydney's Medically Supervised Injecting Centre as a sanctuary. *Geographical Research*, *54*(3), 313–323.
*Re Hull and Selby Railway Co* (1839) 5 M&W 327, 151 ER 139.
Robinson, D., & Raven, M. (2017). Identifying and preventing biopiracy in Australia: Patent landscapes and legal geographies for plants with Indigenous Australian uses. *Australian Geographer*, *48*(3), 1–21.
Serrao-Neumann, S., Crick, F., Harman, B., Sano, M., Sahin, O., van Staden, R., Schuch, G., Baum, S., & Low Choy, D. (2014). Improving cross-sectoral climate change adaptation for coastal settlements: Insights from South-East Queensland, Australia. *Regional Environmental Change*, *14*(2), 489–500.
Sherval, M., & Hardiman, K. (2014). Competing perception of the rural idyll: Responses to threats from coal seam gas development in Gloucester, NSW, Australia. *Australian Geographer*, *45*, 185–203.
Steffen, W., Grinevald, J., Crutzen, P., & McNeill, J. (2011). The anthropocene: Conceptual and historical perspectives. *Philosophical Transactions of the Royal Society A*, *369*(1938), 842–867.
*Southern Centre of Theosophy Inc v South Australia* (1982) AC 706.
Thom, B. (2004). Geography, planning and the law: A coastal perspective. *Australian Geographer*, *35*(1), 3–16.
Thom, B. (2012). Climate change, coastal hazards and the public trust doctrine. *Macquarie Journal of International and Comparative Environmental Law*, *8*, 21–41.
Titus, J. G. (2011). *Rolling easements* (Environmental Protection Agency, 2011). Retrieved from www.flseagrant.org/wp-content/uploads/rollingeasementsprimer_June_2011_Titus.pdf
Turton, T. (2015). Unconventional gas in Australia: Towards a legal geography. *Geographical Research*, *53*(1), 53–67.
Valverde, M. (2015). *Chronotopes of law: Jurisdiction, scale and governance*. New York, NY & London: Routledge.
Vaughan, J., & McDonald, J. (2010). A Byron Bay beach barney. *ABC Radio Interview Transcript*. 9 February. Retrieved 19 May 2015, from www.abc.net.au/radionational/programs/lawreports/a-byron-bay-beach-barney/3107160#transcript
*Vaughan v Byron Shire Council* (2009) NSWLEC 88.
Verschuuren, J., & McDonald, J. (2012). Towards a legal framework for coastal adaptation: Assessing the first steps in Europe and Australia. *Transnational Environmental Law*, *1*(2), 355–379.
*Walker & Ors v Minister for Planning* (2008) 161 LGERA 423.
Watson, I. (2005). Buried alive. *Law and Critique*, *13*(3), 253–269.

Chapter 9

# Property as a technique of jurisdiction

## Traplines and tenure

*Shiri Pasternak*

*This chapter examines how Indigenous subjects are produced and marked as capable of belonging to property law through the apparatus of jurisdiction. It survey some of the ways the machinery of jurisdiction operates through property relations, property law, and discourses of proprietary ownership, unfolding through a range of instantiations and by a variety of institutions, in response to the ongoing valiance of Indigenous tenure, jurisdiction, and proprietary interest in Canada.*

Anishnabe legal scholar Dawnis Kennedy reflects on how when settlers came to these Northern American lands they brought with them their own distant memories of tradition that they wished to find space for. "However," she writes, "since Indigenous peoples already governed these lands, settlers could not create such a space except by way of their relations with Indigenous peoples" (2007, p. 177). Insofar as they pursued peaceful means, settlers needed to establish meaningful relations with Indigenous people. One form of these dealings was by establishing a relationship between the legal orders of settler societies and Indigenous societies. Kennedy recognizes that there was a time of mutual respect between settler societies and many Indigenous nations, when settler law *by agreement* did not apply to Indigenous peoples. This shifted over time, evident, for example, in gradual interpretations of treaties as a "burden" on the Crown. But even where Canadian authorities reject or deny Indigenous legal orders, they must define themselves and their law through this rejection. After all, colonial laws were developed to colonize Indigenous peoples and their lands. Therefore, the role of colonial law in affirming Indigenous orders is still only affirming colonial law. But, as Kennedy explains, this incorporation acknowledges that, "the development of the Canadian state and its legal orders *within Indigenous territories* is at issue" in that it seeks to transform Indigenous law into "forms of relation based on Euro-derived statist models" (2007, p. 179). Nowhere is this enmeshing more clear than in the Western property system.

The meaning of the property right in a settler society, as Kennedy conceives it, is always already in relation to the Indigenous territories on which it is applied. In my chapter, I examine how Indigenous subjects are produced and marked as capable of belonging to property law through the apparatus of jurisdiction. I survey some of the ways the machinery of jurisdiction operates through property relations, property law, and discourses of proprietary ownership, unfolding through a range of instantiations and by a variety of institutions, in response to the ongoing valiance of Indigenous tenure, jurisdiction, and proprietary interest in Canada.

Among other strategies of perfecting settler sovereignty, the imposition of Western property rights onto Indigenous forms of landholding has been pivotal to colonization and has produced a rich field of scholarly attention.[1] When I first began writing about colonialism in Canada, property rights seemed to offer the most cogent explanatory power for how the social relations of land were transformed in the "New World" by settlers. Certainly, there is compelling evidence to support this framework.[2] But through my work with the Algonquins of Barriere Lake – a small Anishnabe community located in the northern region of the Ottawa River watershed in Quebec – I found that the imposition of property rights onto Indigenous lands already presumes the state's authority to govern, whereas it is *the apparatus of jurisdiction* that determines which laws will apply in a given context.

In other words, the problem that colonization introduces is not just the leasehold, the fee simple estate, or the government's regulatory land management system that institute new social relations on the land. The problem is the machinery of jurisdiction that authorizes these proprietary regimes. The utter confusion in the literature around how to define Indigenous peoples' basis of ownership in contrast to Western property rights partly stems from this conflation between property and jurisdiction. Because the issue in property literature has moored on whether property did or did not exist in Indigenous societies prior to contact, what tends to follow is a narrow debate about whether colonialism could actually *dispossess*. Even where the debate comes down on the side that Indigenous conceptions of property pre-existed contact, this approach still fences the debate into a rigid understanding of territorial belonging. Moreover, it elides the fact that in either case Indigenous forms of *jurisdiction* govern the social relations of land on the territory, not a set of property rights or rules. *Just as* on the other side of the ledger, claims to settler jurisdiction authorize Western property regimes.

This chapter illustrates the order-, knowledge-, and space-making practices of jurisdiction on Barriere Lake territory by conflicting land-use patterns produced by provincial regulation and through Barriere Lake's tenure system. The Algonquin tenure system differentiates the landscape into spaces of care to ensure self-preservation and to protect the land base for future generations. Comparing this land tenure system to a provincial beaver preserve system and the introduction of two government-regulated trapline regimes on the territory shows how provincial and Algonquin proprietary systems overlapped to produce a complex interlegal space. These layers, like shifting tectonic plates, eventually crashed into each other in real time, materializing in conflict between Algonquins, park authorities, logging companies, and other visitors to the territory.

I argue that at stake in these conflicts is the way in which jurisdiction is exercised by the provincial state and the band towards different respective ends of comportment: *supply* and *care*. I examine how the production of social scientific knowledge around Indigenous "property" has radically circumscribed, in a range of ways, the Algonquin legal order that governs land allocation and responsibility on Barriere Lake's territory, including the agency of other-than-human beings.

## What is Indigenous territory?

One evening, Clayton Nottaway told stories late into the night about the incredible hunting skills of his grandfather, Joe Ratt. One story involved Joe and his hunting partners, who saw a moose stumbling along, its belly big against the snow, falling a bit, from side to side. One hunting partner thought it was a pregnant moose, but Joe knew it was a healthy moose that was not pregnant, and he shot her. He turned out to be right, and the families feasted. Another time, Joe saw six moose walking together, and one was walking over on the side. This sixth moose was eating different plants than the rest, and Clayton's grandfather knew it must be sick because the leaves he ate were medicine. Joe killed the moose and piled up the meat and bones to leave on the trail as a signal to let others know of the sickness.

These stories that have been passed on to Clayton convey important information for survival in the bush. They also signal the importance of kinship relations in land-use management of the territory. Algonquin tenure is vested in the political community of the band and actualized by the consensual deployment of families and trapping partnerships on the land. Clayton will pass along these stories to his children and their partners and to his grandchildren and extended family. Algonquin kinship is defined by bilateral (blood) kinship; post-marital residence in flexibly constituted extended families and affinal (in-law) alliance that binds the community together through a network of reciprocal relationships (Roark-Calnek, 2004a, p. 4). These networks represent points at which accumulated knowledge is passed along: knowledge passes directly down from grandparents to children to grandchildren, but also across families to cousins, brothers-in-law, or through a woman's new family ties soldered through marriage (Roark-Calnek, 2004a, p. 4). As Fabris writes in his chapter, property relationships do not just embody struggle over the land but bring to light the kinds of relationships that are at stake in the making.

Key characteristics of Algonquin kinship include respect for elders (Algonquin *ketizidjek*), who have authority as tradition bearers. There is also an expectation of sibling solidarity and generational complementarity, where the youth repay the care of their elders through their own contributions of labor and material support. Gender complementarity is a defining characteristic of Algonquin kinship, too. Women and men have different roles, as they are raised to provide specific household and political and ritual roles or to play key roles in community decision making. Relations through marriage are also key, because this is the main form of expansion to the kinship nexus – through marriage Algonquins learn both family territories, matrilineal and patrilineal, and gain affinal access to resources, ecological knowledge, and skills (Roark-Calnek, 2004a, p. 4). These extended family alliances persisted after Barriere Lakers settled at the reserve in the 1970s and 1980s, but there were changes to the kinship nexus: arranged marriages came to an end, there was a greater expansion of kinship through migration to nearby towns, and dense kinship networks were affirmed through housing shortages, where it was not unusual to have twelve extended family members sharing a two-bedroom house. New challenges were also ushered in by changes on the territory, such as the contracting land base, making it more difficult to maintain relations between families, gender, and generations (Roark-Calnek, 2004a, p. 4).

These kinship principles apply to three major components of the Algonquin social regime: household, task group, and territory (Roark-Calnek, 2004a, p. 5). While these social regimes are interlocking, territory is jurisdiction's most visible currency. The family territorial system co-developed with a highly adaptive land management and conservation system. The Algonquin word for hunting territory or ground is *ânokî(w)akî*. In its prepositional forms, -akî is generally understood by Algonquins to mean "an area used by one or *more* persons for one or *more* harvesting purposes, an area that he/they know particularly and for which he/they have particular responsibility" (Roark-Calnek, 2004a, p. 34). Access to areas of the territory is structured through the kinship and friendship nexus: because large game are migratory, hunting parties may ensure individuals access to moose and bears that will not travel through their own family hunting territories that season. But for smaller game, such as marten, rabbit, or fox, that do not tend to migrate far distances, individuals hold and share traplines where they know the land well and where their families may have been trapping for generations. These land-holding practices balance the need for responsibility without requiring exclusive forms of ownership. As Roark-Calnek puts it, the advantages are "social as well as economic/ecological, over *either* a wholly unpartitioned 'commons' *or* the 'unsociable extreme' of rigidly privatized territories" (Roark-Calnek, 2004a, p. 38). Located somewhere between these extremes, a unique system developed over time to accommodate the ecological conditions and the values of Barriere Lake society. It is a system that continues to evolve to this day.

This tenure system also has an external dimension: treaties, agreements, assertions, and mobilizations have secured this tenure across a range of time and against a variety of encroachments. Trespass laws represent what is often the key marker of territoriality from an outsider's perspective, since they conform to Western understandings of property as an exclusive right. Trespass was historically met with a variety of sanctions if interference was detected, such as confiscation of prey or amicable negotiation (Roark-Calnek, 2004a, p. 39).

But Barriere Lake's laws of trespass were also subject to the adaptive technologies of their tenure system. Following the impact on land shortages stemming from the registered trapline system, one hedge against the emergence of a strict ownership regime for the remaining traplines was "free areas" introduced to mitigate against excessively privatized land holdings (Roark-Calnek, 2004a, p. 33). Today, the highways are considered an open access area where anyone can hunt.

Marylynn Poucachiche and Clayton Nottaway told me that a lot of people are afraid to shoot moose on the highway, though, because they are afraid tourists or locals will call the cops. Apparently, game wardens sometimes do charge people. For example, Marylynn reported that Jackie Keyes got lured with a decoy only to have a game warden pull a gun on him and his children and give him a big fine. Jackie fought the charges in court without a lawyer, arguing that hunting is his traditional way of life and that he hunts to survive. He won the case, but Marylynn tells me that everyone wins these cases. Clayton chimed into explain, "We used to hunt moose when we traveled, that's the Algonquin way, now we take the highway instead of the lakes, so that's where we're going to meet the moose. Our travels have changed since they dammed the rivers and built all the roads." Later, they tell me stories about shooting moose in front of tourists, who are invariably shocked, and how the Algonquins try to politely wait until the photos are taken before lifting their rifles and aiming.

Ultimately, family hunting territories ensure conservation and social cohesion; there are social, economic, and ecological advantages to structuring access to territory in this way. The collective survival of the community is ensured through this system, as a knowledge pool of regional experience is passed lineally and laterally throughout the community. A web of intricate relations secures an expansive reach of jurisdictional oversight and responsibility.

## Traplines and maplines

One approach to understanding the differences between Indigenous and Canadian expressions of jurisdiction is through Bradley Bryan's work, which offers insightful reflection on *property as ontology*. Bryan's work stands out in the property literature on colonization because he comes closest to describing the respective social relations of jurisdiction I witnessed at Barriere Lake. He theorizes that English ontologies of property are based on a conception of the world as "standing reserve" (2000, p. 16).[3] As Bryan explains: "Technology . . . makes a demand of nature, and that demand is one of supply" (2000, p. 16). This Heideggerian concept that describes a world of instrumental modern comportment can be contrasted to an Indigenous comportment that I have been calling an ontology of care. To specify for this context, I mean for "standing reserve" to pertain to two interrelated proprietary systems: the provincial leasehold system that permits resource extraction on Barriere Lake lands and the conservation regime that legislates restrictions on extraction and exploitation. Both the leasehold property right and the conservation regime express a technique of provincial jurisdiction whereby Barriere Lake lands are managed as *supply*. Jurisdiction at Barriere Lake is exercised by the provincial state and the band towards these different respective ends of comportment: *supply* and *care*.

Jurisdiction inaugurates property, and through its actualization as care at Barriere Lake, expressed in a proprietary form through land tenure, we can see how jurisdiction embeds the community in particular relations of mutual reciprocity on the land. In contrast to Indigenous jurisdiction, the commodity form of land in liberal capitalist society aims to erase value other than that which can be expressed in market terms (Polanyi, 1957, p. 73). As David Harvey notes, "The exchange process is . . . perpetually abstracting from the specifics of location through price formation. This paves the way for conceptualizing values in place-free terms" (2007, p. 338). Of course, despite the premise of abstraction, value can never actually be disembedded from land. That is what led Karl Polanyi to label land as a *fictitious* commodity at the heart of capitalist crisis: the market seeks to treat it as supply, despite its unpredictable and finite nature. Polanyi recognizes the value of land, irrespective of its fictitious properties. Brett Christophers underscores this point, arguing that perhaps it is time to reevaluate the meaning of "fictitious" in the context of contemporary capitalism, where land is more valuable than ever to the political economy of nations, for example, concerning resource extraction (2016). Land is *real* as a commodity, and it literally *supplies* the geographic context for the political economy of the settler state. Even as a principle of conservation, *supply* is a key goal of maintaining wildlife populations, for the purposes of human consumption, survival of the species, and recreational hunting.

What is the ontological basis of life that property expresses at Barriere Lake? I spent a summer learning Anishnabemowin in the bush at Barriere Lake. Curious about the language of property and jurisdiction in Algonquin society, I asked Toby Decoursay one day if there was a word for ownership in their language. *Kadthaben-duck* or *debendan*, he answered. What about a word for belonging or "to belong"? I asked. "Same thing almost," he said. "*Debendaygayzik* or *debendan*." "To own and to belong are almost the same?" Toby answered affirmatively: "Yep, ours is *tibenindiziwin*, or *debdendan* or *benjigaywaynan*. *Nin-diki-bendan. Debendeegayzik*" (2009). The land is *ni(n)daki* – it means my responsibility/autonomy/belonging while referring to everything there: the moose, the sun, the stars, the trees, the eagle, the beaver, the moon, the earth, and even the planet. Literally, *aki* is "ground" while *nin* would mean "my."

I did not know exactly what a trapline was when I first started working with the Algonquins of Barriere Lake. I thought it was literally a line in the snow, made of rope or something, maybe a long snare. A trapline is a route or circuit along which a series of animal traps is set. There is no word for trapline in anishnabemowin, though nearly every adult in the Barriere Lake community has a designated place to catch mink, rabbit, marten, muskrat, fox, and beaver. One can say, "I am going to set my traps": *inglendo onige* or *on-donige*, and one can even specify what kind of trap one is setting – *wapsheshu onige* if one is going to check a marten trap or *ameku onige* for checking beaver. There is a verb for "trap" (*onige*), but there is no noun to describe the place one traps specifically. It is part of one's hunting grounds, and these hunting grounds are distributed by a system of aboriginal tenure embedded in the Mitchikanibikok Anishnabe Onakinakewin.

The fact that the Algonquins have no word for "trapline" in their language is indicative of their orientation towards land distribution. A trapline is made up of the places where you trap on your hunting grounds, but it was never something that could be calcified in maps, since people cycled through various areas and then areas were left to rest through various seasons. In the 1920s, the word "trapline" entered into the Algonquins' vocabulary. A trapline system was introduced by the provincial government at the insistence of the federal Department of Indian Affairs due to the massive shortage in game and subsequent starvation on the territory. Following a joint federal-provincial conference on Wildlife and Fisheries, two Indian-only game preserves were established on Barriere Lake's territory (Elias, 2002, p. 22). A Quebec Order-in-Council created the Grand Lac Victoria (GLV) Beaver Preserve (6,300 square miles) and Abitibi Beaver Preserve (4,000 square miles) in 1928. These preserves covered much of the hunting and trapping territory in the Algonquin communities of Grand Lac, Lac Simon, some lands from Winneway and Wolf Lake, and some lands of Barriere Lake (Conn, 1942).

The beaver preserves seemed at first to be a positive step towards returning exclusive rights to the Algonquins over their hunting grounds, but the initiative turned out to fall short on meaningful implementation. Quebec had apparently no interest in enforcing these boundaries from settler encroachment. Until 1941, only two game wardens patrolled more than 10,000 square kilometers of land, and so, predictably, the poaching continued unabated (Di Gangi, 1986).[4] That year, a provincial game warden, René Lévesque,[5] was hired to oversee the management of game. He introduced the tallyman system into the beaver preserve, requiring every Indigenous trapper to map their trapline territory along with the numbers and locations of beaver lodges. In return, the residents would receive a license (and later tags) validating their right to trap beaver on the territory within the beaver preserve. Trappers would also receive a nominal yearly payment from the Department in exchange. The tallyman system was designed as an elaboration of a form of Indigenous land tenure, based loosely on the decentralized system of family hunting grounds. But it was based on Cree land tenure, where a system of *Ndoho Ouchimau* – male leaders – were responsible for the land in different areas of their territory (Feit, 2005, p. 278). Barriere Lake land tenure was similar, but decision making was community based, and Chief and Council governed land allocation under the laws of the Mitchikanibikok Anishnabe Onakinakewin – their sacred constitution – therefore the tallyman system conflicted with Barriere Lake customary governance.

The tallyman system had originally been established in 1927 in Rupert's House (now the Waskaganish First Nation) Cree territory, about a fifteen-hour drive north of Barriere Lake's territory. A parallel set of responses to beaver depletion in Cree territory had been adopted there. The Department of Lands gave the Rupert's House Cree an 18,500-square-kilometer beaver preserve, which the Cree would manage under a state-mandated program of beaver conservation. In short, the tallyman system was implemented, and the program was a success: beaver populations were restored, and the government boasted internationally about their management control of the north. But by the 1940–1950s, the tallyman system had developed into a state property and governance system instituted through a new bureaucracy that claimed control over the Cree and James Bay region (Feit, 2005, p. 273).

The gradual government oversight of Cree territory, where previously there had been little, meant that the occasional visits to the territory by doctors and Royal Canadian Mounted Police (RCMP) officers were expanded in the 1940s to include a professional staff of Indian Affairs agents and officers to take charge of the federal and Quebec beaver preserves (Feit, 2005, p. 273). Harvey Feit concludes that

> The beaver reserves were exercises in governance that reduced Cree control of the land and of their hunting, asserted the competing claims of governments and fur trade companies for authority, jurisdiction and control of the region and enhanced the legitimacy of their claims of northern rule more generally.
>
> (2005, p. 273)

He further notes that the more knowledge the government collected about the Cree and their lands, the better they could claim management authority over these lands. The induction of the Waskaganish band into Canadian jurisdiction took only the maplines of a new system of management through which the land could be governed and the people could be surveyed and, ideally, controlled as a population.

Sensing this danger, between the early 1940s and 1950s the Algonquins of Barriere Lake adopted an attitude of non-cooperation with and resistance to the Department of Indian Affairs. Instead of complying with the tallyman system, the Barriere Lake men took out hunting licenses yet refused to make the maps for trapping permits, knowing that this information would cede the remaining control they had over their land base.[6] Resisting the logic of mapmaking, Barriere Lake community members found outside buyers for furs and other ways to circumvent the system that penalized them for refusing to map their territory for the government. They trusted only their own resource management system, and so they ignored designated "seasons" of harvest, and they did not cooperate with game wardens who carried out patrols.[7]

No cooperation meant no beaver tags, and so community members were persecuted for hunting and trapping on their own lands; Barriere Lake members were searched and their spoils of subsistence seized. Despite the consequences, the community fought back with non-compliance and physical resistance. One game warden report documents the fierce resistance of Algonquin women, who hit back with paddles and whatever else they had when attempts were made to search and confiscate their hunting and trapping spoils. Leveque reported, "I was lucky to see one squaw who was getting ready to hit Cont [Constable] Christe [Christie] with an axe and stopped her."[8] The resistance seemed to be effective, even against the threat of RCMP violence. Lévesque found that the RCMP demurred from arresting and charging the Algonquins, concluding that, "in the future, we may as well leave those Indians do whatever they want because if a

Mountie has not got any authority with them it is not safe for a game warden to mix up in their business."[9] The lack of enforcement the RCMP and game wardens could exercise with the Algonquins demonstrates how settler laws lacked authority at Barriere Lake and set the limits of state sovereignty. Exasperated, Lévesque lamented to the Fur Supervisor at Indian Affairs that "we don't seem to be able to control that Barriere tribe" whereas "all the other Indians seem to try to cooperate with us for the protection of their Reserve."[10]

The trouble continued. Another trapline system was established in 1945 for lands just outside of the GLV Beaver Preserve but that still fell inside the border of what is now Parc La Veréndrye. While this attempt to regulate non-Indigenous land use was an overt money grab by Quebec to permit hunting and trapping in the region, attempts at regulation were generally welcomed by the community (Di Gangi, 1986, p. 13).[11] Unfortunately, once again, this effort was undermined by the province's indifference toward the Algonquin land tenure system of the region and its boundaries. The traplines arbitrarily divided Barriere Lake's traditional territory that fell outside of the GLV preserve into fixed territories of no more than 50 square miles. Lands within these registered trapline areas "required payment for annually renewed leases, in return for exclusive trapping rights" (Roark-Calnek, 2004b, p. 21). If the trapper did not trap each year, failed to follow regulations, or defaulted on payments, the license could be lost.[12] In all cases, the GLV preserve was excluded from the registered trapline system, but some Barriere Lake lands outside the preserve were subject to this new registered trapline regime, and many of these lands were eventually lost, leased out to white trappers, or to Algonquins who lost leases, thus family lands, due to defaults in payment.

While Barriere Lake were resentful of white interference, they gradually came around in 1942 and agreed to participate in conservation efforts led by fur conservationist Hugh Conn by estimating the number of beaver colonies in the preserve and promising to count beaver lodges in the spring (Conn, 1942). These compromises, or interlegalities, over trapline jurisdiction meant that authority was being shared between parties, however tentatively. But even efforts by Conn – who tried to ensure some measure of protection for Barriere Lake's tenure system – suffered from the uneasy "pluriverse" of two systems of governance, in Walter Mignolo's terms, "a world entangled through and by the colonial matrix of power" (Mignolo, 2016).[13] Conn was influenced by anthropologist Frank Speck's fairly rigid account of family hunting territories, stating that "each family head is appointed as guardian on his own hunting grounds" and largely ignoring the broader kinship nexus I have described (Conn, 1942). This outside expertise displaced the Algonquins from being the regulators of their own tenure system. As Audra Simpson writes in relation to the anthropological disciplining of her own community of Kahnawá:ke, this production of knowledge is what forms the attention of anthropologists around "culture" rather than "the scene of object formation – ongoing land dispossession" (2014, p. 67). The complicity of anthropologists is a key social process that has had significant agency in shaping the means and matter of colonization in the territory.

## Here come the anthropologists

Whether Algonquin land tenure is a system that reflects nomadic, proprietary, or jurisdictional interests is a question (for outsiders) that has been around for a long time. Placing the discussion of Algonquian land tenure into a disciplinary context, we can see long threads of controversy in the profession of anthropology for almost a century. Frank Speck was an early observer of what he called the Algonquin "family hunting territory" system (*nok'i-'wak'v'*), comprised of fixed tracts of land with natural boundaries to accommodate extended social units of kinship (Speck, 1915). These social units, he observed, were composed of patronymic families, with a system of land allocation distributed across kinship lines (Speck, 1915, p. 4). Speck reports that family territories were pretty rigid, though he goes on to show many examples that break with the strict enforcement of paternal family territories, such as sharing territory in bad years, visiting the wife's territory during poor seasons, and hunting on common lands during the spring gatherings. It is notable in Speck's work that little connection is explicitly made between governance and land tenure. For example, the Chief's responsibilities are not laid out at all in relation to resource and land allocation. There is also a virtual silence on jurisdiction, though implications of a relationship between tenure and jurisdiction exist, for example, through reference to trespass regulations.

Underscoring his interpretation of Algonquian land tenure, Speck's work in the first quarter of the twentieth century challenged the accuracy of Marxist anthropology and argued for a more nuanced understanding of "primitive" societies. Where Marx argued that hunter-gatherer societies held their land and resources communally, Speck and Lowie described "family hunting territories" in Algonquian communities as a direct challenge to this thesis, due to their quasi-private form. Indigenous societies, Speck pointed out, were comprised of decentralized social units of discrete land-holding areas for the purpose of hunting. In 1920, Lowie concurred and strongly advised against the "blunt alternative" between communism and individualism, dismissing as "evolutionary dogma" the teleology of property from collective to private (Lowie, 1920, p. 210).

Speck's work was influential, particularly on D.S. Davidson (1928), John Cooper (1939), and Robert Lowie (1920), but it was by no means universally accepted. As Adrian Tanner notes, many anthropologists were convinced that these territorial allocations resulted from the fur trade rather than from long-standing Algonquian social norms of organization. Tanner explains that Europeans were believed to have infected the Indians with an idea of property that soon took root in their society (1983, p. 312). By far the most influential of these counter-theorists was Eleanor Leacock, who first cast doubt on Speck's conclusions in her monograph *The Montagnais Hunting Territory and the Fur Trade* (1954). Leacock dislodged the influence of Speck in the 1950s with her thesis that the fur trade gave rise to individualized and privatized forms of territoriality on the land. Her work supported anthropologist Diamond Jenness's earlier 1925 criticism of Speck and furthered ideas of Indigenous peoples' tenure system as a sign of assimilation into European modes of production rather than as an Indigenous social form of organization.[14]

Debates continued to wage into the 1970s and 1980s between Leacock and Speck supporter Edward S. Rogers, and the discussion continues with Harvey Feit recently suggesting that pre-contact hunting territories were a distinctly plausible historical theory.[15] The controversy also has ideological traction in non-anthropological political spheres. Right-wing pundit and Conservative Party advisor Tom Flanagan recently used Leacock's work to deny any collective nature to Indigenous society, therefore any basis for sovereignty or self-determination on cultural grounds (Flanagan, Alacantra, & Le Dressay, 2010, pp. 38–39).

Scholars have struggled to defend – ideologically, ethnographically, and historically – cases for *either* a private or communal system of property enacted in Algonquin tenure systems. Perhaps this is because an ambiguity in the definition of property cuts across both Speck and Leacock's camps. After all, do "private" hunting territories mean the same thing as "private" property in Canadian society? Are there any commonalities between fee simple ownership of residential homes in urban centres and the allocation of hunting territories among kinship units on native territory? A major hook for Speck's anthropological work hinges on a faulty brace of ethnocentricity, where property is transformed into ideal types rather than understood in social context. As Tanner writes: "In the cases I am aware of, Algonquian territories are never 'owned' by anyone other than those who work on them; they cannot be sold, accumulated, or used by the owner to accumulate surplus production. Labelling them private property in 'our' sense of the term thus tells us very little and is actually misleading" (1986, p. 28). Though Leacock and her followers move towards an acceptance that hunting territories are a response to external material conditions – ecological, economies of fur trade, coercive influence of traders and missionaries – their methodology is focused more on the "function and operation" of hunting territories post-contact rather than their relation to Indigenous social structures and cultural values (Tanner, 1986, pp. 21–22).

This anthropological knowledge informed conservation regimes on Barriere Lake's territory and continues to inform discussion today on whether Indigenous peoples can actually claim land if they do not possess systems and ideations of "property." Linking Indigenous governance systems to tenure regimes is a crucial step towards understanding how Canadian proprietary regimes can operate as a technology of colonial jurisdiction.

## Property as a technique of jurisdiction

Akin to anthropology, a prevalent tendency in liberal theory has been to subordinate the legal orders of Indigenous societies through a series of typologies concerning property rights, constructed to formulize Indigenous demands into the sovereign claims of the state (Nichols, 2013, p. 175). In brief, liberal theorists conflate *imperium* and *dominion* in social contract theory, which assumes that Indigenous people make demands on society in the register of property rights and ownership rather than in the register of governance and jurisdiction

(Nichols, 2013, p. 175). The danger of the social contract theory is the way it can elide questions of legitimacy around its proprietary regime. In Robert Nichols's incisive critique of what he calls "settler contract theory," he exposes the fictional product of the alleged contract between founding members of society when it is invoked to "displace the question of that society's actual formation in acts of conquest, genocide and land appropriation" (2013, p. 168). In the Rousseauian formulation, the contract is the deliberative procedure that distinguishes modern life from the *state of nature* that preceded agreement and was brought into being the state.

However, as we can see in the case of Barriere Lake, Indigenous people often primarily make demands on the state by calling into question the state's *imperium*. That is, claims *about* property differ from claims *to* property. The conflation between *dominion* and *imperium* presents the question of Indigenous property rights "as though they may be adjudicated *within* the already assumed prevalence of European legal and philosophical *imperium*" (Nichols, 2013, p. 175). This kind of reasoning and argumentation invokes the civilizing discourses of Hobbesian sovereignty that did not acknowledge that Indigenous people could have exercised leadership over their people prior to state formation, but it also echoes assumptions of more recent anthropological work that denies a relationship between governance and tenure, as I have tried to show.

What a closer look at Indigenous tenure arrangements shows clearly is precisely how *proprietary* systems cannot be separated from questions of *rule*. Before the "white man made the counties" or began to subdivide the land into various jurisdictions, it was the customary council that determined the distribution of band lands. In 1991 at Chestnut Lake, community members discussed this practice of allocation:

> The Chief looked at how the land was to be used. Before registered traplines, everyone had a territory. People would rotate use of their territories in partnership with other community members: A would trap his area one season, and then partner with B on B's territory to allow his own to regenerate. Then, the following Season, A and B would go to A's territory . . . Set during the meeting [the feast] the people would decide who to go with, decide who to ask, [say to one another] who are you trapping with?
>
> (Di Gangi, 1996)

Feasts took place in the fall and spring, and it was there that the Chief would deal with issues of over-crowding or shortage of game on the land and move people around accordingly.

Toby Decoursay remembers David Makokos, the life Chief who governed for most of the twentieth century, ensuring that there was not excessive overlap of families on the land. For instance, if two families were already heading towards La Bouchette (an area in the park), Makokos would tell the third family to find another place. There were no property lines, but the territory was clearly delineated by Algonquin place names that contained in their language the geological boundaries and toponymies of a particular area. Toby recalled that people were generally less strict or more respectful of each other's territories in the past. "That's what they say, me I'm going to *kamashgono-gamak* or *gasazibi*, they just say the name of the territory and the Chief is going to take care of that. And they know what direction to go and where is the name of the place. And that's it" (Decoursay, 2009). The traplines at Barriere Lake reflected this governance system, at piece with the tenure regime of land management.

While traplines always existed in practice, their regulation by provincial authorities dug them up from an embedded system of tenure and governance and laid them neatly on the land like two-dimensional lines on a map. In an interview in June 1994 done with Toby Decoursay and Maggie Wawatie, they discussed the marginalization of the Chief by outside agencies in the establishment of registered traplines:

> It was up to the Chief to decide [where people would go]. Everyone would come together in a big feast, make basket[s]. That's where they were told [where] to trap. That's why the Indians didn't fight long time ago among themselves about the trapline. Since the white man made the counties – how big the trapline going to be – that's when the trouble started.
>
> (Di Gangi, 1996)[16]

The government trapline systems mapped over the existing system of aboriginal land tenure and political governance. Dorsett and McVeigh cite maps as one of the easiest technologies of jurisdiction, because one gets an instant picture of the spatial extent of law (Dorsett & McVeigh, 2007, p. 15). The disciplinary strategy of mapping has long been studied as systems of territorial surveillance that assimilate space into Cartesian grids. But the ways these representations overwrite Indigenous ways of knowing and recording space create specific parallaxes of language, place, and law (Goeman, 2013).

Trapline systems formed a new technique of colonial power that scarred the land with such disjuncture. They constituted a complex set of regulations and jurisdictional claims that impacted the Mitchikanibikok Anishnabe Onakinakewin and inculcated novel ideas of propertization into the governance system. As a result, the new tenure system of traplines wrought unprecedented changes in social relations in the territory. Former customary Chief Jean Maurice Matchewan described the impact of the traplines system on the community's communal ethics:

> Families were pretty much fighting over their territory and with their neighbours and neighbouring communities, as well. So that's how the trapline came to be. Before that, they didn't really have a trapline. They just had a territory that they occupied, but it wasn't really specifically given to them, [just] to manage.
>
> (Matchewan, 2009)

What had begun as a conservation effort in fact worked to undermine the jurisdiction Algonquins exercised over their lands. Whereas Barriere Lake traplines could be shared across a number of kinship relations, the government trapline system forced individuals to take ownership of individual traplines in order to secure tenure and avoid confiscation and redistribution of lands to settlers by the government. Essentially, the registered traplines solved a problem of dispossession that the provincial government itself created by creating another mode of dispossession.

At Barriere Lake, much as people did not own individuated plots of property, aboriginal tenure secured some of the advantages of proprietary regimes. As I have described, customary or traditional users of the range would have spent many years on that land, and therefore they would have built up an extensive fund of knowledge about the area, making them more successful hunters and gatherers and building families' historical attachments to particular areas. These historical attachments then led to some measure of responsibility (***tibenindiziwin***) for the areas, ideally managing their resources for other users and future generations, requiring recurrent (not necessarily continuous) occupancy and use. This jurisdiction of care could not be replicated through bureaucratic regimes of ownership.

Partly what outsiders could not perceive was the flexibility in Algonquin social relations of belonging. As Jean Maurice Matchewan illustrates,

> if there's one family, if at their trapline there's no animals there, pretty much, another family will take them into their area when their animals are growing. So those are the kinds of thing they would do to accommodate other families. Cause I remember when I was young my grandfather was a great trapper, he used to go out to somebody else's territories, with permission, and there was no problem that way.
>
> (2009)

The Barriere Lake trapline system represents a set of social relationships between community members that respects boundaries between ecological areas but also corresponds to the dynamics of a hunting and trapping economy and the overarching value of ensuring sustenance for all. This flexibility has invoked what often seems like the central question for settlers studying the land interests of Indigenous peoples: is it property? Bryan contends, however, that the main issue should not be whether Indigenous peoples "have conceptions of property and what those are, but rather how an analysis of other cultures' ways of life, using our own terms, serves to rationalize that other way of conceiving of the human's relationship to the world-at-large in our own terms" (Bryan, 2000, p. 5). The beaver preserves and trapline systems served to re-order Algonquin society along the lines of Western understandings of ownership, even in the best-intentioned efforts. To re-make Algonquin land as individual property was to deny or distort the ways of life that embodied and enacted the community's legal and political order.

The trapline system reveals how the alienation of Barriere Lake lands through multiple regulatory plans and authorities impacted the community's jurisdiction. Unevenly applied and enforced, legislation meant to protect wildlife and habitat for Indigenous use ended up carving up the territory into restrictive zones, eventually facilitating recreational sport, and running up constantly against other planning authorities for the region that built transportation corridors and flooded reservoirs throughout the preserve in pursuit of commercial enterprise and energy generation. Foreign systems of land allocation – even the tallyman system that was based on Algonquin tenure – undermined the traditional roles of the Chief and Council through these new differentiations of space, and perhaps more importantly, through disruption to the expansive kinship nexus that facilitated land use on the territory. It is on this final point on which I would like to focus my final argument on Indigenous jurisdiction.

## Reproducing life

Land use clashes are inevitable and widespread throughout the country precisely because Indigenous land-holding systems are subject to imposition, incursion, and outright denial, violating Indigenous laws and trampling on invisibilized turfs of Indigenous responsibility and belonging. As Peter Usher, Robert Galois and Frank Tough put it so well, "The state system of resource tenure and management exists as an *overlay on*, not a *replacement of*, aboriginal systems – hence the frequency of land and resource conflicts" (1992, p. 122, *emphasis added*). These overlays are not mere lines on a map. They produce the materiality of the region, partially generated through the technologies of settler property rights that attempt to render Indigenous land tenure obsolete.

This act of overlay affects not only human beings but also the "other-than-human" beings on the land (Todd, 2016). Here we uncover another insight into the failure of Conn's good intentions to replicate Indigenous principles of land management that caused the profound loss experienced by the Algonquins. As Kim Tallbear describes, "Indigenous peoples have never forgotten that nonhumans are agential beings engaged in social relations that profoundly shape human lives" (2015, p. 235). "Objects" and "forces" such as stones and thunder form part of this "ecology of intimacy" between all living things on the land.[17] Where Indigenous peoples assert jurisdiction through protection of their tenure system, they are also extending this care to other-than-human "tenures" or ecosystems. In the passage that follows, for example, Jean Maurice Matchewan describes the impact on animals by dams, invoking the problems the animals are having as the community's own:

> There's no beaver once they lower down the water. They lowered down the water 10 feet – that means the beaver has to walk 10 feet to get to the water and it's under ice. And they have no food – the food they store in front of their cabans – it's in the ground it's supposed to be in the water, that's why

they put it in the water, and a lot of time, they're on the ground, especially on the reservoir here. And the moose sometimes, will just go through the ice. Those are some of the problems we have with everything they're doing.
(Matchewan, 2009)

The Algonquins' preoccupation with the impacts of colonization on the animals is a critical intervention into studies of property and jurisdiction. Human–animal interactions are not just objects of colonization: these relations are colonial subjects that enable colonial expansion (Belcourt, 2015). A case in point, the dogged efforts pursued by provincial authorities to collect data on beaver habitat and populations not only enacted a loss of land and subsistence for the Algonquins but radically changed the world of the beaver, whose living conditions were increasingly produced by way of the empirical and scientific knowledge used to manage their homelands.

Vanessa Watts explores these ideas in her writing, where she observes that colonization is not just about dispossession or displacement from their lands but the theft of the "ability to act and govern" when Indigenous homelands are damaged and their epistemic frames are subject to ignorant misinterpretation (2013, p. 23). According to an Indigenous point of view, governance is intimately tied to how agency is circulated through human and other-than-human worlds in the creation and maintenance of society. It is the connections with the living land that form the societies in which Indigenous peoples thrive. These other-than-human lifeworlds "have ethical structures, inter-species treaties and agreements . . . Not only are they active, they also directly influence how humans organize themselves into that society" (Watts, 2013, p. 23). Human thought, in turn, expresses the thinking of particular places, drawing obligations to maintain this balance and remain in communication with its desires, will, intent, and labours. Colonization corrupts Indigenous peoples' capacity to exercise care, but this form of dispossession also affects the other-than-human world in the exercise of its own reciprocal agency.

The kinship system at Barrier Lake has changed a lot over time. Norman Matchewan said it used to be that there were no family territories – people would move around from place to place. I asked when that changed, and he said maybe with the traplines (Matchewan, 2010). Then he showed me his grandfather's trapline on a map where he and his cousin Benjamin Keyes trap together. His uncle gave the trapline to him and showed him all the best places to catch marten when Norman was broke and could not afford to pay his bills. Fortunately, while the rigidity of the government trapline system reified these family territories due to sudden "shortages" of land, trapping has been a flexible system to begin with, containing room for adaptation to changing circumstances, to which the families, Chief, and sub-Chiefs would attend. Today, the trapline system calls less upon the customary government for adjudication and allocation, but it is still entrenched in the territory of Barriere Lake's ecological boundaries and within the purview of the customary government's jurisdiction. It is attuned specifically to the movement of animals and the needs of families. One thing for certain is that control of "populations" – human and other-than-human – is always subject to forces of resistance on the ground. A trapline is only as colonized as the maplines in which its jurisdiction falls.

## Notes

1 See, Joseph Singer, "Re-Reading Property," *New England Law Review* 26 (1991–1992): 719; and Cheryl I. Harris, "Whiteness as Property," *Harvard Law Review* 106:8 (June 1993): 1721.
2 See for example, John C. Weaver, "Concepts of Economic Improvement and the Social Construction of Property Rights: Highlights From the English-Speaking World," *Despotic Dominion: Property Rights in British Settler Societies*, John McLaren, A.R. Buck, and Nancy E. Wright, eds. Vancouver: UBC Press.
3 The shift towards modern conceptions of property took place during a period when Anglo-Norman England was rationalizing its governing structure away from the feudal mode towards a more Lockean model of "use" and exchange" tailored to the market economy (13).
4 Cited in Leigh Ogston, "Algonquins of Barriere Lake Historical Report," November 1987, document unnumbered.
5 Not *the* René Lévesque (founder of the Parti Québécois).
6 See, for example: Diary of field investigation from René Lévesque, Quebec Game Warden, Senneterre. NA RG10 Vol. 6753 File 420–10–4GR-1: Quebec Fur Conservation – Correspondence re: the Grand Lac Victoria Preserve of the Maniwaki Agency (Maps) 1947–1950.
7 See, for example: 1948: Annual Report for Grand Lake Victoria Hunting Reserve, 1948 from Rene Levesque, Quebec Game Warden to Indian Affairs. NA RG10 Vol.6752 File 420–10–1–3 Reel C-8107; NA RG10 Vol. 6754 File 420–10–4GR3 – Grand Lac Victoria Annual Report 1950).
8 See: November 1947: Diary of field investigation from René Lévesque, Quebec Game Warden. NA RG10 Vol. 6753, File 420–10–4GR-1: Quebec Fur Conservation – Correspondence re: the Grand Lac Victoria Preserve of the Maniwaki Agency [Maps] 1947–50.
9 Ibid.
10 Ibid.
11 To recoup millions of the highway costs, Quebec took advantage of the preserve for tourist purposes. No commercial fishing would be allowed.
12 As Stu Herbert notes, "Plans showing the location of the territory were to be submitted for each license. The license could be lost if the territory was not trapped each year or if the trapper failed to follow the regulations. An annual inventory and report was required from each trapper (see: #1641 (14 Sept 67))" (Summary of Quebec Orders-in-Council (1928–1980). September 16, 1988, 6).
13 This pithy definition comes from Mignolo's blog, http://waltermignolo.com/on-pluriversality/ (accessed April 6, 2016), but to read a scholarly book on this subject, see Walter D. Mignolo, *Local Histories/Global Designs: Coloniality, Subaltern Knowledges, and Border Thinking* (Princeton, N.J.: Princeton University Press, 2000).
14 See, for example: Diamond Jenness, "Origin of Copper Eskimos and Their Copper Culture," *Geographical Review* 13:4 (1923): 540–551. Another early and influential critic of Speck was Alfred G. Bailey, *The Conflict of European and Eastern Algonkian Cultures, 1504–1700: A Study in Canadian Civilization* (Sackville,

NB: Tribune Press, 1937). For a good overview of this literature more generally, see Charles A. Bishop and Toby Morantz, "Who Owns the Beaver? Northern Algonquian Land Tenure Reconsidered," *Anthropologica* 28:1–2 (1986): 7–9.

15 See also: Edward Rogers, *The Hunting Group-Hunting Territory Complex Among the Mistassini Indians*, National Museum of Canada Bulletin (Ottawa: Department of Northern Affairs and National Resources, 1963), 195. For a deeper discussion into these debates, please see: Siomonn Pulla, "A Redirection in Neo-Evolutionism? A Retrospective Examination of the Algonquian Family Hunting Territories Debates," *Histories of Anthropology Annual* 7 (2011): 170–190.

16 The feast baskets they refer to here presented food offerings for bush spirits associated with game renewal and change of seasons, customs of the Onakinakewin.

17 The reference to "objects" and "forces" as living is from Tallbear, "An Indigenous Reflection on Working Beyond the Human/Not Human," and the phrase "ecologies of intimacy" was borrowed from Leanne Simpson, "Anishnabe Nationhood," *Nation to Nation Now: The Conversations*. Symposium. Toronto, March 23, 2013. Simpson uses this phrase in her talk to describe Indigenous nationhood.

## References

Belcourt, B-R. (2015). Animal bodies, colonial subjects: (Re)locating animality in decolonial thought. *Societies*, *5*, 1–11.

Bryan, B. (2000). Property as ontology: On aboriginal and English understandings of ownership. *Canadian Journal of Law and Jurisprudence*, *13*(1), 3–31.

Christophers, B. (2016). For real: Land as capital and commodity. *Transactions*, *41*(2), 134–148.

Conn, H. (1942). *Grand lake Victoria Indian hunting system 1942 Annual Report*, submitted to the Department of Indian Affairs, Public Archives Canada, (RG 10, Volume 6751, file 420–410x 5).

Cooper, J. M. (1939). Is the Algonquin family hunting ground system pre-Columbian? American *Anthropologist*, *41*, 66–90.

Davidson, D. S. (1928). *Family hunting territories in northwestern North America*. New York, NY: Museum of the American Indian, Heye Foundation.

Decoursay, T. (2009). In discussion with the author, July 24 2009, Barriere Lake.

Di Gangi, P. (1996). *Barriere lake leadership: Excerpts from oral history and HBCo records*. Prepared for the Algonquin Nation Secretariat.

Di Gangi, P. (1986). *The Barriere lake band: Claims research*, October 1986, Prepared for the Algonquin Nation Secretariat.

Dorsett, S., & McVeigh, S. (2007). Questions of jurisdiction. In S. McVeigh (Ed.), *Jurisprudence of jurisdiction* (pp. 3–19). Oxford: Routledge-Cavendish.

Douglas Elias, P. (2002). *Socio-economic profile of the Algonquins of Barriere lake*, Prepared for the Algonquin Nation Secretariat, January 1996 (Revised August 2002).

Feit, H. A. (2005). Re-cognizing co-management as co-governance: Visions and histories of conservation at James Bay. *Anthropologica*, *47*(2), 267–288.

Flanagan, T., Alacantra, C., & Le Dressay, A. (2010). *Beyond the Indian act: Restoring aboriginal property rights*. Montreal; Kingston: McGill-Queen's University Press.

Goeman, M. (2013). *Mark my words: Native women mapping our nations*. Minneapolis & London: University of Minnesota Press.

Harvey, D. (2007). *The limits to capital*. London: Verso.

Kennedy, D. I. (2007). Reconciliation without respect? Section 35 and Indigenous Legal Orders. In Law Commission of Canada (Ed.), *Indigenous legal traditions* (pp. 77–113). Vancouver & Toronto: UBC Press.

Leacock, E. (1954). *The Montagnais hunting territory and the Fur trade*, American Anthropological Association, Memoir No. 78.

Lowie, R. (1920). *Primitive society.* New York, NY: Boni and Liverlight.

Mignolo, W. D. (2016). *On pluraversality.* Retrieved 6 April 2016 from http://waltermignolo.com/on-pluriversality/

Matchewan, N. (2010). In discussion with the author, June 16.

Matchewan, J. M. (2009). In discussion with author, July 26, Rapid Lake.

Nichols, R. (2013). Indigeneity and the settler contract today. *Philosophy and Social Criticism*, *39*(2), 165–186.

Polanyi, K. (1957). *The great transformation.* Boston: Beacon Hill Press.

Roark-Calnek, S. (2004a). *Algonquins of Barriere lake background reports, Volume 3: The social organization of Barriere lake Algonquin land use*, Prepared for the Algonquins of Barriere Lake.

Roark-Calnek, S. (2004b). *Barriere lake Algonquin family narratives.* A Report to the Algonquin Nation Secretariat, Mitchikanibikok Inik, Algonquins of Barriere Lake.

Simpson, A. (2014). *Mohawk interruptus: Political life across the borders of settler states.* Durham, NC & London: Duke University Press.

Speck, F. (1915). *Family hunting territories and social life of various Algonkian bands of the Ottawa valley.* Canada Department of Mines – Geological Survey – Memoir 70 No. 8, Anthropological Series, Ottawa, Government Printing Bureau.

Tallbear, K. (2015). An indigenous reflection on working beyond the human/not human. *GLQ: A Journal of Lesbian and Gay Studies*, *21*, 2–3.

Tanner, A. (1986). The new hunting territory debate: An introduction to some unresolved issues. *Anthropologica*, *28*, 1–2.

Todd, Z. (2016). An indigenous feminist's take on the ontological turn: 'Ontology' is just another word for colonialism. *Journal of Historical Sociology*, *29*(1) (March), 4–22.

Usher, P. J., Tough, F. J., & Galois, R. M. (1992). Reclaiming the land: Aboriginal title, treaty rights and land claims in Canada. *Applied Geography*, *12*, 109–132.

Watts, V. (2013). Indigenous place-thought and agency amongst humans and non-humans (First Woman and Sky Woman go on a European world tour!). *Decolonization: Indigeneity, Education and Society*, *2*(1), 20–34.

Chapter 10

# Decolonizing neoliberalism?

## First Nations reserves, private property rights, and the legislation of Indigenous dispossession in Canada

*Michael Fabris (Krebs)*

*This chapter focuses on contemporary proposals to implement private property regimes on First Nations reserves. First, I examine the arguments used by proponents of the First Nations Property Ownership Act to motivate support for this legislation, demonstrating how it represents a rearticulation of past proposals, albeit as a 'restoration' of precolonial property rights regimes. Second, I discuss how this legislation informs contemporary discussions within academia concerning Marx's theory of primitive accumulation. Finally, I discuss how disputes over First Nations property rights demonstrate that both settler colonial subjection and continued assertions of Indigenous identity are inseparable from relationships with land.*

In recent years there has been increased momentum to implement private property regimes on First Nations reserves in Canada. In 2006, for example, the First Nations Tax Commission launched a new project to expressly advocate for federal legislation, the proposed First Nations Property Ownership Act (or FNPOA), to establish fee simple property rights on reserves (the form of tenure that allows for the sale or transfer of property under British-derived common law). This project, known as the First Nations Property Ownership Initiative (FNPOI), is headed by Manny Jules, former chief of the Kamloops Indian Band, and receives direct financial support from Aboriginal Affairs and Northern Development Canada (also known as the Department of Indian Affairs and Northern Development, or DIAND).

To date, the most concrete action taken by a federal government towards supporting the FNPOA involved mentioning the legislation in the 2012 federal budget, where the then-Conservative government announced its intent to 'move forward with legislation that would allow private property ownership within current reserve boundaries' (Flaherty, 2012, p. 171). The Ownership Act was also discussed in the Conservative Party's 2015 platform, and, if they had been re-elected, their stated plan was to make this a key part of their Indian policy (Conservative Party of Canada, 2015, p. 149).

The proposed FNPOA faced strong opposition from First Nations communities and individuals. Leaders from the Assembly of First Nations (AFN), the national organization representing First Nations in Canada, condemned the legislation and in July 2010 passed a resolution to reject the FNPOA (Assembly of First Nations, 2010). Numerous Indigenous activists and writers also expressed concern and outright opposition to the legislation (Cuthand, 2014; Manuel, 2010; Palmater, 2012; Vowel, 2012). However, even though widespread opposition played a significant role in halting the FNPOA, the legislation is indicative of a trend towards redefining First Nations–state relationships in ways that implement or lean towards the establishment of private property regimes on reserve lands, such as the Nisga'a Final Agreement, the Tsawwassen Final Agreement, and similar treaties negotiated through the British Columbia (BC) Treaty Process (Blomley, 2014).

Two major advocates for the proposed FNPOA are Tom Flanagan and Chris Alcantara. Flanagan is a prominent conservative political activist in Canada, retired political science professor at the University of Calgary, and former campaign manager for Stephen Harper's 2004 election campaign. He is also a frequent writer on First Nations issues for major newspapers in Canada and conservative think tanks such as the Fraser Institute ('Tom Flanagan', n.d.). Alcantara is currently a political science professor at Western University ('Chris Alcantara', n.d.). Flanagan and Alcantara have authored and co-authored numerous pieces outlining their major arguments for private ownership on reserves (Alcantara, 2007; Flanagan, 2010; Flanagan & Alcantara, 2002, 2004). Their most comprehensive treatment of this proposal is *Beyond the Indian Act*, a book they co-authored with André Le Dressay, which was explicitly written to help motivate support for the FNPOA.

Taken on their own, *Beyond the Indian Act* and other writings advocating for the FNPOA might be easily dismissed as ideological right-wing diatribes. However, as the aforementioned developments demonstrate, the previous federal government was seriously considering legislation to implement the proposals contained in *Beyond the Indian Act*; and for the Nisga'a, Tsawwassen First Nation, and other communities that have signed 'modern' treaties through the BC Treaty Process, fee simple property on their reserves is already becoming a reality. For Indigenous peoples in Canada, it is therefore important for us to understand how FNPOA supporters are attempting to motivate support for the legislation, paying special attention to their attempts to differentiate this proposal from past, more overtly assimilationist attempts at privatizing Canadian reserves or US reservations, such as the Dawes Act in the US and the 1969 White Paper. Thus, I critique the proposed FNPOA with a focus on the central arguments contained in *Beyond the Indian Act*, demonstrating how the FNPOA provides an important avenue from which to explore questions of property, dispossession, and subject formation that are specific to settler colonial contexts.

This chapter is comprised of three parts. In the first section, I analyse how the FNPOA represents the continued ascendency of 'recognition' politics in Canada (Coulthard, 2007, 2014). I demonstrate how, despite its similarity with past attempts to privatize First Nations reserve lands, the FNPOA represents a re-articulation of these older proposals as a type of recognition, where the implementation of fee simple property regimes is cast as 'restoring' precolonial property rights regimes. Building upon existing critiques of the FNPOA (Dempsey, Gould, & Sundberg, 2011; Fabris, 2013; Pasternak, 2015), I then focus on the economic character of Canadian settler colonialism, arguing the FNPOA must be viewed in light of past and present manifestations of dispossession. Intervening in academic discussions concerning the continued utility of Karl Marx's theory of primitive accumulation, I explore how this theory applies to the FNPOA while in turn suggesting ways the proposal of this legislation can inform the broader discussion concerning the continued workings of 'accumulation by extra-economic means' (Glassman, 2006). Third, I analyse the relationship between property, land, and subject formation in settler colonial contexts, arguing that assimilationist forms of Patrick Wolfe's (2006) 'logic of elimination' are inherent to the proposed FNPOA. Through these three lenses of inquiry, this chapter argues that the FNPOA provides a key example of the Canadian state's need to continuously redefine its settler colonial strategies against Indigenous peoples, which in turn demonstrates the role Indigenous struggles play in forcing these redefinitions.

## *Beyond the Indian Act* and the politics of recognition

I start with a brief summary of the arguments used by supporters of the FNPOA to motivate support for the legislation. These arguments are important in illustrating how the Canadian government's efforts to facilitate increased capitalist accumulation on First Nations reserves have shifted discursively from a 'property rights as assimilation' narrative to one of 'property rights as restoration.' As I mentioned, *Beyond the Indian Act* was written by some of the legislation's key architects, and with the explicit purpose of generating support for the FNPOA; further, because the legislation was never tabled, this book provides the most comprehensive account of the legislation's objectives and justification.

In *Beyond the Indian Act*, Flanagan, Alcantara, and Le Dressay argue for the establishment of fee simple regimes on First Nations reserves in Canada. The authors discuss the various socioeconomic problems on First Nations reserves, arguing these problems stem from the absence of the 'legal, governmental, and fiscal framework' that other Canadians 'take for granted' (2010, p. 125). In the present era, there is 'almost an explosion of aboriginal entrepreneurship,' which includes 'opening casinos, shopping centres, industrial parks, golf courses, and residential developments' (pp. 3–4). Unfortunately, at least in the minds of Flanagan, Alcantara, and Le Dressay, these potential economic opportunities are constrained due to the lack of formalized private property rights on reserves. As they argue, this economic potential for First Nations is

> handicapped by an inadequate framework of property rights. Investors are deterred by uncertainty; legal work and litigation multiply; projects take

> longer than they should, and many potentially profitable developments never happen because all these factors raise the cost structure.
>
> (Flanagan, Le Dressay, & Alcantara, 2010, p. 4)

The solution, according to *Beyond the Indian Act*, is the creation of Aboriginal property rights, creating 'certainty' over reserve land titles and eliminating the 'bureaucratic red tape' within existing regulations for reserve land developments as encoded in the Indian Act, the main body of federal legislation in Canada governing Status Indians and First Nations reserves (The Indian Act, 1985). Influenced by the thinking of Peruvian economist Hernando de Soto, they argue the FNPOA would give both First Nations people and potential investors the necessary tools to unlock the 'dead capital' awaiting on reserve lands, opening up the space for economic potential that will apparently be for the benefit of First Nations people (De Soto, 2001). The FNPOA will thus make it possible to 'enhance economic activity on reserves, create more jobs and business opportunities for First Nations people, and improve both the quantity and the quality of housing on reserves' (Flanagan et al., 2010, p. 8).

In many ways, the FNPOA as outlined in *Beyond the Indian Act* is not a new or original policy, as the Canadian and US governments have both proposed and enacted past legislative attempts to impose private property regimes on reserve/reservation lands. In the US, the most notorious example is the Dawes Act of 1887, whereby many American Indian communities had their reservation lands allotted into individual parcels, eventually resulting in 'extreme land loss' (Stremlau, 2005, p. 266). In Canada, both British and later Canadian colonial governments have repeatedly advanced proposals for individual property rights on reserve lands, up to and including the 1969 White Paper, the infamous legislative proposal that recommended establishing fee simple title for reserve lands (Chrétien, 1969, p. 22). At the same time, the authors of *Beyond the Indian Act* argue their proposal contains an important difference that distinguishes it from these previous proposals. Aware of criticisms of the Dawes Act and the resultant loss of Indian reservation lands in the US, the authors devote an entire chapter to their own assessment of why the Dawes Act was 'a failed project', and repeat several times throughout the book that the FNPOA is directly opposite to the Dawes Act 'because it recognizes and protects the inalienable reversionary right to First Nations title' (p. 177). With the FNPOA, the underlying title to reserve lands will be transferred to First Nations as a new, third form of Crown title. Under current Canadian law, the underlying title to all lands is held by the Crown and can be in the right of either the province or the federal government (Flanagan et al., 2010, pp. 161–162).

This difference in how private property rights are proposed under the FNPOA, with underlying title granted to First Nations, should be understood in light of what Glen Sean Coulthard refers to as the colonial politics of recognition. In *Red Skin White Masks*, Coulthard (2014) argues that for 'the last forty years, the self-determination efforts and objectives of Indigenous peoples in Canada have increasingly been cast in the language of recognition' (p. 1). Here Coulthard is describing

> the now expansive range of recognition-based models of liberal pluralism that seek to "reconcile" Indigenous assertions of nationhood with settler-state sovereignty via the accommodation of Indigenous identity claims in some form of renewed legal and political relationship with the Canadian state.
>
> (p. 3)

According to the authors of *Beyond the Indian Act*, the recognition of underlying title is the most important way the FNPOA is a modification of previous proposals, even distinguishing it from the proposal Flanagan advanced in his notorious book *First Nations? Second Thoughts* (Flanagan, 2000). Apparently, since the writing of this book, Flanagan 'has come to realize that making property rights functional for First Nations requires *recognition* of their underlying title to their lands' (p. 7, emphasis added). The FNPOA is therefore presented by its supporters as different from previous schemes to privatize reserve lands, because, by granting underlying title to reserve lands, it amounts to the 'recognition' of First Nations land claims.

According to *Beyond the Indian Act*, however, the FNPOA isn't just about *recognizing* underlying title, but – as they imply in the book's subtitle, *Restoring Aboriginal Property Rights* – would entail the 'restoration' of First Nations property rights. Taken at face value, this argument appears as a discursive shift from the arguments used for the Dawes Act and 1969 White Paper, under which property rights were framed as a part of the civilizing, assimilationist project of settler colonial states (Stremlau, 2005, p. 266). To represent the FNPOA as a 'restoration' of Indigenous property rights, however, the authors of *Beyond the Indian Act* must first manufacture a very particular historical narrative of British and Canadian colonialism. First, they anachronistically project capitalist market forms back through time as essential components of precolonial societies. In the foreword to the book, Manny Jules writes that, as Indigenous peoples, '[m]arket economies were not foreign to us,' arguing Indigenous trade relations are proof of the existence of finance systems, and, prior to contact, Indigenous societies 'had individual property rights' (Flanagan et al., 2010, p. ix). The authors proceed further with this line of argument in a chapter called 'The Panorama of Indian Property Rights' (pp. 30–41). Here they dispute arguments, which they attribute to Vine Deloria Jr. and other Indigenous rights advocates, that portray 'Indians as natural collectivists, indeed proto-communists' (p. 30). Instead, 'aboriginal people everywhere in North America practiced personal ownership of possessions' and combined a 'collective sense of territory [. . .] with specific use rights of families and individuals' (p. 40). They consider it 'both ironic and tragic that this originally European conception of Indians as natural communists has now been accepted by many aboriginal leaders and thinkers,' as it is now 'a barrier to native participation in the modern economy' (p. 31). According to this narrative, private property rights are not necessarily a colonial imposition on First Nations communities but formed a significant part of precolonial Indigenous economic relations.

How, then, were these Indigenous private property rights lost? Continuing with their particular historical narrative, Indigenous private property rights were lost due to colonial policy, which was mainly about the exclusion of First Nations people and their reserve lands from the ability to participate in the capitalist free market. This 'exclusion' model of colonialism, *and apparently only this*, is what explains contemporary poverty on First Nations reserves. As Jules explains: 'We (First Nations) became the poorest of the poor because after contact the governments of Canada and the United States passed legislation that removed us from the economy' (Flanagan et al., 2010, p. x). Elsewhere, *Beyond the Indian Act* describes how, due to not understanding or recognizing existing property systems, 'the British and Canadian governments intended the introduction of property rights to lead to the integration and assimilation of aboriginal peoples into mainstream society' (p. 71). Originally intended as temporary measures, these governments created the reserve system and its associated forms of limited property rights, such as Certificates of Possession (CPs), which has led to the present-day situation in which 'the basic reality of Indian reserves in Canada is government ownership of land' (p. 28). For the authors of *Beyond the Indian Act*, current property regimes are a matter of unfinished business, and in the current political climate there is now 'an opportunity to make fee-simple ownership, both collective and individual, available to First Nations' (p. 72). Therefore, an understanding of precolonial Indigenous societies as 'proto-communist' constituted a form of misrecognition on the part of early European observers, and the proposed FNPOA is an attempt to correct this colonial mistake of excluding First Nations from active involvement in the Canadian capitalist economy.

This key argument of *Beyond the Indian Act*, that the FNPOA represents a 'restoration' of precolonial property forms that will rectify past mistakes on the part of the Canadian state, exemplifies precisely how narrowly the authors must define the terms of discussion and analysis for their legislative proposal to maintain a modicum of intelligibility. As Jessica Dempsey et al. (2011) argue in a book chapter critiquing previous works by Flanagan and Alcantara on the subject of reserve property rights, their arguments 'rest upon a full-scale bracketing of history and geography' (p. 254). As we have just seen, *Beyond the Indian Act* doesn't so much completely ignore colonial history but rather constructs its own peculiar historical imaginary. Nonetheless, there are several forms of 'bracketing out' involved in constructing the central arguments of *Beyond the Indian Act*, three of which I explore here in greater detail.

First, in *Beyond the Indian* Act, both Canadian sovereignty and present-day reserve boundaries are presented as fixed, legitimate, and not up for discussion. The authors argue existing underlying title to reserve lands in Canada – and all lands in Canada for that matter – were established under the 'international-law doctrines of discovery and (sometimes) conquest,' whereby 'Canadian sovereignty over the whole of Canada is recognized both internationally and by Canadian courts' (p. 27). Though *Beyond the Indian Act* does briefly acknowledge the projection of Canadian sovereignty 'happened without any consultation with the native people of North America [and] may be cause for regret,' the book generally treats the history of colonial dispossession as a sequence of large real estate transactions, albeit potentially unfair ones (p. 27). Regarding reserve boundaries, the authors do not spend much time elaborating on how reserve lands were formed, be it as a type of property or in terms of their specific borders. The authors' assertion that Canadian sovereignty underlies all lands in Canada does not address this gap, as underlying sovereignty doesn't explain why some lands are First Nations reserve lands and some are not, nor how their boundaries came to be. The argument of the book is thus narrowly defined both spatially and discursively, reinforcing what Sarah Hunt (2014) refers to as the *colonialscape*, whereby 'reserves become the natural space of "Indians", as Indigenous territorialities are rendered an impossibility in order to facilitate the reception of Canadian sovereignty' (p. 72). I argue the authors are proposing the FNPOA in order to achieve 'certainty' over title on First Nations land by a redrawing of property lines and forms *within* reserve boundaries, where much of the larger discussion and contestation in contemporary Indigenous struggles and scholarly works pertain to interrogating the very nature of these boundaries (Egan, 2012; Harris, 2002; Thom, 2009). As Shiri Pasternak (this volume) argues, 'the imposition of property rights onto Indigenous lands already presumes the state's authority to govern,' an imposition which ignores Indigenous forms of jurisdiction. This reification of both Canadian sovereignty and reserve boundaries should be understood as a deliberate strategy of attempting to contain and reframe the contemporary aims and tactics of Indigenous political action, a strategy of containment I suggest is crucial to understanding the ascendency of recognition approaches to Indigenous struggles on the part of the Canadian state.

This leads me to the second major 'bracketing out' found in *Beyond the Indian Act*: neither the historical narrative of the book nor any of the discussion around the benefits of the FNPOA contain any reference to gender. However, the Indian Act historically discriminated against women with Indian Status, and this had a distinctly spatial component. Prior to the passing of Bill C-31 in 1985, Status women who married non-Status men had their Status revoked and were subsequently denied the right to live on reserves. Property rights on reserves have always been inseparable from attempts by the Canadian settler state to implement heteropatriarchal relationships in Indigenous communities. For example, part of the proposed FNPOA involves converting existing forms of title over reserve lands as allowed under the Indian Act, such as Certificates of Possession (CP), which the authors of *Beyond the Indian Act* argue were 'meant to be the final step before the introduction of fee simple ownership' (p. 69). However, as Joanne Barker (2008) points out,

> by the 1960s, only 6 percent of elected council chiefs and council members were women; and certificates of possession, or the legal documents granting status Indians permission to live in reserve housing, were issued by bands and DIAND officials almost exclusively to men.
>
> (p. 263)

Thus, even if we were to accept that the conversion of these titles to fee simple might create an economic benefit for those holding CPs (which is admittedly a dubious claim), this benefit would serve to reinforce already existing colonial structures of heteropatriarchy.

However, to critique the FNPOA for not discussing gender is not about demanding a recognition of the specific circumstances of Indigenous women in the legislation, especially when neoliberal strategies have proven a certain level of adaptability in accommodating claims for inclusivity. More crucially, the kinds of human–land relationships dictated and presumed by the Ownership Act are imbued with fundamentally patriarchal notions about how Indigenous people ought to relate to and utilize land: as property with value that is only commensurable in economic terms. These notions are in sharp opposition to what Mishuana Goeman (2013) refers to as 'remapping discourses' within Native women's geographies, discourses which mark a 'move toward geographies that do not limit, contain, or fix the various scales of space from the body to nation in ways that limit definitions of self and community staked out as property' (p. 11). I argue the further enshrinement of private property regimes on reserves would directly undermine the remapping discourses of Indigenous women that Goeman discusses.

Third, returning to the notion that the FNPOA represents a restoration of aboriginal property rights, the authors of *Beyond the Indian Act* make a fundamental mistake in equating property rights with capitalism and the market. It is a huge stretch to equate twenty-first-century, distinctively capitalist property rights with any of the Indigenous property rights regimes the authors discuss. Rather, the creation of private property regimes across the vast majority of non-reserve lands in Canada entailed a blatant, pervasive form of colonialism much more significant than the 'exclusion' framework the authors of *Beyond the Indian Act* narrowly deploy. As Cole Harris (2004) argues regarding the projection of settler colonialism across what is now BC, 'the rights of property embedded in the common law tangibly legitimated the dispossession and repossession of land for which assumptions about civilization, savagery, and the progressive use of land had provided a more abstract justification' (p. 177). Thus, the various tools of Canadian state administration, jurisdiction, and power discussed in *Beyond the Indian Act* are built on a history of dispossession. At best, a large leap of faith on the part of First Nations is required in order to presume that land and property rights of First Nations would be protected by a state founded on achieving the exact opposite end.

Therefore, when one considers past and present manifestations of dispossession, the argument that colonialism has predominantly entailed the 'exclusion' of Indigenous people from the capitalist economy really starts to break down. Rather, for Indigenous people, dispossession entails an intimate, 'inclusive' experience with the workings of capitalism, its reconfiguration of human–land relationships, and the imposition of private property regimes vastly different from Indigenous, non-capitalist forms of property tenure. As a manifestation of recognition politics, then, the proposed FNPOA is inherently unable, and, by design, unwilling to reconcile this experience of dispossession. As Coulthard (2014) argues, 'the politics of recognition in its contemporary liberal form promises to reproduce the very configurations of colonialist, racist, patriarchal state power that Indigenous peoples' demands for recognition have historically sought to transcend' (p. 3). How the FNPOA reproduces settler colonial hegemony by facilitating the continued dispossession of Indigenous people is the subject of the next section.

## Settler colonial property rights and primitive accumulation

The proposed FNPOA points to the dynamic of dispossession as a permanent feature of Canadian settler colonialism. Further analysis of this dynamic entails drawing from contemporary discussions concerning Marx's theory of primitive accumulation, which he defined in *Capital: Vol. 1* as 'nothing else than the historical process of divorcing the producer from the means of production' (1981, p. 875). Within geography, David Harvey's interventions have figured heavily in these discussions, especially his concept of 'accumulation by dispossession,' whereby 'the features of primitive accumulation that Marx mentions have remained powerfully present within capitalism's historical geography up until now' (2003, p. 145). Similarly, in Indigenous studies, Coulthard discusses the continued relevance of Marx's theory to the political economy of Canadian settler colonialism as part of his critique of the liberal politics of recognition. Coulthard points out, however, that Marx's theory needs to be 'transformed *in conversation* with the critical thought and practices of Indigenous peoples themselves' (2014, p. 8). Coulthard then identifies three problematic features of Marx's primitive accumulation thesis: its rigid temporal framing, its normative developmentalism, and the ways in which 'colonial relations of power are no longer reproduced primarily through overtly coercive means, but rather through the asymmetrical exchange of mediated forms of state recognition and accommodation' (pp. 8–15). Coulthard also highlights the need to shift, when discussing settler colonial contexts, from focusing on the 'capital-relation to the colonial-relation' (p. 11). Crucially, this means that 'the history and experience of dispossession, not proletarianization, has been the dominant background structure shaping the character of the historical relationship between Indigenous peoples and the Canadian state' (p. 13). With this key insight in mind, I want to first demonstrate how the proposed FNPOA is a form of primitive accumulation and then suggest ways this legislation might inform contemporary discussions concerning the continued role of dispossession as a form of accumulation outside of the point of production.

The proposed FNPOA is a blatant example of primitive accumulation's continued operation and is presented by its advocates as essential for further incorporating First Nations lands into the capitalist market. The FNPOI website explains why the inalienable nature of reserve land creates a 'barrier' to economic development: because reserve land 'is held by the Crown for the use and benefit of Indian bands, a trust or fiduciary responsibility lies with the Government regarding its management of the land' (First Nations Property Ownership Initiative: The Proposal in Summary, n.d., para. 2). Since reserve land is governed by federal law and is inalienable except from the band to the government, it is outside provincial property rights law, creating what the FNPOI website describes as 'an extensive "regulatory gap"' (para. 2). According to advocates of the FNPOA, then, the inability to alienate reserve lands is a barrier to the full functioning of capitalist markets on First Nations reserves, and private property rights on reserves will serve to 'unlock' their economic potential.

The FNPOA also aims to provide specific mechanisms for First Nations governments in enforcing property rights and attracting investment that would directly facilitate the dispossession of First Nations individuals from reserve land when applied. Despite the aforementioned claims by the authors of *Beyond the Indian Act* that the FNPOA would recognize and protect 'the inalienable reversionary right to First Nations title,' this only appears to hold true based on the very narrow definition of 'First Nations' implicit throughout the book (p. 177). For example, under the FNPOA, First Nations governments would acquire increased powers to evict members who default on their housing mortgages or do not pay their housing charges. The authors of *Beyond the Indian Act* advocate for these powers by citing the current non-payment rates of housing charges on various reserves: 'At Cowichan Tribes, fifty of four hundred members living in rental homes were not paying in 2002; at Siksika, the nonpayment rate was 60 percent; and at Blood, approximately 75 to 80 percent. At Piikani, 97 percent of members living in rental housing were not paying' (p. 89). The inability to enforce payment of these housing charges is decried for not existing under current on-reserve property arrangements, creating problems such as diminishing 'the amount of capital available to First Nations to build more housing and engage in repairs' (p. 89). As Dempsey et al. (2011) argue, advocating for greater eviction rights for non-payment of mortgages and rent payments is dismissive of alternate conceptions of reserve housing as a treaty right that might explain why members choose not to pay, not to mention 'whether the people living in those houses actually can pay their mortgages and rent' (p. 245). Ignoring these considerations, the proposed FNPOA instead provides what I refer to as the 'right to evict' as an essential mechanism for the removal of First Nations members from reserves.

With investments and developments not related to housing, both the current realities and potential impacts of the FNPOA are even more troubling for First Nations members living on reserves. Throughout *Beyond the Indian Act*, the types of property developments upon which the authors bestow the highest praise include the Sun Rivers Golf Course on Tk'emlups (Kamloops) reserve land, the Great Canadian Superstore on the Squamish Seymour Creek reserve, and the 'economic success story' of the Westbank First Nation where, as part of the Westbank implementation agreement, they have residential developments represented by more than 10,000 non-members living on Westbank reserve lands (p. 156). The authors discuss these examples to demonstrate the numerous forms of economic development that are currently taking place on First Nations reserve lands, which implicitly could flourish more broadly under the FNPOA. What they don't discuss are the implications for First Nations if much of what is already scarce reserve land is unavailable for occupation and use by its members. As Pasternak (2015) argues, the FNPOA 'is discursively framed to acknowledge Indigenous land rights while the bill simultaneously introduces contentious measures to individualize and municipalize the quasi-communal land holding of reserves' (p. 180). One of the implications of this 'municipalizing' is that the FNPOA only guarantees the collective jurisdiction of the First Nation *as a government entity* over its reserve lands. As for guarantees of physical occupancy of those lands by First Nations people and communities, under the proposed FNPOA it appears these would be subordinated to the forces of the newly established on-reserve private property markets.

These examples, both with and without the proposed FNPOA, of creeping encroachment onto First Nations reserves by non-Indigenous commercial and housing developments are very significant for contemporary discussions concerning the nature of contemporary forms of primitive accumulation. The role of struggle in helping to understand the continued working of primitive accumulation is central to Jim Glassman's (2006) intervention in the debate concerning primitive accumulation, whereby class struggle provides 'one basis for the likelihood [. . .] of primitive accumulation remaining a fixture within capitalist development' (p. 615). This aspect of the contemporary discussion concerning primitive accumulation, whereby historical struggles against enclosures are key to understanding the continued operation of primitive accumulation, is extremely valuable in understanding the specific context within which the FNPOA arises. At least as early as the Bagot Commission of 1844, representatives of the British Crown preferred to encourage individual property ownership of reserve lands (Erasmus & Dussault, 1996, p. 247). This was opposed by Indigenous communities at the time, who, along with an overall opposition to the Commission's assimilationist approach, exhibited 'strong resistance to the notion of individual allotment of reserve lands, as many feared – rightly – that this would lead to the loss of these lands and to the gradual destruction of the reserve land base' (Erasmus & Dussault, 1996, p. 247). Opposition to individual titling was also clearly expressed by the Indigenous leaders who participated in the Conference of Orillia, a meeting organized by the superintendent of Indian Affairs to consult with official Chiefs in Eastern Canada in 1846. According to Miller (2000), the chiefs in attendance 'wanted no part of provisions that would allow the conversion of lands that bands held in common to individual plots held in freehold tenure' (p. 141). These examples of opposition are significant in understanding the complexities in how First Nations reserves and collective property rights are still defended by communities despite their colonial nature. Further, as much as both the Indian Act and the reserve system are blatant colonial impositions, the current form of property tenure means that reserve land is both collectively held and inalienable, therefore providing a beneficial protection, however limited, for First Nations reserve communities. Therefore, as a legislated form of dispossession, the FNPOA's proposal draws attention to the role of Indigenous struggle, whereby the 'unfinished business' of establishing private property rights on reserves points to past efforts by Indigenous communities to resist their implementation.

Nicholas Brown (2014) provides an important contribution to the discussion on the role of Indigenous struggle in understanding the workings of primitive accumulation. He presents his own intervention as seeking to answer a set of related questions: 'is the *continuous character* of primitive accumulation contingent on and enabled by the *failure* of settler colonialism? In other words, does failure allow processes of primitive accumulation to endure?' (p. 7). By failure, Brown is referring to Audra Simpson's (2011) characterization of settler colonialism as a 'failed project' in which continued Indigenous presence in North America means having 'survived this acquisitive and genocidal process and thus to have called up the failure of the project itself' (p. 205).

From the vantage point of Indigenous people, I worry it is setting the bar a bit low if the inability of the Canadian or US states to execute a 100% genocidal elimination is the criterion for declaring the 'failure' of these settler colonial projects. Nonetheless, Brown and Simpson point to the role of Indigenous struggle in ways that imply the continued existence of non-capitalist spaces and relations. The continued existence of these spaces has important implications for theorizing contemporary processes of primitive accumulation, whereby the assertions of existence by Indigenous people are made as people who exist at least in part outside of both the political and economic spaces of Canada. Further, struggles against dispossession inherently foreground struggles over subject formation: as Ngai-Ling Sum and Bob Jessop (2013) argue, class struggle 'is first of all a struggle about the constitution of class subjects before it is a struggle between class subjects' (p. 187). In other words, the question of property forms on reserves doesn't point to strictly a struggle over control of particular parcels of land but the kind of relationships that are at stake in the further entrenchment of private property regimes within First Nations communities. These communities are thus also the site of a struggle between assertions of Indigenous identity and attempts by the Canadian state at colonial *resubjection*, a struggle which I will now discuss.

## The FNPOA and settler colonial subjection

For both the Canadian settler state and Indigenous peoples, the struggle over subjects is inherently spatial: in conflicts over land and property rights there is a direct connection between land, property forms, and subject formation. In 'The Subject and Power,' Michel Foucault (1982) suggests the term *subject* has two meanings: 'subject to someone else by control and dependence; and tied to his own identity by a conscience or self-knowledge' (p. 781). Foucault argues both definitions 'suggest a form of power which subjugates and makes subject to' (p. 781). Here, Foucault defines struggles against subjection as struggles 'against forms of subjectivity and submission' (p. 781). For the purposes of this analysis, I use the term *resubjection* to describe the ways the proposed FNPOA involves a reconfiguration of the kinds of colonial subjects that have already been produced through the Indian Act.

Drawing from Franz Fanon's notion of 'colonized subjects', Coulthard argues,

> the maintenance of settler-state hegemony requires the production of [. . .] the specific modes of colonial thought, desire, and behaviour that implicitly or explicitly commit the colonized to the types of practices and subject positions that are required for their continued domination.
>
> (2014, p. 16)

Shifts towards politics of reconciliation and recognition therefore mean that not only do the structures of domination change over time but along with them the colonizer's preferences for the reconstitution of Indian subjects. Thus, the ideal Indian subject is no longer one that is presumed to assimilate and disappear but joins and prospers within Canadian society guided by an 'Indigenous entrepreneurialism,' or what Dempsey et al. refer to as 'property-owning entrepreneurial subject-citizens' (2011, p. 239). As I explain, the FNPOA thus presumes a very narrow subjectivity for Indigenous people, one that excludes the possibility for Indigenous ways of relating to land. If taken to its logical conclusion, this vision still embodies an assimilating, disappearing subject.

The authors of *Beyond the Indian Act*, along with other supporters of the FNPOA, assume an inherent relationship between subject formation and property relations. This is especially the case when the authors discuss the virtues of private home ownership on reserves, in which 'there must be owners who take pride in their own homes and see them as a savings vehicle' (pp. 6–7). The authors of *Beyond the Indian Act* also use anecdotes to provide examples of the ideal entrepreneurial First Nations subject whose individual aspirations for personal advancement are thwarted by existing property regimes. For example, the authors cite a legal case involving one couple, the Johnstones, who had acquired control over roughly one-sixth of the entire Mistawasis First Nation reserve land base in a combination of CP and 'ad hoc' holdings. The authors decry the fact that, despite a court ruling stating that the Johnstones had 'improved, maintained, nurtured and sustained the lands in their occupation and possession,' they were forced by the band council to give back the lands for which they had not acquired any sort of CP (pp. 73–74). This is emblematic of the kind of assumptions held by the authors of *Beyond the Indian Act* concerning subjects and the proper relations one should have with land. Within this particular model, which Nicholas Blomley (2004) refers to as the 'ownership model' of land relations, 'private ownership is seen as good to the extent that it fosters valued behaviours, including responsible citizenship, political participation, and economic entrepreneurship' (pp. 3, 4). Further, according to Blomley, viewing property

> as a spatialized thing, rather than a bundle of relationships, locates its central relationship as that between the owner and the thing owned. The effect is to suppress our understanding of the undeniable and often differential relations between the owner and other people.
>
> (p. 6)

David Cohen and Allan Hutchinson (1990) also critique the constraining effect of world making as it is enacted through what they refer to as the 'normative authority of law' (p. 21). For Cohen and Hutchinson, this means the 'essential and creative act of world-making' always occurs with 'the equally unavoidable act of world-ending. To make one world is to abandon, at least temporarily, other potential worlds. Sight and blindness are simultaneously experienced. A way of seeing is always a way of not seeing' (p. 23). Extending this to property law, if other worlds are precluded by certain views of property relations, we can also presume the same dynamic concerning their corresponding forms of subjectivity. And, as I will explore, the notion that the FNPOA represents a 'restoration' of Indigenous land relations is difficult to sustain when such narrow limits on property forms and subjectivities are inscribed.

Discussing the relationship between property forms and colonial subjects, Dempsey et al. (2011) characterize the work of Flanagan and Alcantara as constituting 'boundary-making practices,' through which they 'draw boundaries around appropriate land management regimes and subjects, and how these, in turn, script other forms as in-appropriate' (p. 235). This 'appropriate' subject is inseparable from their ideal forms of property regimes, because, for Flanagan and Alcantara, appropriate land management regimes 'are those that facilitate the acquisition of credit, and the ideal Canadian subject is one who is self-sufficient and enterprising, and who never makes special demands based on history/geography/culture' (p. 235). As a project of resubjecting Indigenous peoples through the adoption of 'appropriate' land management regimes, Dempsey et al. also characterize Flanagan and Alcantara's argument as 'one that seeks to place rigid boundaries around both Aboriginal land management and subjectivity' (p. 241). However, I want to expand on the analysis of the relations between land and subject formation in settler colonial contexts. Here, I draw from Wolfe's two key contributions to theorizing settler colonialism:

first, it is guided by a logic of elimination, and second, it should be understood as a structure and not an event (2006, p. 390).

I argue the FNPOA points to the act of settler colonial *resubjection* as part of the larger, continued Canadian project of genocide. For Nelson Maldonado-Torres (2007), the eliminating tendency is an ever-present aspect of what he refers to as 'coloniality,' whereby '[t]he imperial attitude promotes a fundamentally genocidal attitude in respect to colonized and racialized people. Through it colonial and racial subjects are marked as dispensable' (p. 246). Simpson (2014) also points to this genocidal tendency in her critique of the politics of recognition. She argues, 'settler colonialism structures justice and injustice in particular ways, not through the conferral of recognition of the enslaved but by the conferral of *disappearance in subject*. This is not seeing that is so profound that mutuality cannot be achieved' (p. 23, emphasis added). Therefore, in settler colonial contexts, the process of producing colonial subjects isn't just about the creation of 'rigid boundaries' around Indian subjectivity but is also about eliminating Indigenous peoples as a subject position altogether.

The proposed FNPOA is an example of the continued applicability of the 'logic of elimination' because of the ways in which it seeks to reconfigure Indigenous relationships with land and place that are central to the continued existence of Indigenous people and Indigeneity itself. As Aileen Moreton-Robinson (2003) argues, these ways of relating to land are essential to Indigeneity, where the 'ontological relationship to land, the ways that country is constitutive of us, and therefore the inalienable nature of our relation to land, mark a radical, indeed incommensurable, difference between us and the non-Indigenous' (p. 31). This is crucial because the threats to Indigenous land relationships posed by the proposed FNPOA point to the inherent limits of the liberal politics of recognition, whereby for Canada the agenda is still ultimately an assimilationist one. Whereas Coulthard (2014) argues the era of recognition has been characterized by 'a significant decoupling of Indigenous "cultural" claims from the transformative visions of social, political, and economic change that once constituted them' (p. 52), I would add that this decoupling is only possible by eliminating aspects of our 'cultural claims' that are incompatible with capital accumulation. Thus, perhaps the greatest threat that the proposed FNPOA poses to us as Indigenous people in Canada is an entrenchment of new forms of assimilation that are more insidious than previous ones, albeit just as impactful.

## Property rights and Indigenous struggles in Canada

Throughout this chapter I have tried to emphasize the role of Indigenous struggle against dispossession, in understanding the proposed FNPOA as well as more broadly in influencing how the Canadian state must continuously adapt its own strategies and tactics for perpetuating colonial domination. To me this is crucial in situating the specific form that the proposed FNPOA takes in the current era of recognition politics. FNPOA advocates have been forced to mobilize a 'property rights as restoration' discourse as a response to Indigenous opposition that is informed, among other experiences, by the results of the Dawes Act in the US. The proposed FNPOA also helps us understand that dispossession and genocide, two of the historically definitive characteristics of Canadian settler colonialism, remain very much on the agenda as fundamental threats to the continued existence of Indigenous people, which we in turn continue to resist. Thus, the settler–Indigenous relationship in Canada continues to be fundamentally defined by struggle.

Centring the role of struggle also helps us understand why, to date, there has been no move towards tabling, let alone implementing, the proposed FNPOA at the legislative level since the 2012 draft federal budget. During the time the Conservatives formed the majority federal government, the FNPOA was only one of several pieces of legislation they either passed or attempted to pass, including the omnibus Bill C-45 and the First Nations Education Act (Flaherty, 2012, p. 149). The Idle No More movement was initially launched by its founders as a specific response to Bill C-45 (Kino-nda-niimi Collective, 2014). The Idle No More movement also mobilized opposition to the Education Act, and after years of negotiation between the Harper government and then-AFN leader Shawn Atleo, the Education Act faced strong opposition by First Nations and was never passed (Rennie, 2015). The FNPOA was thus part of a larger legislative agenda of the Conservative government that was ultimately thwarted due to Indigenous opposition. Flanagan himself later credited Idle No More for halting the FNPOA, suggesting the legislation was never introduced 'because of opposition from the Idle No More movement' (2015, p. 5).

Despite the attempts by FNPOA to frame the legislation as representing a 'restoration' of Indigenous forms of property tenure, the proposal has very little support from First Nations communities, and at the time of this writing it is fair to say the momentum for the FNPOA is gone. At the same time, since the FNPOA was itself a re-articulation of previous proposals to implement private property regimes, it is unfortunately safe to predict the legislation will return in a different, repackaged form. The implications of my critique of the FNPOA are also important because, even without the FNPOA, fee simple regimes are becoming a reality on reserves through the BC Treaty Process. Further, the new Liberal government has also discussed ways it might seek to eliminate the Indian Act. In 2016, new Justice Minister Jody Wilson-Raybould (2016) delivered a speech to the AFN, where she referred to the new Liberal government's 'renewed Nation-to-Nation relationship with Indigenous peoples,' a relationship based on 'recognition of rights, respect, co-operation and partnership' (para. 10). According to Wilson-Raybould, this renewed relationship 'includes mechanisms to negotiate modern treaties under new mandates' and facilitating 'self-government beyond the Indian Act band' (para. 31). As I previously outlined, in the current framework 'modern treaties' all stipulate the conversion of reserve lands into fee simple. Though Wilson-Raybould specifies the need for new mandates in treaty negotiations, it is not clear from this speech whether this might include removing the requirement for fee simple from future treaty negotiations.

I think it is thus very possible that the return of a repackaged FNPOA will happen even during the era of the current Liberal government, and if not is very likely to return in the future. However, regardless of whether this most recent attempt to rebrand former proposals is successful, the dynamics of dispossession, colonial *resubjection*, and other forms of elimination continue to structure Indigenous–settler relations in Canada, and the struggle over property forms is but one of them. Therefore, the larger theoretical questions I explore using the FNPOA as an entry point are still important to analyse given their political implications for Indigenous peoples in Canada.

## References

Alcantara, C. (2007). Reduce transaction costs? Yes: Strengthen property rights? Maybe: The first nations land management act and economic development on Canadian Indian reserves. *Public Choice*, *132*(3/4), 421–432. Retrieved from https://doi.org/10.1007/s11127-007-9168-7

Assembly of First Nations. (2010, July). *First nations' rejection of a 'property ownership act'*. (Resolution No. 44/2010). Annual General Meeting, Winnipeg, MB. Retrieved from www.afn.ca/uploads/files/2010-res.pdf

Barker, J. (2008). Gender, sovereignty, rights: Native women's activism against social inequality and violence in Canada. *American Quarterly*, *60*(2), 259–266. Retrieved from https://doi.org/10.1353/aq.0.0002

Blomley, N. (2004). *Unsettling the city: Urban land and the politics of property*. New York, NY: Routledge.

Blomley, N. (2014). Making space for property. *Annals of the Association of American Geographers*, *104*(6), 1291–1306. Retrieved from https://doi.org/10.1080/00045608.2014.941738

Brown, N. A. (2014). The logic of settler accumulation in a landscape of perpetual vanishing. *Settler Colonial Studies*, *4*(1), 1–26. Retrieved from https://doi.org/10.1080/2201473X.2013.784236

Chrétien, J. (1969). *Statement of the government of Canada on Indian policy (The White Paper)*. Ottawa: Queen's Printer. Retrieved from http://ejournals.library.ualberta.ca/index.php/aps/article/viewFile/10138/7950

Chris Alcantara – Political Science – Western University. (n.d.). Retrieved from http://politicalscience.uwo.ca/people/faculty/full-time_faculty/chris_alcantara.html

Cohen, D., & Hutchinson, A. C. (1990). Of persons and property: The politics of legal taxonomy. *Dalhousie Law Journal*, *13*(1), 20–54. Retrieved from http://heinonline.org.ezproxy.library.ubc.ca/HOL/Page?handle=hein.journals/dalholwj13&collection=journals&id=20

Conservative Party of Canada. (2015). *Protect our economy: A conservative plan to protect the economy*. Retrieved from www.poltext.org/sites/poltext.org/files/plateformes/conservative-platform-2015.pdf

Coulthard, G. S. (2007). Subjects of empire: Indigenous peoples and the 'politics of recognition' in Canada. *Contemporary Political Theory*, *6*(4), 437–460. Retrieved from https://doi.org/10.1057/palgrave.cpt.9300307

Coulthard, G. S. (2014). *Red skin, white masks: Rejecting the colonial politics of recognition*. Minneapolis: University of Minnesota Press.

Cuthand, D. (2014, 5 September). Reserve land a birthright, not mere real estate. *Star – Phoenix*. Saskatoon, Sask., Canada, p. A.11.

De Soto, H. (2001). *The mystery of capital: Why capitalism triumphs in the West and fails everywhere else*. London: Black Swan.

Dempsey, J., Gould, K., & Sundberg, J. (2011). Changing land tenure, defining subjects: Neoliberalism and property regimes on Native reserves. In A. Kobayashi, L. Cameron, & A. Baldwin (Eds.), *Rethinking the great white north: Race, nature, and the historical geographies of whiteness in Canada* (pp. 233–255). Vancouver: UBC Press.

Egan, B. (2012). Sharing the colonial burden: Treaty-making and reconciliation in Hul'qumi'num territory. *The Canadian Geographer/Le Géographe Canadien*, *56*(4), 398–418. Retrieved from https://doi.org/10.1111/j.1541-0064.2012.00414.x

Erasmus, G., & Dussault, R. (Eds.) (1996). *Report of the royal commission on aboriginal peoples*. Vols. 1–5. Ottawa: Minister of Supply and Services.

Fabris, M. (2013). *Beyond the Indian act: Restoring aboriginal property rights*. Unpublished book review. Burnaby, Canada: Department of Geography, Simon Fraser University.

*First nations property ownership initiative: The proposal in summary*. (n.d.). Retrieved from www.fnpo.ca/Proposal.aspx

Flaherty, J. (2012). *Jobs growth and long-term prosperity: Economic action plan 2012*. Ottawa: Public Works and Government Services Canada. Retrieved from www.budget.gc.ca/2012/plan/pdf/Plan2012-eng.pdf

Flanagan, T. (2000). *First nations? Second thoughts*. Montreal: McGill-Queen's University Press.

Flanagan, T. (2010, 22 March). First nations property rights: Going beyond the Indian Act. *The Globe and Mail*. Retrieved from www.theglobeandmail.com/opinion/first-nations-property-rights-going-beyond-the-indian-act/article1209790/

Flanagan, T. (2015). *Clarity and confusion? The new jurisprudence of aboriginal title*. Retrieved from www.fraserinstitute.org/sites/default/files/clarity-and-confusion-new-jurisprudence-of-aboriginal-title.pdf

Flanagan, T., & Alcantara, C. (2002). Individual property rights on Canadian Indian reserves. *Public Policy Sources*, *60*, 1–60. Retrieved from www.fraserinstitute.org/sites/default/files/PropertyRightsonIndianReserves.pdf

Flanagan, T., & Alcantara, C. (2004). Individual property rights on Canadian Indian reserves: A review of the jurisprudence. *Alberta Law Review*, *42*(4), 1019–1046. Retrieved from http://heinonlinebackup.com/hol-cgi-bin/get_pdf.cgi?handle=hein.journals/alblr42&section=44

Flanagan, T., Le Dressay, A., & Alcantara, C. (2010). *Beyond the Indian act: Restoring aboriginal property rights*. Montreal: McGill-Queen's University Press.

Foucault, M. (1982). The subject and power. *Critical Inquiry*, *8*(4), 777–795. Retrieved from www.jstor.org/stable/1343197

Glassman, J. (2006). Primitive accumulation, accumulation by dispossession, accumulation by 'extra-economic' means. *Progress in Human Geography*, *30*(5), 608–625. Retrieved from https://doi.org/10.1177/0309132506070172

Goeman, M. (2013). *Mark my words: Native women mapping our nations*. Minneapolis: University of Minnesota Press.

Harris, C. (2002). *Making native space: Colonialism, resistance, and reserves in British Columbia*. Vancouver: UBC Press.

Harris, C. (2004). How did colonialism dispossess? Comments from an edge of empire. *Annals of the Association of American Geographers*, *94*(1), 165–182. Retrieved from https://doi.org/10.1111/j.1467-8306.2004.09401009.x

Harvey, D. (2003). *The new imperialism*. Oxford & New York, NY: Oxford University Press.

Hunt, S. E. (2014, 3 March). *Witnessing the colonialscape: Lighting the intimate fires of Indigenous legal pluralism*, Thesis. Simon Fraser University, Burnaby, BC. Retrieved from http://summit.sfu.ca/item/14145

The Indian Act (An Act Respecting Indians), Statutes of Canada, I-5 c §. (1985). Retrieved from http://laws-lois.justice.gc.ca/eng/acts/I%2D5/

Kino-nda-niimi Collective (Ed.) (2014). *The winter we danced: Voices from the past, the future, and the Idle No More movement*. Winnipeg: Arbeiter Ring Publishing.

Maldonado-Torres, N. (2007). On the coloniality of being. *Cultural Studies*, *21*(2), 240–270. Retrieved from https://doi.org/10.1080/09502380601162548

Manuel, A. (2010). *Re: DIA letter on reserve land and First Nation development* (Open Letter). Coldstream, BC: Indigenous Network on Economies and Trade.

Marx, K. (1981). *Capital: A critique of political economy: Vol. 1*. London & New York, NY: Penguin Books in association with New Left Review.

Miller, J. R. (2000). *Skyscrapers hide the heavens: A history of Indian-white relations in Canada* (3rd ed.). Toronto & Buffalo: University of Toronto Press.

Moreton-Robinson, A. (2003). I still call Australia home: Indigenous belonging and place in a white postcolonizing society. In S. Ahmed (Ed.), *Uprootings/regroundings: Questions of home and migration* (pp. 23–40). Oxford: Berg Publishers.

Palmater, P. (2012, 7 August). Flanagan national petroleum ownership act: Stop big oil land grab. *Indigenous Nationhood*. Retrieved from http://indigenousnationhood.blogspot.com/2012/08/flanagan-national-petroleum-ownership.html

Pasternak, S. (2015). How capitalism will save colonialism: The privatization of reserve lands in Canada. *Antipode*, *47*(1), 179–196. Retrieved from https://doi.org/10.1111/anti.12094

Rennie, S. (2015, 9 February). Harper to AFN Chief: No movement on education plan. *The Huffington Post*. Retrieved from www.huffingtonpost.ca/2015/02/09/stephen-harper-afn-first-nations-education-plan_n_6646832.html

Simpson, A. (2011). Settlement's secret. *Cultural Anthropology*, *26*(2), 205–217. Retrieved from https://doi.org/10.1111/j.1548-1360.2011.01095.x

Simpson, A. (2014). *Mohawk interruptus: Political life across the borders of settler states*. Durham, NC: Duke University Press.

Stremlau, R. (2005). 'To domesticate and civilize wild Indians': Allotment and the campaign to reform Indian families, 1875–1887. *Journal of Family History*, *30*(3), 265–286. Retrieved from https://doi.org/10.1177/0363199005275793

Sum, N-L., & Jessop, B. (2013). *Towards a cultural political economy: Putting culture in its place in political economy*. Cheltenham, UK: Edward Elgar.

Thom, B. (2009). The paradox of boundaries in Coast Salish territories. *Cultural Geographies*, *16*(2), 179–205. Retrieved from https://doi.org/10.1177/1474474008101516

Tom Flanagan. (n.d.). Retrieved from www.fraserinstitute.org/content/prof-tom-flanagan

Vowel, C. (2012, 23 August). *First nations property ownership act just White paper lite*. Retrieved from http://rabble.ca/blogs/bloggers/apihtawikosisan/2012/08/first-nations-property-ownership-act-just-white-paper-lite

Wilson-Raybould, J. (2016, 21 July). *The Honourable Jody Wilson-Raybould's remarks at the Assembly of First Nations Annual General Assembly.* Retrieved from http://jwilson-raybould.liberal.ca/news-nouvelles/the-honourable-jody-wilson-rayboulds-remarks-at-the-assembly-of-first-nations-annual-general-assembly/

Wolfe, P. (2006). Settler colonialism and the elimination of the native. *Journal of Genocide Research*, *8*(4), 387–409. Retrieved from https://doi.org/10.1080/14623520601056240

Chapter 11

# Contesting claims to gardens and land

## Gendered practice in post-war northern Uganda

*Julaina A. Obika, Ben Adol Otto, Sulayman Mpisi Babiiha, and Michael Whyte*

*This chapter explores how, in a patrilineal and patriarchal society recovering from two decades of war, women and men frame arguments about entitlement. Here claims to gardens (plots of land for cultivation) become a contested conversation about women's rights of belonging to family and community, revealing transformations in ideas and practices about land rights and land ownership. Drawing on extended cases we follow claims through a variety of legal and social fora as men and women mobilise allies and seek to draw on goodwill and the ideal of harmonious co-existence (ber bedo).*

### Introduction

For two decades the Acholi and Langi regions of northern Uganda formed the primary war zone in a complex conflict between the Ugandan government and the insurgent Lord's Resistance Army (LRA). At the end of the war, in 2006, more than 1.8 million people, about 90% of the population, had been forced into camps for the internally displaced (Mabikke, 2011). Camps were degazetted and, impoverished and marked by 20 years of armed conflict, Acholi and Langi began to return to homes that had been abandoned for years. Houses were rebuilt, bush cleared, and communities began to re-establish themselves. With return came conflict – and the era of 'land wrangles' began. Boundaries were debated and contested, land sales were attempted and contested, and, above all, issues of social belonging were raised and contested.

These events form the context for this chapter. We explore contested property claims that have become a hallmark of the period of return and, in particular, what these contested claims have come to mean for patrilineality and patrilocality, gender relations and land governance. We draw on the Acholi language distinction between kinds of land, *ngom kwaro* as clan or ancestral land and *poti* as land in use, usually translated as 'gardens.' *Ngom kwaro* discourse highlights collective ownership and rights of use by clans and patrikin; *poti* discourses, particularly relevant for women, highlight land use as a recognition of belonging to a community. Drawing on case studies, we show how men and women make use of these discourses to claim and contest access to and use of land in different contexts.

## Dilemmas of return

Filda and her partner, Peter, were staying in the Awach internally displaced people's (IDP) camp, where they had been interned. After the war, they planned to go and settle on his ancestral land in Aswa, some 7 km away. Peter's father had died, so he asked his father's brother, who was taking care of their ancestral land at Aswa, to 'show' (give) him his portion so that he could start constructing a home for his family. However, the father's brother refused, pointing out that, in addition to her sons with Peter, Filda was caring for two other sons from her earlier relationship with a man from another clan, now dead. If these sons were allowed to live with their mother, the father's brother worried that they might, in the future, claim ownership over the gardens that their mother would be assigned as Peter's wife. A condition was set: if Peter wanted to live with Filda and his biological sons on his ancestral clan land, she would have to take the two older sons back to their father's family. Peter's father's brother was not prepared to share his ancestral land with strangers.

Filda, 48, had started living with Peter while both were interned in Awach IDP camp, one of the many camps for what were called internally displaced persons, into which the national army forced all people at the height of the war in 2002. Filda and Peter were not formally married but by 2008, two years after hostilities ceased, they had two sons, aged 6 and 4. Filda's other two sons from her late husband (also an informal marriage) were 16 and 14 years old. Peter was initially ready to settle down with Filda and all four children but now he was in a dilemma. Everybody was moving home, and he did not want to miss his chance to secure a portion of his ancestral land and to settle in the newly re-established community at Aswa. But at the same time, he loved his wife, the mother of his two young sons.

Peter tried to persuade her to take the two older sons to their father's relatives. Filda did not want to try; she knew that the only two sisters of her deceased husband were married, and their husbands would not be willing to take on more responsibility. She did not even ask her own brothers, who had a customary obligation to help, since they had not been willing to assist her in Awach. Instead, Filda separated from Peter and moved to a nearby trading centre, where she could rent land to build a hut, care for all the children and establish gardens – at least for a while. She and Peter continue to see each other, and Filda hopes that in time Peter may find a way to bring her and all her sons to his home. If this plan fails she can continue renting her plot on the outskirts of the trading centre for a while. Ultimately, she could return to her own natal home with all her children. Here she believes she can, as a clan daughter, be given gardens and space to build a house.

Land conflicts are widespread in post-war northern Uganda after the years of war and displacement. The simple assumption that everyone could return to 'where the war found them' was, in reality, problematic. As we shall see, access to land for Acholi is largely through social relations, not certificates of tenure. Contested claims to land, as Peter and Filda's case illustrates, are also disputes about belonging and attachment. Peter and his sons can claim clanship, and Filda, as the mother of clansmen, has a potential claim to belong and to be 'shown' garden land that she may cultivate. But her other sons can be seen as a threat – or at any rate an excuse to avoid attaching the family. The threat comes from the implication that Filda's older sons (who belong to the clan of their deceased biological father) may in future make a claim to portions of Peter's clan land.

The issue for Filda was not simply where – and from whom – she could claim land but where she could be recognised as a wife (or even a widow) or where she was a daughter or where her children might come to belong. In the patrilineal system that obtains among the Acholi people, sons claim land on the basis of descent from their fathers, while women claim land both on the basis of marriage and, should that fail, on the basis of descent. This basic formula of descent, gender and generation has been complicated by the war and displacement, as we see in Filda's case. Her eldest sons had lost their father, to whom their mother had not been formally married. Like many others, they had 'missing links' to family and land (Whyte, Babiiha, Mukyala, & Meinert, 2014).

## Land, gardens and 'ownership'

Acholi culture has long dictated that landed property is a social relationship shaped by clanship and affinity. Land is – or at least many people say that it still should be – about belonging. But men and women seem to belong differently, the one as clansmen and the other as the mothers of clan children. And, as we can see from Filda's case, people have a range of potential options to claim to belong in different social contexts. Land tenure in such systems, as Bohannan (1963) recognised long ago, is not necessarily about landed property at all. We examine how women and men use arguments about entitlements in an ostensibly patrilineal and patriarchal system. Here land claims depend on appeal to 'customary' principles but also, in this post-war era, on their ability to seek legal fora, mobilise allies, and draw on goodwill and the ideal of a community of harmonious co-existence, *ber bedo*.

In northern Uganda, 93% of the land is held under 'customary tenure' (Nakayi, 2013). It is generally accepted that land is held collectively by patrilineal kin groups (*kaka*, translated as clan or lineage), allocated to specific households for their use but not owned by individuals in the Western sense of private property. This land is supposed to be kept in trust from generation to generation; ideally it should not be sold (Shipton, 2009). Senior men in the kin group have authority to take decisions about its use and allocation. Sons inherit rights to ancestral land (*ngom kwaro*) through their fathers and can transmit such rights to their own sons. Daughters should be able to use it as well, especially if they do not have access to a husband's land. But in principle they cannot transmit claims on their fathers' land to their children, since those children belong to the kin group (*kaka*) of *their* fathers.

*Ngom kwaro*, which relates to patrilineal descent, may be contrasted with a family of Acholi terms for different kinds of land-in-use. Words such as *tim dwar* (hunting grounds) and *olet* (grazing land) point towards *use* as a fundamental characteristic of an area. While hunting and grazing are traditionally male occupations, two terms are particularly important for understanding women's land use. 'Garden' (*poto, pl. poti*) is used by Acholi when speaking English to indicate a field used for cultivation in one season or over years. Food security in households, families and communities is still the burden of women (see Gärber, 2013; Moyo, 2008), and women have a strong attachment to the gardens where they invest their labour and grow food. *Okang*, on the other hand, refers to garden use-history and denotes a garden opened by a particular woman on virgin land. Creating a new garden out of bush is demanding, and when people speak of a piece of land as the *okang* of their mother or grandmother, they implicitly recognize the work she did to establish a new garden.

Often when people make reference to gardens they will say something like, '*eni poto pa min Okello*' – this is the garden of Okello's mother. A wife is allocated gardens by her husband or his mother and ideally passes them on to her sons and their wives. Women also receive garden access from their brothers or fathers, especially after a marriage has been dissolved or when they remain single. Filda's plan to take her children to her father's home and obtain gardens there is a common strategy for women in Acholi today. In one sense, men are most concerned with claims to ancestral land (*ngom kwaro*), while women claim gardens (*poti*). However, gardens are also relevant to men in intergenerational transmission. Sons have particular claims on the portion of *ngom kwaro* where their mothers had made *poti*. Thus Peter's uncle was worried that Peter's stepsons might try to claim their mother's (Filda's) gardens if they were allowed to stay at Peter's home.

Even today, after two decades of conflict and disruption, male discourse about land is very often a discourse about lineality. Here land is perceived broadly and strategically, in terms of territory and corporate groups. Such discourse is in the first person plural: '*ngom wa*' – *our* land. Women, on the other hand, will often speak tactically about '*poto/poti na*' – my garden/gardens – a discourse more specific to their individual position, identity, belonging and shared history with that particular piece of land within a patrilineal system of land access.

Acholi women usually do not consider themselves (or are indeed not considered) as 'owners' of *ngom kwaro* in the sense of being custodians or stewards. Their reference to *my* gardens is a claim to another kind of tenure security, and one that is by and large respected as customary (Hopwood [2015] offers some important insights into changing practice and cultural continuity.) The cultivation of *poti* over several years gives Acholi women both a sense of attachment to *ngom* (land) and entitlement to the land that bears fruits of their labour (*poti*).

The literature on gender and property in East Africa is extensive. Women's changing right to secure tenure, often in the context of the introduction of land titling, has been examined (see Cotula, Toulmin & Hesse, 2004; Englert & Daley, 2008; Paradza, 2011; Tripp, 2004), as has the gendered impacts of HIV/AIDS on land access (Izumi, 2007; Drimie, 2003) and the gender implications of large-scale land deals on land rights and tenure systems (Behrman, Meinzen-Dick & A Quisumbing, 2012; Doss et al., 2014). In this chapter we draw on ethnography and case studies to examine land contestation at a more micro level. We focus on exploring the gendered practice of contestation, in which men and women present their claims and their positions.

In our cases, claims to land are primarily argued in terms of two dimensions: use and social relations. In land conflicts, evidence of use is important; the remains of house foundations, signs of old gardens, graves and fruit trees show that someone has physically engaged with the land. Such signs offer evidence of belonging and attachments to land, but they must be corroborated by memories of community members. A second line of argument draws on claims of affinity and consanguinity, of being a descendent of someone or a mother of lineage children or a wife or even a friend who was welcomed to stay on the land many years ago.

Acholi remind us that gardens are an especially 'tricky' form of property; claims to them are both specific to a bounded plot that can be seen to be in use and also general, involving the social acceptance as part of a settlement, practicing agriculture over many seasons, perhaps supporting many dependents. Gardens are linked to a discourse about tenure security that is literally 'grounded.' The labour invested in gardens has a moral status as well as an economic logic. This shapes the nature of conflicting claims in important ways and can make the claims themselves take on social and moral overtones. Specific conflicts between men and women over gardens and land rights are often about more than boundaries. They are disputes about status, identity, even legitimacy; to borrow Christian Lund's phrase, they draw on 'competing normative orders' (Lund, 2011, p. 72).

It was a premise of the Contested Property Claims Project that contesting claims can compel social actors to 'reason about the institution of property.' Our cases suggest that what our interlocutors 'reason about' are the social and historical links that mark their ability to have access to property. Here we are inspired by Ribot and Peluso, who, in 'A Theory of Access' argue that: 'focusing on *ability*, rather than *rights* as in property theory, . . . brings attention to a wider range of social relationships that can constrain or enable people to benefit from resources without focusing on property relations alone' (Ribot & Peluso, 2003, p. 154).

Under customary tenure in Acholi, the levels of security to be enjoyed by each individual woman cannot be discussed outside the larger realm of social relations and belonging. Both men and women have claims under customary tenure, but in most patriarchal societies in northern Uganda, the responsibility of ensuring women's access to land comes from her natal or her marital family. Filda's case suggests that she is attempting to secure access to land through different kinds of links through men: Peter, her father's clan and the male landlord of the plot she rents. These relationships may provide access to the gardens she needs and will also, if and when they are accepted, serve to define further her own social positions and possibilities.

As we shall see, gendered claims on land have become fraught in the post-camp period. War and internment prevented the use of land and gravely disrupted patterns of social relations. Despite the ideal that *ngom kwaro* is to be kept in trust, informal land sales appear to be relatively common, albeit often problematic. As custodians of land, senior men are in a position to sell it, apparently converting *ngom kwaro* into property in the Western sense.

In the subsequent sections we use two more cases to discuss the questions about position and belonging that arose in connection with land conflicts after people left the camps. The answers depend on remembered residence and land use (Rose and Korina case, in what follows), but also on confirmation of memories through social relationships and recognised assertions of identity (Filda case, earlier), backed up by accepted personal history (Betty and Margaret case, in what follows). The power to interpret and reinterpret historical events in order to legitimise claims (Shipton & Goheen, 1992) is critical ten years after armed conflict, when people return to (re)claim their land.

## The changing conditions of land claims

Economically, if not politically, Uganda flourished in the early days of independence. But the Idi Amin coup in 1971 marked the beginning of an era of violence and economic decline for the country as a whole. The Acholi region certainly did not escape the brutality of the 'regimes,' but land was plentiful, food generally in good supply and customary wealth, in cattle and children, was still available. Then, starting in 1986, the region became the centre of two decades of armed conflict by the Lord's Resistance Army (LRA) led by Joseph Kony (Doom & Vlassenroot, 1999). From 1986 to 2005/6, northern Uganda witnessed violence, abductions, murder and mass crimes against humanity carried out by the LRA but also by government soldiers. Villages and homesteads were looted, gardens destroyed and cattle, which had profound symbolic social, economic and cultural significance, were stolen by the protagonists as well as by the Karimojong cattle rustlers who border Acholiland to the east.

In 2006, a Cessation of Hostilities Agreement was signed between the government of Uganda and the LRA, which officially marked the end of the war, though sporadic violence continued until 2008 when the last LRA forces withdrew into the Central African Republic. In 2008, the camps were decommissioned, an announcement made that 'the war was over' and people told to 'return to where the war found you.' The people who returned, however, returned to an economy and a society in ruins. Poverty was widespread; houses needed to be repaired or rebuilt and fields to be prepared for cultivation after years in fallow. For most people, claims to land were their most significant remaining asset.

In many ways it was women, especially the 'new' social category of single mothers and the ambiguously married, who were most challenged. The theft and loss of most of the cattle and other livestock – the most traditionally treasured asset in rural Acholi society – was an economic catastrophe, essentially removing the store of wealth of most men and with it, at least some of their authority. It also had major social and symbolic implications for Acholi society during the conflict and, especially, in the post-war period. With no cattle for bridewealth exchange, customary marriage had not been possible. The decades between 1986 and 2006 saw partnerships being formed (and dissolved) and children being born, all without formal recognition of the relationships between male and female partners and their families – and between children and their fathers. This is a radical shift from the pre-conflict pattern. Evidence from research in the late colonial period (Foster, n.d.) suggests that recognized marriage was near universal (though separation and divorce were also not uncommon); accounts from senior generations collected in the post-war period agree that marriage was the rule and the norm in the 1960s and 1970s.

The status of wife is still recognized and valued; the status of 'partner,' while perhaps ambiguous, seems not to be a major point of contention in resettled communities. However, at the time of resettlement, as people returned home, marital status had implications for women and thus for their children. At this point, many Acholi needed to affirm the social links that marked belonging to groups and thus to territory and to social position. Young men with a clear clan identity might accuse their lineage elders of denying – or more often delaying – their access to *ngom kwaro*. Nonetheless cultural ideology and practice are on the side of these young men and their claims. 'Be patient,' they are told.

The situation is more precarious for women, especially 'wives' and 'widows' who have been rejected or are unable or unwilling to join 'husbands' and their affines. Many can choose to settle (as Filda planned) with their own paternal kin, claiming membership in local communities and garden access. However, their acceptability is subject to 'good behaviour' and their ability to live in harmony (*ber bedo*) with members of their extended families.

In the post-war era, mothers and widows, who seek access to gardens and thus to recognition in a family, may face 'attachment' issues from several directions: (a) As we saw in Filda's case, their partners' lineages may question their status as 'wives,' especially if they bring children from other 'marriages' who might stay and make property claims in the future; (b) other, older 'wives' may see younger mothers (whether new wives or returning daughters and sisters) as competitors for gardens and resources; (c) resident clan women ('daughters') who have children but no partners have become common after the war; they have the right to return home and access gardens and they, too, may see new 'wives' as competition. Difficulties in becoming 'attached' – for women with children – is of course a problem in many parts of Uganda today. What is special in the north is the war experience, the decades without cattle and thus bridewealth and – most of all – the suddenness of the peace and the scramble for belonging.

Issues of belonging are intimately connected to relationships, history and place. However, with the increased emphasis on land as the only remaining 'wealth resource' that the Acholi have left after the war, the notion of customary tenure seems to be undergoing rigorous transformations in post-war Acholi. A popular discourse, often repeated in interviews, holds that customary lands are being sold off, that there is an increased gap between the youth and elders, that more widows are becoming landless and that the 'nephew' question (claims on maternal clan land by men raised in their mothers' homes) is becoming a threat to lineage stability. The same interlocutors also claimed that the formal (and sometimes the traditional) institutions that handle land are either uncoordinated or corrupt or lack the requisite capacity to handle the current land claims.

Uganda has several courts and fora that handle land conflict resolution. They are both formal and informal; they operate in parallel but with unofficial and unclear links – a situation which Rugadya (2008) argues creates duplication in role and legal jurisdiction. The Local Council (LC) II and LC III courts, Magistrates and High Courts in order of hierarchy are all statutory. They co-exist with traditional institutions (comprised mainly of family heads, village chiefs, councils of elders, clan structures and chiefs – *Rwodi kweri* and *Rwodi moo*) and apply customary rules and norms to resolve customary land disputes. The structural and normative procedures of these institutions are not dictated by the state, though decisions and agreements may, and often are, appealed to the formal system. Forum shopping (K. von Benda-Beckmann, 1981) is often described in narratives of land contestations (Mabikke, 2011; Hopwood, 2015). Researchers have found that local-level fora, whether statutory like LCs or traditional like clan elders, tend to be more successful in resolving disputes (Atkinson & Hopwood, 2013; Kobusingye, Van Leeuwen & Van Dijk, 2016). The large and very relevant literature on legal pluralism (F. von Benda-Beckmann, 2002; von Benda-Beckmann, von Benda-Beckmann, & Griffiths, 2009), legal hybridity (Kyed, 2009) and legal dynamism in property rights (Meinzen-Dick & Pradhan, 2002) explores the ways in which the existence of diverse legal fora can shape the course of conflicts over land. While this chapter builds on insights drawn from the field of legal pluralism, we focus here particularly on local practices and explore how contested claims over land are shaped by arguments from custom, gender and local history. In particular, we highlight how social as well as legal fora are chosen by women (and by men) and how land cases reflect the kinds of arguments that they are able to make.

## Contesting male claims to land

The extreme poverty in the post-war period had fostered an awareness of land as property, a commodity asset that could be sold for money. In this case, we focus on a dispute between Betty and Margaret, widows who had been married to two brothers, and Henry, their late husbands' classificatory son and the leader of the local lineage (*dog-gola*). Betty and Margaret claim that Henry is misusing his position by taking gardens (*poti*) that had been passed to them by their now deceased husbands. The gardens that Betty and Margaret had used as wives, before they were interned in the camps, were, in Henry's view, *ngom kwaro*, and as the senior man of the *dog-gola* he was able to dispose of them. For Betty and

Margaret, their *poti* was land achieved through marriage and labour. In general, selling *ngom kwaro* for cash is seen as problematic in Acholiland. Such sales are opposed by traditional leaders and often unrecognised by formal institutions; the transactions, however, may be accepted locally.

During the period of active conflict, many families and communities were split apart. Betty, Margaret and Henry went to different IDP camps, but all returned to their land in Ogom after the camps were closed down, albeit at different times. Henry was the first to arrive back in Ogom. Betty, who returned before Margaret, found that her gardens, which are still readily recognisable, had been sold off. On asking Henry, he told her that she had taken too long to return, and he had not thought that she was still alive or coming back. Later, when Margaret returned and asked him the same question, he replied that the two women did not belong on the land anymore.

Both women have sons and daughters. Their sons, who in Acholi kin terminology are younger brothers to Henry, had left the Acholi region during the war; two are now settled in Bweyale, south of the Nile, and one is married and working in Kenya. The absence of resident sons with lineal claims to residence *ngom kwaro* seems to have made it harder for Betty and Margaret to sustain their claims to their gardens and even to their rights of residence as widows.

The two women have involved many legal fora in their attempts to re-access their gardens. They first tried mediation at the community level to regain their gardens and their status as widows. There is a virtue attached to mediation, compromise, and restorative justice in Acholi, which seeks to promote *ber bedo*, but Henry remained dismissive. Later they involved other fora, including clan leaders and elders, the LCI chairman (whom we later discovered was one of the people to whom Henry sold land), the Uganda Land Alliance (an NGO that works on land rights issues in northern Uganda) and FIDA, an association of women lawyers who provide legal aid for disadvantaged women in Uganda. Henry attended a few of the mediation meetings but was often hostile and adamant about his position on the land. Recently, Betty and Margaret's sons came from Bweyale and tried to talk to Henry about their mothers' claims. At first, Henry seemed to welcome the idea of all three working together to resolve their issues, but he later changed his mind and even threatened to harm the two men if they tried to cultivate their mothers' former gardens.

The end of the war and Henry's early return to Ogom as a senior man gave him the opportunity to sell off – as 'land' – gardens (*poti*) that did not belong to him. It is generally agreed in the community that he misused (and abused) *kaka* customs and his position to sell land for personal benefit. Although married and with children, he was only a child when the war began, and much of his adult life has been in the camps. He was not well grounded in the rules and norms of the Acholi patrilineal system before the war, where the *dog-gola* or *kaka* elders, using mediation in order to promote community harmony, resolved conflicts. Camp life gave him little opportunity to see this system in practice. Betty and Margaret always refer to him as a young man.

This is a case in which arguments based on *ngom kwaro* by a young man seem tendentious and self-serving, ignoring other recognised Acholi values, in particular garden rights and maintaining community harmony in the *dog-gola*. All parties, including other clan elders, agree that the land in question can be considered to be *ngom kwaro* for the *dog-gola* where Henry is now the senior man. But by refusing to also accept the rights of senior women like Betty and Margaret to gardens that they created and cultivated for many years, Henry (their classificatory son) rejects compromise and introduces discord into the community he claims to lead. His actions challenge the special status of gardens, also part of Acholi tradition.

One strategy that Henry has used to strengthen his position locally has been to sell off land to influential people in the neighbourhood who will support, or at least not oppose, his claims. Some of the land in this case has been sold to the Local Council chairman, making it difficult for the two women to get 'justice' from his 'court'. Henry regularly ignores summons from the Magistrate's Court and has also sent false information to the court hearing the case; he seems to maintain enough local support to continue doing this with impunity. He ignores his younger clan brothers' (Betty and Margaret's sons) requests to divide the land so that their mothers could live peacefully and their own (non-resident) interests could be preserved.

Betty, Margaret and Henry are now locked in a land conflict at the Magistrate's Court that has been on-going for more than three years, after exploring all other non-formal legal fora. The Magistrate's Court is part of the formal legal structure in Uganda, whose jurisdiction overrules all decisions of informal legal structures such as *dog-gola* and *kaka*. However, there have been instances where a Magistrate will send complainants back to the *dog-gola* and/or the *kaka* to resolve (mediate) land disputes because of the increased understanding of the social embeddedness of most land (claims). We argue that the emergent climate of land wrangles challenges traditional leaders, statutory authorities and even the plural legal system itself. It is a climate in which contested claims, appropriate to one context, can be moved into other legal and political contexts. In this case Betty and Margaret, financed in part by their sons, have pushed their claims beyond the *dog-gola* in the hope that they would regain access to their gardens. The process of following mobile claims about land and identity is on-going and open-ended, and they may not in the end be successful. But contesting claims in different fora helps to widen the space in which locally grounded claims about practice and history and identities can be heard.

In his work in northern Uganda, Hopwood (2015) has argued that 'the notion of claims may have more traction than that of rights,' an idea that can productively complicate law-based approaches to land disputes. He repeats Johan Pottier's call for analysts and policy makers to go beyond the restrictive view of women's land rights as being secondary to men's and endorses Pottier's suggestion that 'we must abandon such evolutionary thought, and instead pay full attention to the proliferation of claims and counterclaims that can be made – and are being made – in the name of custom' (Pottier, 2005). The claims, and indeed counter-claims, made in the arena of gardens (*poti*) illustrate contrasting customary principles and practices and the multiple discourses and fora that have emerged. Equally important, cases and claims reveal today's real-life tangle of motives and strategies among claimants, as well as the uses and misuses of personal and cultural authority.

## Whose gardens?

Rose, 36, a mother of five, has been separated from her husband Tom for more than a decade. Her eldest son (now 16 years) was fathered by another man before she met Tom and now lives with Rose's brothers. During encampment, Rose stayed with her (step) mother-in-law Korina, with whom she had an amicable relationship. When the war ended, Rose opted to remain in the town where the camp had been located; from there she could easily run her small business and also cultivate her gardens in the village, while Korina and other family members returned to the village. Tom, who lives far away in another city, wrote a letter to the sub-clan leader stating that he wished formally to divorce Rose, citing irreconcilable differences. To this day, however, divorce proceedings have not been pushed any further. Tom's bridewealth has not been refunded by Rose's family to effect the divorce as required in Acholi tradition, and Rose continues to look after their children.

Later, Korina made an allegation that Rose was in a relationship with another man with whom she (Rose) would go to cultivate the gardens that Korina had passed on to her. Korina argued that this man (a 'stranger') would later make a claim to those gardens if Rose insisted on bringing him along. Gardens (*poti*) are generally considered to mark a kind of property claim reflecting use over time. Korina enforced her decision by forcefully planting crops in the gardens already prepared by Rose. When Rose sent her children to the contested gardens, Korina threatened them with a knife and vowed to kill them the next time they returned to the gardens – an action which angered clan members.

Two of Korina's sons are already married and have their land allocated to them. Her youngest son, who is still in secondary school, is considered a family heir, and Rose believes he is the reason Korina wants to take the gardens away from her so he could inherit in future. Uncertain of how the bitter conflict would end, Rose's brothers agreed in a family meeting to allocate eight gardens to her at her natal home, which she could use to raise her children. In the event that Rose succeeds in reclaiming access and use of the five gardens at her marital home, her eldest son living with his uncles would inherit the eight gardens. Rose, meanwhile took the case, first to the LC1 chairman, then to the Community Development Officer (CDO), the sub-clan leader, the Magistrate's Court, and to the higher clan leadership, who finally granted her full access and use of the gardens.

Women try to cope with the current situation and the confusion that resulted from the war and displacement by employing different strategies to maintain access to land (Burke & Kobusingye, 2014). In Acholi today, people are attempting to reach back to try and establish what used to be in the past. However, the normative *kaka* (clan) rules and arguments drawing on autochthony (Geschiere, 2009) that may serve in inter-clan disputes are seldom relevant for women. Indeed, their situation could easily become precarious if current marital status alone is considered. Rose claims status as a 'wife' in the clan because she and Tom are not formally divorced despite their ten-year separation, but also – and primarily– as a 'mother of sons' and a good neighbour. This case expands our understanding of how women can contest for gardens within the *kaka* system and highlights how their claims to land are granted by a responsive *kaka* leadership. In order to regain her access, Rose had to 'navigate' (Vigh, 2006) through the plural legal system that is characteristic of contested land claims in northern Uganda today.

Hopwood's (2015) argument that local authorities in Acholi support kinship and marital claims to land by women is well articulated here, and the presence of children (especially sons) provides a 'backup' to land claims, irrespective of a woman's social status. Rose went directly to the LCI and then to the CDO before going to the *dog-gola* and *kaka* leaderships. In the end, however, she had to go back to the *kaka*, which confirmed her access to her gardens, basing their decision on the fact that she was raising the clan's children (i.e. Tom's children).

Being the mother of recognised clan children cements a woman's claim to garden land. This is a widespread entitlement in Uganda (Gärber, 2013; Rose, 2002) and takes on special significance in post-war Acholi; recognising paternity has become an issue. For Filda (our first case), her sons from another genitor worked against her moving with Peter to his ancestral land. Rose, on the other hand, has recognised children from her formal marriage with Tom; her claim to gardens is both as a wife and as a mother of clan children, who will in turn have garden claims. Her status as a mother with children is her strongest argument for repossessing her gardens, even though she has been separated from Tom for a long time. For Betty and Margaret, the absence of their grown sons works against their claims to their gardens. Henry argues, with some basis in Acholi custom, that women are given gardens to cultivate and feed their children; sons will eventually receive these gardens and insure *dog-gola* continuity. But their sons chose to settle elsewhere during the time of the war and have not been willing to return as permanent residents, and Henry used this argument to dispossess them of their gardens.

The goal of maintaining and preserving *ber bedo* – harmonious living – is often mentioned by our interlocutors. It is recognised (though not always and not by all) that secure access to gardens can promote harmony; women's (and indeed some men's) successful land claims reflect this concern. And, of course, *ber bedo* relationships cultivated over time allow women to navigate through their social network to gain support for their claims to gardens. Land access is maintained by continuously living together in harmony, by practicing cooperation and showing willingness to avoid disputes. A woman may be living in an ambiguous relationship/partnership with a man yet can often legitimize her continuous access to gardens by being a good neighbour. A divorced woman can be allocated gardens at her home, especially if she is 'well behaved' and 'knows her place' in the home. Rose originally had a good relationship with Korina while they were in the camps because Rose supported Korina economically and socially.

When Rose opted to remain in the town, her relationship with Korina changed. Korina grabbed some of the gardens Rose had been using, arguing both that she was no longer a good wife and that her liaison with a man from another clan turned garden use by a wife into a potential threat to the *ngom kwaro* status of the garden land in question. Korina was both challenging her status as a good wife in the community and accusing her of potentially alienating clan land. It is not enough to be a 'woman,' but one has to be a 'good woman' in order to be able to access land within a certain community and remain there harmoniously.

It is not unusual for women, too, to use male-centred arguments (against other women or men) in contesting land claims. Korina's use of *ngom kwaro/kaka* arguments for detaching Rose from her gardens and from the community is essentially the argument that Filda faced. But here the outcome is different because Rose, already well integrated in the community and well-respected by her own brothers, is able to mobilise support from both clan and community.

## Conclusion: navigating claims and rights in post-war Acholiland

Gendered discourses on land continue to be of utmost interest and relevance in Africa and particularly in sub-Saharan Africa, where global economic shifts are shaping institutional land reforms, land markets and large-scale commercialised agriculture. This chapter, we argue, is relevant to broadening our understanding about property claims from rural women's point of view, where customary land tenure is predominant and arguments are made around patrilineal systems of land governance. Our exploration of gardens as a tricky form of property reveals very pertinent ideas about land rights and land ownership that are transforming and changing in post-war northern Uganda.

Formal and customary institutions are beginning to collaborate more effectively, and this is possible because of an increased sensitivity to gender positions and to issues of access. From the point of view of access, *poto/poti* are central, and from the point of view of rights and ownership, *ngom kwaro* is central. When women are given access to land by men, it is not just about garden access; it is also a claim to an identity and a place in a community. The implication of gardens for community belonging is significant. Patrilineal clanship remains the dominant model for conceiving community, landed property (*ngom kwaro*) and identity, but a women's language of land, focused on gardens and access, is heard and respected.

When the property being contested is land, itself socially constructed, contestation is very often about placing oneself in a strategic position, in effect choosing the best forum or context for contesting with others. People, as social beings, have options, possibilities for taking alternate identities.

In this chapter, we have seen that to ask, where is our land? (or where are my gardens?) is to ask both about a specific plot and also, in adding the personal pronouns, to claim a social history, a set of relationships with and through others. This point is also brought out by Pasternak (Chapter 6, this volume) when she describes the Algonquin of Barriere Lake and their reaction to government attempts to reconceptualise hunting practices as specific property rights. Here, as in Uganda, indigenous land practices cannot simply be taken as reflecting Western legal concepts; these practices are embedded in local knowledge of people and the land as well as conceptions of kinship and gender that are, these days, also culturally contested.

For Acholi, who you choose to be has implications for how (and even when) you may claim access to land and gardens. Answers, for Rose, depend on skilful social manipulation but also on remembered residence and land use (how long have I been here?) and the confirmation of memories through social relationships and recognised assertions of identity (who am I?). For Betty and Margaret, their answers have not swayed Henry. As widows without resident sons, and perhaps above all as late returners, claims based on accepted personal history are at the moment trumped by Henry's aggression and local contacts. Yet when their sons address him as elder brother and remind him that Betty and Margaret are mothers, there seems to be a softening that might lead to conciliation.

Filda, as a mother of sons, has in principle the traditional right – but not the social ability – to access gardens in the homes of her deceased partner as well as her present partner. As a mother of children without recognised fathers she may find support in NGO programs that focus on single mothers. As a clan daughter, she has a right and, it seems, the ability to return to her birth home with all of her children. At the moment, all these alternatives are at least potentially open. Finding *her* gardens will involve 'navigating' (Vigh, 2006) in the complex sea that is the post-war Acholi region.

This social dimension of property allows for different kinds of claims and different arenas for contestation. Our case studies reveal not fixed social identities but rather social identities in play. As we came to learn more about our cases, as we expanded the life stories in time and space, we have seen how some of the actors have claimed different social positions and undertaken what begins to look like a forum-shopping expedition (see K. von Benda-Beckmann, 1981). When our actors contest property claims in different fora, they must also present appropriate – and at times different – social identities.

Claims and disputes about land and gardens reflect claims to position, with implications for social relations. But the materiality of the property also helps to shape its social and historical status. Gardens have histories that can be read in heaps and ridges of soil. Agriculture leaves signs in the ground, and these can be recognised and remembered, even after years in IDP camps. These signs can, of course, also be overseen, forgotten and ignored.

We have drawn on cases to discuss the dynamics of conflict and to emphasise both the significance of encampment and the (relatively) sudden mass return, with almost no resources, to a home area unfamiliar to many. The power to interpret and reinterpret historical events in order to legitimise claims (Shipton & Goheen, 1992) remains critical and contested ten years after the cessation of armed conflict. This sudden return gives birth to key questions about land, questions that, for men and for women, are as much about social position as they are about cartography.

## References


Atkinson, R., & Hopwood, J. (2013). *Land conflict monitoring and mapping tool for the Acholi sub-region*. Kampala: United Nations Peacebuilding Programme in Uganda/Human Rights Focus.

Behrman, J., Meinzen-Dick, R., & Quisumbing, A. (2012). The gender implications of large- scale land deals. *The Journal of Peasant Studies*, *39*(1), 49–79.

Bohannan, P. (1963). 'Land', 'tenure', and 'land tenure'. In D. Biebuyck (Ed.), *African Agrarian systems* (pp. 101–115). London: Oxford University Press.

Burke, C., & Kobusingye, D. (2014). *Women's land rights in Northern Uganda (West Nile, Acholi, Lango, Teso and Karamoja)*. Kampala: United Nations Peacebuilding Program in Uganda/Oxfam.

Cotula, L., Toulmin, C., & Hesse, C. (2004). *Land tenure and administration in Africa: Lessons of experience and emerging issues*. London: International Institute for Environment and Development.

Doss, C., Meinzen-Dick, R., & Bomuhangi, A. (2014). Who owns the land? Perspectives from rural Ugandans and implications for large-scale land acquisitions. *Feminist Economics*, *20*, 76–100.

Drimie, S. (2003). HIV/AIDS and land: Case studies from Kenya, Lesotho, and South Africa. *Development Southern Africa*, *20*(5), 647–658.

Doom, R., & Vlassenroot, K. (1999). Kony's message: A new Koine? The lord's resistance army in Northern Uganda. *African Affairs*, *98*(390), 5–36.

Englert, B., & Daley, E. (Eds.) (2008). *Women's land rights and privatization in Eastern Africa*. Rochester, NY: Boydell & Brewer Inc.

Foster, Paula Hirsch. (n.d.). Unpublished draft of PhD thesis. Located in Foster Archive, African Studies Library, Boston University.

Gärber, B. (2013). Women's land rights and tenure security in Uganda: Experiences from Mbale, Apac and Ntungamo. *Wiener Zeitschrift für kritische Afrikastudien*, *13*(24), 1–32.

Geschiere, P. (2009). *Perils of belonging: Autochthony, citizenship and exclusion in Africa and Europe*. Chicago, IL & London: University of Chicago Press.

Hopwood, J. (2015). Women's land claims in the Acholi region of Northern Uganda: What can be learned from what is contested. *International Journal on Minority and Group Rights*, *22*(3), 387–409.

Izumi, K. (2007). Gender-based violence and property grabbing in Africa: A denial of women's liberty and security. *Gender and Development*, *15*(1), 11–23.

Lund, C. (2011). Property and citizenship: Conceptually connecting and rights and belonging in Africa. *Africa Spectrum*, *3*, 71–75.

Kobusingye, D., Van Leeuwen, M., & Van Dijk, H. (2016). Where do I report my land dispute? The impact of institutional proliferation on land governance in post-conflict northern Uganda. *The Journal of Legal Pluralism and Unofficial Law*, *48*(2), 238–255.

Kyed, H. M. (2009). The politics of legal pluralism: State politicies on legal pluralism and their local dynamics in Mozambique. *Journal of Legal Pluralism*, *59*, 87–121.

Mabikke, S. B. (2011). *Escalating land grabbing in post-conflict regions of northern Uganda: A need for strengthening good land governance in Acholi region*. Paper presented at the International Conference on Global Land Grabbing, 6–8 April 2011, University of Sussex.

Meinzen-Dick, R., & Pradhan, R. (2002). *Legal pluralism and dynamic property rights*. Washington, DC: International Food Policy Research Institute (IFPRI).

Moyo, S. (2008). *African land questions, agrarian transitions and the state: contradictions of neo-liberal land reforms*. Dakar: CODESIRA.

Nakayi, R. (2013). The role of local council courts and traditional institutions in resolving land disputes in post-conflict northern Uganda. *Malawi Law Journal*, *7*, 119–138.

Paradza, G. (2011). *Innovations for securing women's access to land in East Africa*. Working Paper 13. Rome: International Land Coalition.

Pottier, J. (2005). Customary land tenure in Sub-Saharan Africa today: Meanings and contexts. In C. Huggins & J. Clover (Eds.), *From the ground up: Land rights, conflict and peace in Sub- Saharan Africa* (pp. 66–75). Nairobi & Pretoria: ACTS and ISS.

Ribot, J. C., & Peluso, N. (2003). A theory of access. *Rural Sociology*, *68*(2), 153–181.

Rose, L. (2002). Women's strategies for customary land access in Swaziland and Malawi: A comparative study. *Africa Today*, *49*(2), 123–149.

Rugadya, M. A. (2008). *Analysis of post conflict land policy and land administration: A survey of IDP return and resettlement issues and lessons: Acholi and Lango regions*. Kampala: World Bank/Associates for Development.

Shipton, P. (2009). *Mortgaging the ancestors: Ideologies of attachment in Africa*. New Haven: Yale University Press.

Shipton, P., & Goheen, M. (1992). Introduction: Understanding African land-holding: Power, wealth, and meaning. *Africa*, *62*(3), 307–325.

Tripp, A. (2004). Women's movements, customary law, and land rights in Africa: The case of Uganda. *African Studies Quarterly*, *7*(4), 1–19.

Vigh, H. (2006). *Navigating terrains of war: Youth and soldiering in Guinea-Bissau*. New York, NY: Berghahn Books.

von Benda-Beckmann, F. (2002). Who is afraid of legal pluralism? *Journal of Legal Pluralism*, *47*, 37–82.

von Benda-Beckmann, F., von Benda-Beckmann, K., & Griffiths, A. (Eds.) (2009). *Rules of law and laws of ruling*. Farnham & Burlington: Ashgate.

von Benda-Beckmann, K. (1981). Forum shopping and shopping forum: Dispute processing in a Minangkabau village in Western Sumatra. *Journal of Legal Pluralism and Unofficial Law*, *19*, 117–159.

Whyte, S. R., Babiiha, S., Mukyala, R., & Meinert, L. (2014). Urbanization by subtraction: The afterlife of camps in northern Uganda. *Journal of Modern African Studies*, *52*(4), 597–622.

# Afterword

## Prophecies on property's probability: climate change and smart contracts in the Anthropocene

*Bill Maurer*

*In his afterword. Bill Maurer speculates about the future directions of property regimes and how new technologies of accounting and greater societal changes like climate change are reconfiguring how to own, what to own, how to manage and distribute property.*

One of the premises of the chapters collected in this volume is that "becoming-world" in the twenty-first century centrally involves contested property claims.[1] We see such contests in the context of massive human displacement caused by conflict and climate change. We see them in the discovery and colonization of new commons, from recently emptied spaces (think: Detroit, New Orleans) to our digital data trails, and by popular, artist and activist groups as well as states and capital, as discussed by several contributors to this volume. We see them in the reconfiguration of age-old struggles over property in different timescales, from that of the family to colonial occupation to world epochs. Humans living in the first decades of the twenty-first century are arguably the first at a species level to have to deal with the consequences of human-caused planetary change (see O'Donnell, this volume). As cities sink, temperatures rise, diseases spread and resources wane, the basic fact of the Anthropocene can no longer be denied.

I borrow the phrase "becoming-world" from J. K. Gibson-Graham, who writes that the Anthropocene "calls us to recognize that we are all participants" in these changes, "where everything is interconnected and learning happens in a stumbling, trial and error sort of way. In the spirit of this participation, many offer the experiment as the only way forward" (Gibson-Graham, 2011, p. 4).

Consider for a moment this notion of the experiment. One conducts an assay, modifying a variable from a presumed steady state. One compares the results against a control in which that variable has not been changed. And one assesses whether or not there is a difference based on that change. This judgment is made probabilistically: you take the mean of the observations of the experimental group and compare it to the mean of the observations of the control group and then you test whether and to what degree any observed difference might be the product of chance.

Probability is central to experimentation. If we heed Gibson-Graham's call, we experiment with what they call "adventures in living" and see what we end up with, whether it's significantly different from what we have now or where we think we might be headed if we do nothing at all. The evaluation of our adventures, in other words, would be done probabilistically. We want to test new options, perhaps continuously, in this unpredictable world we seem to have entered, especially since we do not know its parameters yet – or even if it will have them.

Probability is also central to property. In the lawyers' refrain, property is a relationship among persons with respect to things (Cohen, 1927, p. 12). It also depends on the spatial surround of those relations. Sarah Keenan argues, "property happens when a space holds up a relationship of belonging" (Keenan, 2010, pp. 423–424). And it depends on time, too, as the editors point out in their introduction. Keenan chooses her verb deliberately: property *happens*. It requires a temporality in which the future can be projected as a probabilistic extension of the present. Property is thus a way to mitigate uncertainty – uncertainty against potential future claimants and conflicts. It is a form of insurance. An actuarial mode of governance (O'Malley, 2000) – again, a probabilistic claim.

The early-twentieth-century legal realist, Morris Cohen, argued that as a form of insurance property is also in the same instance a form of rule over others. As he put it, "the essence of private property is always the right to exclude" (Cohen, 1927, p. 12). This means, for him and as echoed by Keenan, "dominion over things is also *imperium* over our fellow human beings" (Cohen, 1927, p. 13), that is to say, a sovereign claim.

If Gibson-Graham in the early twenty-first century made an argument for experimentation in light of the becoming-world of the Anthropocene, Cohen in the early twentieth made an argument for an invigorated state in light of an economic world in the process of becoming-market.[2] He repeatedly stressed the increasing complexity and uncertainty of "modern life" and made a case for public action the benefits of which would flow to all: "[A]s modern life is becoming more and more complex it is dangerous to give too much sovereignty to those who are after all dealing with the rather simpler aspects of life involved in economic relations" (Cohen, 1927, p. 29).

Today, such calls for government action and public goods are as quaint as they are comforting. While it remains vital to build a case for public goods, the world transformations documented in this volume, which always proceed on top of and through the accretions of durable colonial, gender and racial histories and hierarchies (see, for example, Nelms, 2015, as well as chapters in this volume such as Pasternak's, Krebs's and Obika, Adol, Babiiha and Whyte's) may compel another experimental move. This is because of the nonparametric nature of the world we now inhabit. That is, the classic assumptions about the normal distribution of variation or error no longer hold. We witness both the creation of new asset geographies (Leyshon & Thrift, 2007) in the financialization of everything from parking meter revenue to the weather itself (Pryke, 2007), as well as the unravelling of the same; Lifeworld, Inc. and its ungrounding in new forms of association and occupation (Thrift, 2011); the enclosure of the "sea of data" (Thrift, 2011, p. 29) that is our new spatiotemporal surround, and its dispersion and distribution in more hopeful (Gibson-Graham, 2011) or more or less libertarian or mutualistic (Swartz, 2017) networks.

The early-twentieth-century American jurist Oliver Wendell Holmes wrote that we should understand law not through the application of rules but through the desires of the "bad man," the actor who makes judgments about whether to undertake a nefarious deed not based on logic but based on his (sic) prediction of what the courts will do to him if he is caught:

> [I]f we take the view of our friend the bad man we shall find that he does not care two straws for the axioms or deductions, but that he does want to know what the Massachusetts or English courts are likely to do in fact. I am much of this mind. The prophecies of what the courts will do in fact, and nothing more pretentious, are what I mean by the law.
>
> (Holmes, 1897)

Felix Cohen extended this line of reasoning to contract: "any answer to the question 'Is there a contract' must be in the nature of a prophecy, based, like other prophecies, upon past and present facts" (Cohen, 1935, p. 839). Contracts then, like property, are probabilities. This understanding wended its way into the United States' Uniform Commercial Code, in which the determination of the existence of contract depends on "agreement" made "in any manner" based on "commercial standards": the commonplace, that is to say statistically average practice of merchants (see UCC §2–204(1), §2–609(2); Maurer & Richland, 2012).

Holmes's bad man has a contemporary analog, but the mathematics is different. Arjun Appadurai (2015) implies that for certain financial players in the years before and after the global financial crisis of 2007–2008, uncertainty lent both economic profit and charismatic authority. They had an orientation that did not seek to tame chance through risk calculations but instead to ride this uncertainty. If we take Appadurai's suggestion seriously, which is in accord with my assessment of a nonparametric world, then what happens to property or contract when we can no longer assume the probabilities of the future based on the experience of the past and present? This is of signal importance for the becoming-world with which I am concerned here and which this volume takes up. What happens when the bell curve distribution of observations and outcomes shifts, morphs into something much more bimodal, with fatter tails or no central tendency at all (see El-Erian, 2016)?

Property's probabilities are made redundant in two increasingly important domains of life – not just human life, but whatever life itself may be becoming as it is transformed, first by climate change and second by novel computational agencies. The former exemplifies the spatiotemporal rootedness of property claims by highlighting what happens when the certainties of their coordinates evaporate, slosh away, burn, desiccate, collapse. The latter exemplifies an attempt to abolish probability, eliminate contingency and automatize contract and property in computer code, abolishing the need for any communicative or human agency in the process – so that things can run themselves without our intercession and even after we as individuals or species are gone (assuming, somehow, the lights are still on).

Two brief examples:

One. After Hurricane Katrina flooded New Orleans in 2005 and led to the death of more than 1,200 people, property's certainties were newly placed in question. People abandoned their property, water and wildlife taking their places. City and community efforts to deal with the new landscape led to experimentations with property. Sean Mallin shows how during the poststorm aftermath critical perspectives on property became popular common sense and strategy. New Orleans residents "not only see private property as social, but also are actively reconstituting the social through property – though questions remain about what kind of social will be created, and who will be included in it" (Mallin, 2016, p. 10). City officials used auctions and other techniques of the market but not simply to revalue property, expropriate it or "return" it to the market but also to develop new government interventions and hybrid forms of public–private ownership. The flood de-abstracted "market logic" or, rather, revealed it as always thoroughly material and mucky (p. 191), much like the city itself after the flood. Despite any attempt to restabilize the coordinates, the flood created a spatiotemporal breach in property. Property's future probability is no longer something that can be extrapolated from the present.

Two. With so-called big data and predictive analytics a growing area of business and scientific attention – including for extrapolating the effects of climate change – my second example is inspired by the fascination with autonomous computational agents. The artificial intelligences of self-driving automobiles (finally literalizing the term's nineteenth-century French meaning) are one example. Smart contracts are another. First envisioned in the late 1990s, smart contracts were modelled on the coin-based vending machine: a simple set of mechanical devices ensures that a sale is concluded and goods dispensed once the correct number and denomination of coins is inserted into the machine (Szabo, 1997). The machine actualizes a contract for the sale of goods. As computer scientist Nick Szabo wrote, we can imagine a similar process enabled by digital technology that would disable an automobile if its owner fails to make a loan payment. The vision was to "embed contracts in all sorts of property" (Szabo, 1997). Szabo further argued that smart contracts, embedded in property, would obviate (human) interpretation or intermediation (Szabo, 2002). One goal was "augmenting legal enforcement with technological constraints" (Szabo, 2002). Another is obviating uncertainty altogether – coding it away.[3]

Of course, property is itself a contract, so there is a tautology in the idea of embedding contracts "in" property. Nevertheless, smart contracts are an effort to abolish the contingency of property, to remove the probability, to get rid of those merchants' commonplace practices invoked in the Uniform Commercial Code. One programming language developed to write and execute smart contracts, Solidity, even eliminates the possibility of randomness at the level of the code.[4] It does not contain the ability – common to programming languages – to generate random numbers, and it blocks access to external databases that might introduce randomness. It does this because it depends on a network of computers all arriving at the same conclusion about the state of the world before executing a contract. As one commentator explains,

> We cannot have any randomness in the contracts processing, because if we did, the network would never get into consensus as to their results. So for example, we can't have [Internet] access from the contracts, because what my computer sees on the internet is probably completely different from a user in say, China.
>
> (StephanTual, 2014)

If you need a random number for some reason in a smart contract written in Solidity, you need to approximate it in another way (leading to much discussion in online forums over whether this exposes the system to vulnerabilities, as such a number would not be truly random).[5] Solidity is focused above all on providing an environment within which a network of agents (computers, corporations, people) can arrive at consensus about a particular event. For the way its developers designed it, Solidity accomplishes this by removing contingency from the world around that event.

Science fiction scenarios aside, there are a number of provocative aspects to the design of contingency-free computational agents. One is simply at the level of application: since we have to worry about things like nuclear waste, which will retain its poisonous properties for organic life long after we as a species have become extinct or have transformed into something radically different from what we are today (Callon, Lascoumes, & Barthe, 2009), it might make sense to develop smart contracts to manage and monitor such waste into the indefinite future. Another, however, is whether smart contracts represent the epitome of the formalization of contract and thereby property or its demise. For rendering contract automatic and removing uncertainty once and for all would seem to set aside the *lex mercatoria* at its heart, the hurly-burly (Kockelman, 2010) of a riotous market – whether comprised of human, nonhuman or computational agencies in tumultuous combination (see Pasternak, O'Donnell, this volume, for examples).

I think climate change and smart contracts raise another fundamental question, which also animates the contributors to this volume. If property is a set of relations among persons/things/agents with respect to persons/things/agents, who or what now gets to enter into such relations and with respect to who or what? This is a political question. Computational agents and the unmooring of property from its spatiotemporal coordinates may signal the need for a new politics of probability for the becoming-world in which we – an expansive we now, agents of all types – are complicit and, in varied ways, responsible for.

## Notes

1 I would like to thank the conveners of the Contested Property Claims conference at Aarhus University, Patrick Cockburn, Bjarke Skærlund Risager, Mikkel Thorup and Maja Hojer Bruun. I would also like to thank Nils Ole Bubandt in the Department of Anthropology, Aarhus University, as well as Nicholas Blomley and Sarah Keenen for comments on the remarks I delivered at the conference. Taylor C. Nelms and Sean Mallin provided critical commentary, and Melissa Wrapp and Caitie Lustig provided research assistance on smart contracts. Research on smart contracts was supported by the US National Science Foundation (SES 1455859). Any opinions, findings and conclusions or recommendations expressed in this material are those of the author(s) and do not necessarily reflect the views of the National Science Foundation.

2 I owe this Deleuzian-infused nod to Karl Polanyi to Taylor C. Nelms.

3 Szabo has become the touchstone for programmers as well as financial industry actors experimenting with smart contract systems. These include startups as well as the NASDAQ exchange, IBM and consortia of large investment banks.

4 Solidity is the programming language for Ethereum, a programmable distributed database or blockchain system inspired by Bitcoin. It was released in 2015 and became an often-cited model for industry experiments with blockchain systems. For more on blockchain systems, smart contracts and the law, see DuPont & Maurer, 2015.

5 This has also caused a small degree of consternation among those who would use Solidity to create online gambling games.

## References

Appadurai, A. (2015). *Banking on words: The failure of language in the age of derivative finance*. Chicago, IL: University of Chicago Press.

Callon, M., Lascoumes, P., & Barthe, Y. (2009). *Acting in an uncertain world: An essay on technical democracy* (G. Burchell, trans.). Cambridge, MA: MIT Press.

Cohen, F. (1935). Transcendental nonsense and the functional approach. *Columbia Law Review*, *35*(6), 809–849.

Cohen, M. (1927). Property and sovereignty. *Cornell Law Quarterly*, *13*(1), 8–30.

El-Erian, M. (2016). *The only game in town: Central banks, instability, and avoiding the next collapse*. New York, NY: Random House.

DuPont, Q., & Maurer, B. (2015). *Ledgers and law in the blockchain* [Blog post]. Retrieved from http://kingsreview.co.uk/magazine/blog/2015/06/23/ledgers-and-law-in-the-blockchain/

Gibson-Graham, J. K. (2011). A feminist project of becoming for the Anthropocene. *Gender, Place and Culture*, *18*(1), 1–21.

Holmes, O. W. (1897). The path of law. *Harvard Law Review*. Retrieved from www.gutenberg.org/files/2373/2373.txt

Keenan, S. (2010). Subversive property: Reshaping malleable spaces of belonging. *Social and Legal Studies*, *19*(4), 423–439.

Kockelman, P. (2010). Enemies, parasites, and noise: How to take up residence in a system without becoming a term in it. *Linguistic Anthropology*, *20*(2), 406–421.

Leyshon, A., & Thrift, N. (2007). The capitalization of almost everything: The future of finance and capitalism. *Theory, Culture and Society*, *24*(7–8), 97–115.

Mallin, S. (2016). *Becoming blight: Property and belonging in post-Katrina New Orleans*, Doctoral dissertation, Irvine, CA: University of California, Irvine.

Maurer, B., & Richland, J. (2012). *Lex Llewellyn and the tribal tax status act: 'Fallible gropings' in law and society*. UC Irvine School of Law Research Paper No. 2012–2078. Retrieved from http://dx.doi.org/10.2139/ssrn.2175674

Nelms, T. C. (2015). *Making popular and solidarity economies in dollarized Ecuador: Money, law, and the social after neoliberalism*, Doctoral dissertation, Irvine, CA: University of California, Irvine.

O'Malley, P. (2000). Uncertain subjects: Risks, liberalism and contract. *Economy and Society*, *29*(4), 460–484.

Pryke, M. (2007). Geomoney: An option on frost, going long on clouds. *GeoForum*, *38*, 576–588.

Swartz, L. (2017). Blockchain dreams: Imagining techno-economic alternatives after Bitcoin. In M. Castells (Ed.), *Another economy is possible* (pp. 82–105). Cambridge: Polity Press.

Szabo, N. (1997). *The idea of smart contracts*. [Blog post]. Retrieved from http://szabo.best.vwh.net/smart_contracts_idea.html

Szabo, N. (2002). *A formal language for analyzing contracts*. [Blog post]. Retrieved from http://szabo.best.vwh.net/contractlanguage.html

Thrift, N. (2011). Lifeworld, Inc. – and what to do about it. *Environment and Planning D: Society and Space*, *29*, 5–26.

Tual, S. (2014). Post to the Ethereum Community Forum, "Solidity vs JS [JavaScript]" thread. Retrieved from https://forum.ethereum.org/discussion/1622/solidity-vs-js

# Index

For Product Safety Concerns and Information please contact our EU representative GPSR@taylorandfrancis.com
Taylor & Francis Verlag GmbH, Kaufingerstraße 24, 80331 München, Germany

www.ingramcontent.com/pod-product-compliance
Ingram Content Group UK Ltd.
Pitfield, Milton Keynes, MK11 3LW, UK
UKHW011002180926
475701UK00004B/520
*9780367264376*